ANOTHER WORLD: Central America

Another World:

CENTRAL AMERICA

HILDA COLE ESPY

with LEX CREAMER, JR.

NEW YORK / THE VIKING PRESS

TO JEFFERSON AND PENNY

"Though we travel the world over to find the beautiful, we must carry it with us or we find it not."

—RALPH WALDO EMERSON

Copyright © 1970 by Hilda Cole Espy and Lex Creamer
All rights reserved

First published in 1970 by The Viking Press, Inc.
625 Madison Avenue, New York, N.Y. 10022

Published simultaneously in Canada by
The Macmillan Company of Canada Limited

SBN 670-20986-4

Library of Congress catalog card number: 76–83252

Printed in U.S.A.

Second printing June 1971

Acknowledgment: Little, Brown and Company: For "The Turtle" from *Verses from 1928 On* by Ogden Nash. Copyright 1940 by Ogden Nash. By permission of Little, Brown and Company.

Maps by Evelyn Curro

Foreword

We of these Central American travels are friends—agronomist and writer. Lex lives in Managua, Nicaragua, but works in Guatemala, El Salvador, Honduras, and Costa Rica as well, with growers of rice, coffee, cotton, sugar cane, rubber, cacao, bananas, lemon grass, and other crops associated with that beautiful Eden.

Leaning on Lex's experience of living and working for years in the five Central American republics, we hope we have been able to avoid the impulsive conclusions of the fleeting visitor. I, the writer, have proxied for the newcomer, seeing these mountains and lakes and seashores, plants and flowers and birds and people, whose native land this is, with new eyes.

Yet, during months of exploration, I have noticed that Lex constantly marvels over the land as if he had never seen it before. So many kinds of beauty keep perceptions keen and, however long a visitor remains in Central America, he will perhaps always have the joy of new eyes.

HILDA COLE ESPY

Gracias to Central Americans and North Americans who have shared their experiences and given us information with unfailing generosity. Their affection for this wonderful little bridge between the continents of North and South America is reflected on every page.

H.C.E.
L.C.

Contents

Illustrations follow page 24

Maps: Guatemala, 138–39 · El Salvador, 172–73 · Honduras, 200–201 · Nicaragua, 226–27 · Costa Rica, 254–55

I / On the Scene

Isthmian Customs and Culture

1 / The Approach

To most North Americans, Latin America, which is always coming up in the news, means Mexico and South America. What has been missed is the isthmus that bridges North and South America, sometimes known as Middle America.

Stateside neighbors are generally vague about the location, climate, culture, indigenous flora and fauna, contemporary accomplishments and aspirations of the Central American republics —Guatemala, El Salvador, Honduras, Nicaragua, and Costa Rica. (Although British Honduras and Panama share the isthmus, they are not considered part of the Central American family.)

In a day when scenically dramatic, historically interesting, recreationally exciting sites are eagerly sought and increasingly hard to find, Central America is a world that awaits discovery almost as completely as it did when Columbus anchored offshore in the sixteenth century.

Here a traveler will find ruins of one of the great civilizations of all time, the Mayan Old Empire, which left a legacy in sculptured stone of temples, palaces, ball courts, and observatories. For centuries these were hidden in the jungle.

The scenery is extraordinary, from the beaches to the craters

3

of 12,000-foot volcanoes. There are colorful villages and cities with exotic names: Masaya, Choluteca, Quezaltenango, Teguci-galpa. Indians dressed in hand-woven garments follow customs honored for centuries, and up in the highlands you can still hear the reed pipe and drum. Crafts are interesting and can be bought inexpensively at village markets. You can dig for your own pre-Columbian artifacts and, so far, finders are keepers. In the miles of wilderness there is hunting for game animals and birds. The fishing is excellent off both coasts. Bird-watching is exciting, and very little of it has been done by qualified people; a visitor can go off on botanical safaris, collect butterflies, seashells, stamps, coins, antique jewelry.

The first-class hotels and motels hold their own with any in the world. Less expensive hotels and pensions, which Lex de-scribes as "nothing fancy but real," are fun and often offer more local color. Everywhere the food is good, and you have your choice of American cooking, international menus, or adventures in local dishes. The climate—except in humid jungle areas—is delightful.

A young sociologist who spent a season in El Salvador follow-ing his graduation from Harvard said, "Today kids are looking for a simpler way of life. If they ever find out about Central America they'll jam the place. It's one of the few parts of the world they can visit on a very low budget."

One Canadian student we met was traveling with a knapsack and sleeping bag and having a beautiful trip on fifty cents a day.

The appeal of this world is not only to those who love un-tamed nature and primitive people. We talked to an advertising man whose firm had just finished a survey in the States to deter-mine the predilections of prosperous American travelers. It was found that the sophisticated ones have mined out the famous "tourist attractions"; now they want to be charmed and amazed; they seek unique experiences. Above all, the jaded traveler relishes surprises, and we can't think of anything more charac-teristic of Central America.

The element of surprise is expressed perfectly in the way you come upon a sudden, bright patio. The house you're visiting may be flush on the sidewalk and appear rather forbidding, with its thick wooden door and shuttered, grilled windows. But then the door swings open and you look through the immediate shadows to the patio, to the dazzling sunshine, the green, the blossoms, the birds, the sparkling fountain. It's like opening at Christmas a rather unprepossessing package that turns out to hold the loveliest present of all.

Or take the roosters. They are supposed to crow at daybreak, and in most of the world they do. But the roosters of Central America begin to crow at dusk—and they keep it up all night too, in an incessant yodeling that you soon learn to tune out. There seems to be a competition as to which can be the loudest and which can come in with a big cock-a-doodle when everybody else has given up. Just as the chorus seems to be mercifully exhausted, one rooster will seize its chance and raucously solo. This will bring on the competition all over again. During fiestas the roosters are joined by cathedral bells, howling dogs, and firecrackers.

Central American gestures are turn-abouts too. When a Central American looks as if he were imperiously beckoning, arm up high, he is actually waving good-by. When he means "Come here," however, a gringo might easily mistake the motion for "*adiós.*" And you won't get any bus to stop in Managua (Nicaragua) by holding up your hand like a cop. The driver will think you're trying to find out if there's any breeze. To get him to stop, make a patting motion in the air, palm down, exactly as if you mean, "Come sit by me here on the sofa." Nicaraguans have a way of asking a question with their noses, meanwhile making such a face that it looks as if they had just run over a skunk. If a Nicaraguan walks up to somebody's secretary and, while making a face, points his nose at the boss's office, it means, "Is he in?" The secretary can make another face, point her nose toward the exit, and answer, "He's out."

You never know when even a dull statue of a hero in a park may turn out to have an unexpected history. Once I was walking in Tegucigalpa (Honduras) with a friend who was born there. We were coming from the beautiful golden and pastel cathedral through the park and we paused before the statue of Francisco Morazán, the Honduran leader whose life was dedicated to the unity of Central American nations. A bronze plaque, under the figure on horseback, declared itself in memory of "The hero of Los Charcos, Espíritu Santo and San Pedro Perulapán."

"But we all know this is not Morazán," our friend said. "It may even be the Duke of Wellington."

Some years ago, she told me, a Honduran had been sent as an emissary to Paris to commission a monument to Morazán. The young man had never been to Paris; he lost his head, his heart, and his Honduran funds. It is thought that he probably bought the statue in the flea market. The magnitude of the hoax was not immediately appreciated; then some scholar noticed that the uniform was not in keeping with Morazán's period. Also Morazán had lost an ear in battle, and this statue showed no such injury.

Hondurans don't fret over the hoax. Newcomers are more vulnerable to surprises. Lex tells about a friend who was visiting him in San Salvador during the earthquake in 1963.

Larry Cecil had just arrived in Central America on a trouble-shooting mission for his firm's international division. That day he had driven from Guatemala City to San Salvador with Lex. After checking in at the Gran Hotel he had gone to bed. Lex had then driven home.

The first tremor occurred at about 4 A.M. Lex was awakened by the sound of a mirror shattering as it crashed to the floor near his bed. The motion, something like that of a boat on a sudden sea, was so lively that he could not get out of bed. He thought about Larry Cecil and resolved to reach him somehow—as soon as he could move.

Meantime he heard the confused sound of all the breakings and fallings and groanings and creakings in the city. And there was the gabbling of people who had managed to reach the streets.

"Like frightened chickens," Lex says.

By now there were no lights; the wiring had been severed. When the shaking stopped he groped for his clothes and his shoes. He later discovered that he had put on two right shoes.

Then the quaking started again. "You wonder if the world is coming to an end," he says.

A couple of blocks away Jimmy and Sonny Simpson, proprietors of a popular pension, the Casa Clark, weathered it out in their bedroom. Sonny screamed and fainted. Jimmy sat on the edge of their wide bed, which was going around the room like the wooden piece on a Ouija board. As the bed moved he paddled his feet, as if he were a tot on a Kiddie Kar.

Outside the Gran Hotel, the night watchman fell down on the sidewalk and noticed, as he gazed upward, that the buildings swayed and looked as if they were "knocking their heads together."

Larry Cecil, meantime, had been awakened in his room at the Gran Hotel by the ding-dong of the church bell, set in motion by the swaying of the bell tower. As the earthquake grew more intense the bell rang louder, describing the motion as it tolled.

He had a great struggle getting out of bed. Then he lurched toward the door, but it was jammed and he could not budge it. He was still pounding on it when he became aware that the motion had stopped and that Lex was calling him from somewhere outside. Larry put his head out the window. He could just make out Lex in the muddle of people on the street below.

"How you doing?" inquired Lex in what must have seemed a comically understated Missouri voice.

"Okay," Larry said. Then, to Lex's great delight, he added dolefully, "But no more surprises!"

There were surprises all over town though. At the Casa Clark there were three antique ceramic angels sitting on the top of a tall bookcase. While the earthquake toppled and smashed heavy pottery planters around the patio, the angels did not fall.

Fortunately a traveler is more likely to be involved with other kinds of Central American surprises, such as the changes that occur in the people and the scenery from one country to another. The dignified Guatemalan of direct Mayan descent, wearing the costume of his village, is not at all like the merry Nicaraguan in shirt sleeves, shaping a new society. The palm-thatched huts that stand on stilts by the sea in San Juan, Honduras, are as unlike the European, chalet-inspired wooden homes of Turrialba, Costa Rica, or the tile-roofed colonials of San Miguel, El Salvador.

Isthmians are insistently individual; from country to country they even like different kinds of beans. Costa Ricans eat little black beans, Nicaraguans prefer big black ones. Each country is proudly parochial and tends to look down on its neighbor as living in something less than paradise. The favorite put-down is that, unfortunately, one's neighbor is "lazy." The usual phrase is, "All they do is lie around in their *hamacas*." (Whereas the denouncer to hear him tell it, comes from a nation that looks on the siesta as a degrading colonial custom.)

You don't get bored with driving in Central America as you do on monotonous throughways at home, where you go rocketing through and machines take your quarters and your dimes and serve you a cup of coffee.

Down there crops grow close to the highway, a few feet from the wheels of your car. You learn to recognize coffee, sugar cane, rice, cotton, pineapple, bananas, African palm. The off-white plumes of ripened cane against a pure blue sky or flaming sunset seem almost phosphorescent. Sorghum is rusty; rice is spears of Killarney green. In all seasons there is a profusion and variety of blossoming trees and vines. This is especially miraculous during the dry season. Trees that incongruously burst into blossom at that time burn in the dusk; their yellows and oranges and pinks and blues and reds are more vivid when the sun, which dazzles out color, is gone. Even when they are not blossoming they are beautiful, as graceful as Japanese bonsai. Their black limbs are sooty and strike beautiful attitudes as if individual artists had finished and said, "There."

South on the Inter-American Highway from San Salvador, El Salvador, just short of kilometer 84, to your right in a wide empty field is a tall, silvery fountain, its height fluctuating slightly. This is a very dramatic geyser and the only one we have seen in Central America.

Human life, too, comes up close to the highway. Near your car there are children playing, meals cooking, bells ringing, roosters crowing, cattle mooing, horses smartly clopping, women doing the wash, volcanoes smoking. Once we paused in a village where everybody wore an odd headdress, one I took to be a quaint localism; a scarf was looped under the chin and tied at the top of the head. Then one of the children thus attired explained to me that they all had the mumps.

On every journey there are unforgettable vignettes. We saw a bride walking along with her wedding procession; a white goat with gamboling triplets; an Indian using a big leaf for an umbrella in the rain. During a fiesta we passed a religious procession —a statue of the Virgin was being carried, followed by serenading guitar, drums, and flute. We saw a nun near an earth-colored bell tower that was etched against the brightness of a morning sky. She wore a white habit, a black veil, and a blue apron, and three small barefooted boys were looking up into her smile. We noticed children selling big yellow birds in homemade wicker cages at a Sunday market under a tree. And one day there was a party under a crude palm-thatched shelter; two women were swinging a bright paper toy, a *piñata* filled with candy, while a blindfolded child tried to hit it with a stick; when he did, it burst open and the candy spilled out for him and his cavorting friends. Once we saw a proud-looking woman in a red dress and a green kerchief carrying a blue parasol and riding a Tennessee walking horse into mountains that were the color of terra cotta.

Every single trip that we have taken over long-familiar roads has been different. There was the afternoon when, halfway up a mountain, we saw a rainbow arch right down into the valley below us and mingle its shimmering prisms with the translucent green of the rice. And the evening we came upon the little harbor of San Juan del Sur in Nicaragua, at a magic moment between sunset and starlight. The dusk was deepening as we got out of the car and stood for a moment on the crescent beach. There was just enough light to make the water a faint robin's-egg blue, to silhouette the shrimp boats gently jouncing offshore. But in the sky, directly overhead, was a bright three-quarter moon, and crowding impatiently behind it were stars, exactly as if the moon were leading them into the night on the heels of the sunset.

Because there is a great deal of unbroken wilderness, one's

first glimpse of a capital city is more thrilling than in parts of the world where the endless megalopolis, a glacier of cement and glass, has covered the last empty meadow and wooded hill. The five Central American capitals are all secluded in valleys, surrounded by giant volcanoes or mountains. At night their lights have the brilliance and intensity of jewels. The miles of night around them are challenged only by the early-extinguished candles or dim lamps of farm families.

Soon, the area of lights will widen everywhere, sparkling beyond the present edges of cities. And as the countries are "developed" there will be a more sophisticated courting of tourism than there is now.

Today there are still the old and the new. In certain ancient cities in Nicaragua—Masaya, Granada, and Chinandega—horse-drawn black *coches* with red wheels still serve as taxis on cobbled streets, and there has been no altering of the colonial character of the buildings. In other cities, such as San Pedro Sula, in Honduras, you can feel a tide coming in. San Pedro Sula is beginning to be a boom town.

Since the original brilliant Central Americans, the Mayas, sank back into mediocrity ages ago, there has been no momentous creativity in the land. But there are now signs of a renaissance in art and science, appropriate to volcano country, where a long-quiescent mountain may become vigorously *activo*.

With every journey we have found that the land and the people have taken a closer hold on our affections, becoming at once more familiar and more remarkable. We envy prospective visitors their upcoming adventures on a calendar whose pages have not yet been flipped into yesterday.

2 / Border Crossers' Briefing

Central America is ridiculously easy to reach. You can fly in, drive your own car, travel by bus, or take a tramp steamer or banana boat to one of the numerous Atlantic or Pacific coast ports. Once there, you can rent a car, use the local bus lines, or fly from capital to capital.

BY COMMERCIAL AIRLINER

A non-stop jet flight from "gateway" cities in the United States —Miami, New Orleans, or Houston—to any of the five capitals takes about two and a half hours and currently costs $152 round trip. Pan American now has a non-stop flight from Kennedy Airport to Guatemala City; there will be more direct flights soon to Isthmian capitals.

If you are flying with a guided tour, which is best arranged through a travel agent, thirteen days to two and a half weeks is usually allowed to cover the high spots of Central America. Should you prefer to arrange your own journeys from capital to capital, flying time between the major cities is twenty minutes to half an hour and costs about $32.

Flying in is an exciting and geographically orienting experience. You will be aware of how close together the Atlantic and Pacific Oceans are, of the narrowness of the land that separates them. You will see the miles of tumultuous green below, its convolutions expressed in glowing light and deep blue shadow; no sign of civilization except one thread of a road, as the Inter-American Highway appears from the sky, crazily twisting as if it had been poked about by a restless child. You see islands, the hundreds of green *isletas* in Lake Nicaragua, Nicaragua, or those rising in the Gulf of Fonseca off the El Salvador-Honduras border on the Pacific coast. You can see some of the thousands of crater lakes, blue-green gems in wilderness settings. And there are wide rivers shining; you notice different shades of blue and green and rich mud-tones, swirling and mixing as on a painter's palette. From up high you get the feeling of the extent of the undeveloped areas, and you are introduced to heart-stabbing surprises, such as mountain peaks jutting up above the clouds outside your plane window. You look deep into the craters of volcanoes. You may see a rainbow, plain as a striped ribbon, lying flat on the cirrus cloud ceiling below.

BY PRIVATE PLANE

The isthmus is comfortable territory for the small-plane flier, despite the mountains and the sometimes uncertain weather; every *finca* (large farm) has its own landing strip, which can be used if the going becomes difficult.

The Flight Department of the Aircraft Owners and Pilots Association reports a dramatic increase in flights to the isthmus. Many privately owned planes bound for South America use Central American airports as way stations.

The AOPA (P.O. Box 5800, Washington, D.C., 20014) provides its members with reliable charts and routes, information about weather, landing charges, local aero clubs, the latest State Department recommendations, changes in regulations, and so forth. The association will even forward the necessary advance notice of a member's arrival to the proper authorities in each country. (It provides the necessary forms which the pilot fills out and returns to AOPA.) Before a member leaves, he is sent an International Flight kit with copies of his official papers and all pertinent data.

(See Part II for how to obtain permission to land in each country.)

BY CAR

If you drive from the States, you must first pass through Mexico from the Texas border, allowing four to five days for a comfortably paced trip. Or you may ship your car from Miami to Puerto Matías de Gálvez, Guatemala, via Coordinate Caribbean Transport, Inc. Sailings are now on Fridays. The charge is $115 for a car weighing less than 3350 pounds, $165 for one weighing more. For information or reservations, write P.O. Box 631, Miami, Florida, 33101.

At one time the C.C.T. transported passengers as well, but you must now fly to Guatemala and pick up your car at the port, using papers furnished you by the C.C.T. to establish your ownership.

It is possible, but very expensive, to ship a car to Central American ports from major east or west coast ports in the United States. (From New York, N.Y., to Puntarenas, Costa Rica, shipping a small compact car costs about $400 and takes approximately ten days.) Except for the C.C.T. service, you must work through a forwarding agent to arrange for shipment by freighter. Certain vessels, such as "banana boats" operated by the United Fruit Company, still carry passengers as well as their cars.

Insurance

Maritime insurance for car shipment is reasonable; it can be purchased in the United States; so can a "floater" policy to cover expensive personal goods during travels by plane, car, ship, or bus in Central America.

It is possible to purchase an automobile insurance policy for isthmian travels through a broker in the United States. American companies work through foreign subsidiaries. However, you must buy a year's policy, refundable after a minimum of 73 days in Central America. On an annual basis the costs are: $108 for $300,000 liability, $87 for comprehensive insurance (fire, theft, etc.), and $118 for collision. Fifty-five per cent will be refunded if you return to the United States within six months.

It is cheaper to buy automobile insurance at the Mexico-Guatemala border (contact Compañía de Seguros Generales, Tapachula). A $50-deductible policy of $26,000 costs from $16.58 for five days to $47.77 for fifteen days, and will cover you from Guatemala through Panama. You can also buy insurance in the capitals and major cities of individual Central American countries.

Border officials do *not* require a tourist to show evidence of insurance. Incredible as this may seem to residents of the United States, many Americans living in Central America are not covered by car insurance. They simply take the calculated risks (not that we recommend it).

Road Conditions, Maps, Traffic Signs

For the entire length of the isthmus the Inter-American Highway, coastal routes, and most of the side roads to beaches, mountains, and lake resorts are in first-rate condition. You drive on the right-hand side of the road, as in the United States.

Pueblo (small village) streets are usually dirt-surfaced or paved with ancient cobblestones. Driving through a tiny village in El Salvador on one of our early excursions, Lex said seriously, "Do you know that Santo Tomás is the only pueblo in Central America where all the streets are paved?" After a slight pause he added that the only street in town was the Litural, down which we were hurtling.

Though roads are generally in good shape, it is best to proceed at a moderate speed because of the frequent crossing of cattle, horses, dogs, pigs, and chickens; always slow down if you see men on horseback driving a herd along the roadside. The impulsive peregrinations of livestock are why you should not, unless it cannot possibly be avoided, travel after dark. Also, buses and trucks may break down and be abandoned without flares. In the mountains there is often fog, and during the rainy season washouts and landslides may occur.

If you are traveling from capital to capital, allow six to eight hours—a day's drive. It is hard to get lost between capitals, for there are relatively few alternate routes.

However, it is important to carry good maps for side trips. Excellent isthmian road maps are available in the United States through the American Automobile Association, and fine maps are also distributed free by the major international oil companies, such as Texaco and Shell.

A paperback, *Mexico and Central America,* is published by the American Automobile Association. Its detailed maps include sites and names of volcanoes that can be seen from the highways; it offers complete information for touring in this area. We consider it a must for the newcomer.

The most familiar guideposts along the major routes throughout Central America are the short white kilometer posts, successively marking each kilometer from the capital city of any country to its border. (If you have passed kilometer 15 and the next post reads kilometer 14, you know you are getting closer!) All distances in Central America are measured in kilometers. To convert kilometers into miles, multiply by six-tenths. Thus 30 kilometers equals approximately 18 miles.

Among the familiar road signs are DESPACIO (slow), ALTO (stop), and PELIGRO (dangerous). We advise carrying a Spanish-English dictionary which should be handy at all times, not only for reading signs but for asking information in small towns along the highway where English is not spoken. Often a single word, uttered with a rising inflection, will serve as a question: *"Mecánico?"* (mechanic), *"La carretera?"* (highway), etc.

Modern service stations can be found at convenient intervals on the highways. Gas costs approximately 50 cents a gallon. Service stations have toilets (*servicios*); some approach the usual

American standards of cleanliness, but many do not. Soap, paper towels, and toilet paper are frequently missing. Best to carry them along. Cold Cokes and bottled "pop" of all flavors can generally be bought at service stations.

Mechanics are numerous, able, and cheap. In every pueblo you will find a *mecánico;* his workshop may also be his home, little more than a roof over an earth floor, with his wife cooking in the corner and a child asleep in a hammock, but he will know how to get your car back on the road. *Mecánicos* are scarce on Sunday, however. Then it is difficult to find one on the job, even in a city.

The average Central American driver is a competent mechanic. Having grown up in a place where formerly garages were few and far between, he learned to be self-sufficient. He will usually cheerfully stop and help you if you are in trouble on the highway. It doesn't matter if your Spanish isn't fluent; he and your car speak the same language.

Restaurants, Motels, Hotels, Trailer Parks

Excellent restaurants can be found along Central America's highways. However, we suggest carrying a Thermos, sandwiches, and fruit for a day's drive, and picnicking along the way. Resident Americans who constantly travel by car know exactly where to go for good and trustworthy food; they time their trips so that the lunch hour will find them parking outside a favorite restaurant. The newcomer is apt to be inaccurate in his time and to become madly hungry at the wrong kilometer, with an hour or two to go before he reaches a restaurant. (For specific suggestions as to where to eat in each area, see Part II.)

Attractive motels, many with swimming pools and air-conditioning, are available in all sections, and their numbers are increasing. (For present accommodations in each country, see Part II.) Mistrust hotels except in the capitals, the larger cities, and the resorts. They can be dishearteningly old-fashioned and run down, with swaybacked bedsprings and thin, lumpy mattresses. One such hotel, where we stopped in an emergency several years ago, had no electric lights; the short remains of a candle were placed on a rickety bedside table.

First-class hotels in the capitals and major cities of the isthmus can be equated with those anywhere in the world. The rooms are attractive, comfortable, and always air-conditioned in climates where air-conditioning is necessary. (San Pedro Sula, Honduras, and Managua, Nicaragua, for example.) The average cost of a room is from $8 to $10 single, $12 to $14 double. You can use electric toothbrushes, razors, traveling irons in any country but Honduras (and this may change tomorrow). All hotels have laundry and dry-cleaning services. However, any drip-dry clothes you wash will be ready to wear in the morning.

Pensions are much cheaper, ranging from $3 to $5 single and from $5 to $8 double, with three meals a day as well as bed in the bargain. Usually you share a bathroom with a small complex of tenants and there is no tub, only a shower. Often the shower is cold.

Trailer parks are just beginning to be developed on the isthmus. The ones that now exist are ill equipped as a rule, affording parking space with a marvelous view, perhaps, but little more. We advise against hauling a trailer for other reasons; regulations for the entry of trailers vary from country to country. But Central America is changing fast, and this may not be true tomorrow. For up-to-the-minute information about facilities for trailers, write to the tourist bureaus of the countries you plan to visit.

Border Crossings

It is important to arrive at border stations of Central American countries during normal working hours in order to avoid overtime charges. You can pass through border stations without charge daily from 8 A.M. to 12 noon and from 2 P.M. to 6 P.M. The exception is Costa Rica, where hours terminate at 5 P.M. and at 12 noon on Saturdays. At every border you will be checked by immigration, customs, and police officials. This normally takes from ten to twenty minutes, depending on the traffic.

NECESSARY DOCUMENTS

Whether you drive in, fly in, or arrive by ship, you cannot get past customs officials without certain documents. Your passport when shown must be stamped with a visa (or official permission to be admitted), obtainable at the nation's consulates in another country. The average tourist visa is good for thirty days and for only one entry, but you can request a multiple-entry visa if you contemplate crossing and recrossing at a particular border; you can even request a visa that will permit multiple entries for two years. This will not be offered unless you ask for it, but since most tourists plan to visit any given country for a short time only, the most flexible visas are not of general interest. Since the usual thirty-day visa is good for only one entry, you must arrange to have a new visa stamped in your passport if you leave and later return.

Central American consulates in the United States are located in key cities, in those from which flights to the isthmus originate (Miami, Houston, New Orleans), and in those next to border crossings to Mexico. You can also have your passport visaed for Central American countries in Mexican cities and, as a last resort, at Tapachula or Ciudad Cuauhtémoc, Mexico, where border stations to Guatemala are located. Each of the five Central American republics has a consulate in the capital cities of her sister republics—if you are in Guatemala and decide to go to El Salvador, you can have your visa stamped by the Salvadoran consulate in Guatemala City.

The alternative is a tourist card, available at any Central American consulate for $2.

You are required to carry a smallpox vaccination certificate; this internationally familiar yellow card must be signed by the doctor who vaccinated you, then stamped by your nearest Board of Health office. This card is not a must at isthmian border stations, but you cannot re-enter the United States without one.

If touring by car, a driver must show his operator's license and his car registration. At each border station in Central America he will be provided with a temporary permit; he must carry this form with him at all times; it is the equivalent of a registration license for the country he is visiting.

CUSTOMS

Each country's regulations as to what can be imported vary slightly. We therefore advise against bringing pets along. In Costa Rica, for instance, a dog in a car will not be admitted.

In general, your luggage is given a once-over-lightly inspection, and there are liberal allowances for personal possessions, such as camera and films, tape recorder, typewriter, musical instruments, and sports equipment (except for firearms, for which some countries require a special permit).

CONVERTING DOLLARS INTO LOCAL CURRENCIES

Each of the Central American republics has a different currency: as you travel through the isthmus you will be spending Guatemalan *quetzales,* Salvadoran *colones,* Honduran *lempiras,* Nicaraguan *córdobas,* and Costa Rican *colones.*

In each country you must learn to cope with the local currency. There is no bank at border stations to convert dollars into local currency; you can buy it from vendors along the sidewalks, who wave large wads of bills at you, but this is not advisable. You are likely to be too tired for quick computing, dazzled by the strangeness, and unable to judge how ruthlessly the vendor may be taking advantage of your all-too-obvious innocence.

Handily, an American dollar bill is acceptable anywhere in Central America, no matter how small the community, so, until you reach your destination, dollars will serve. For change you will receive local currency. (To convert local currency into dollars, or dollars into local currency, see under Driving Through section for each country in Part II.)

For a trip of two to six weeks, we advise carrying a backlog of from $50 to $100 in dollar bills, and a pad and pencil with which to do quick arithmetic so that you will know how much is being charged and what change you should be receiving.

Traveler's checks can be cashed at any hotel, motel, restaurant, or shop in the big cities; internationally established credit cards are honored at hotels, first-class restaurants, travel agencies, and airlines offices.

It is impossible to cash personal checks in Central American banks.

BY SHIP

A very pleasant and inexpensive way to see high spots of Central America is to take a cruise on a banana boat or a freighter that calls at east and west coast ports. Passenger accommodations are limited; there may be as few as six double staterooms. You live aboard ship, never need a hotel. You may disembark in ports and fly to sites inland that are interesting scenically or historically. The meals aboard are excellent; you eat with the ship's officers. The chief steward is bartender.

For a sampling of rates, a 12-day cruise from New York to Honduran ports through the Caribbean costs $360 for a single cabin, $325 per person when sharing a double cabin. An 18-day cruise from New Orleans to Honduras, Costa Rica, and Panama costs from $475 for space in a double cabin, to $530 for a single cabin.

Many lines that offer "tramp trips" call at Central American ports. Your travel agent can offer you a wide choice of cruises.

BY BUS

Buses crisscross Central America. Spacious modern buses, such as those of the Tico Line, are preferable for capital-to-capital junkets. But the little local buses are more fun. Each bus has its own jaunty personality; its windows may have flowered curtains, the steering wheel may be decorated with braided plastic of all colors, and diverting hand-lettered graffiti can be read wherever there is wall space. Invariably the backs of these stubby buses bear the injunction *Guarda su distancia* (keep your distance), but other, less businesslike remarks from the bus to the public can be found on the rear. We recently followed one where "Tarzan's mother wears panties" was the most conspicuous legend.

The driver is always accompanied by another driver who not only collects the fares but treats each customer in a courtly manner. As you board the bus he eagerly seizes your luggage or your bundles and stows them away; if you are a woman he takes your arm and boosts you aboard. If there isn't a seat he gives up his own and rides on the back step. It is his special job to sing out the destination of the bus at every stop, and he really socks it out, "Managua, Managua, Managua." Sometimes, when the name of the next town on the route is too long, he gets a swingier effect by calling out its nickname, "Chichi, Chichi, Chichi" for Chichicastenango or "Guate, Guate, Guate" for Guatemala City. Sometimes, by announcing the names of two towns at once, he can get a birdlike effect, "CholuTEC, CholuTEC, Teguc, Teguc, Teguc" (Choluteca, Tegucigalpa).

A Central American bus *never* says no to a passenger and therefore can get terribly jam-packed. In desperation a skinny young Indian in his twenties once sat on my lap. Everybody took a deep breath, moved over, and made space for him on the edge of the seat.

A bus ride can be quite exciting, as a farmer from Tennessee, who was prospecting for land, recently discovered. The driver spotted some wild turkeys on the highway ahead. He braked the bus, shouted out the glad tidings, and all aboard with guns— which are carried as casually as gringos carry fountain pens— piled out and banged away.

TRAINS

Many of the trains that travel from the ports to the interior through the hinterlands of Central America are incredibly antique, often drawn by ancient chuffing steam engines discarded a half-century or more ago in other countries. Railroad buffs might not be able to tear themselves away from this living museum of ancient coaches and locomotives. There is a trip by train that should not be missed, however, railroad buff or no. (See Part II, p. 265.)

TAXIS

These are always available in Central American cities, cruising constantly down the main streets; it's a buyer's market—most of the cabs are empty. The charges are relatively reasonable; for instance, you can take a cab anywhere within the city limits of San José, Costa Rica, for the equivalent of forty cents. Taxis can be hired for sightseeing trips around the cities; ask your hotel manager for the going rates. Confer with your cab driver *in advance of the trip* to find out what he plans to charge; then make a deal. Most cab drivers speak English. They know their way around and are generally entertaining and informative guides.

ON FOOT

You can't help missing a lot when you travel around a city in a car; you may catch a fleeting, tantalizing glimpse of a beguiling scene—a child walking along with a pet parrot on his arm, a woman weaving under a tree, bright flowers behind an iron grille—but you are helplessly caught in the flow of traffic and cannot back up. Walking is a treat. You can really soak up the atmosphere. We suggest planning at least one walking tour of an interesting section of each city you visit. The tourist bureau will give you a map of the city, tell you the interesting high spots, chart the streets to follow, and indicate a good restaurant to wind up at for lunch.

CAR RENTALS

All Central American capital cities have at least one car-rental agency. Sometimes it's fun to take a day's side trip at your own pace. A sample of prices: from an agency in Tegucigalpa, Honduras, with a wide range of cars for rental, a VW sedan costs $7.50 per day, a Mercedes-Benz $11. You get a discount for longer rentals: 10 per cent for seven days, 15 per cent for twenty, 25 per cent for thirty. Rates include insurance coverage, maintenance, and repairs. They will ask to see your passport and driver's license.

GUIDED TOURS

Especially for a woman traveling alone, a tour may be the best introduction to Central America. Pan Am has been very active in developing air tours with isthmian travel agents. Contact Pan Am for currently available packages. The over-all price of a tour usually includes overnight stays in luxury hotels, sightseeing trips, transportation to and from airports, and handling luggage. Sample, based on current prices: an eleven-day air tour originating in San Francisco and covering the high spots of Guatemala and El Salvador costs $662.

Up to now, tours have tended to concentrate on archaeological ruins, especially those at Tikal, Guatemala, and Copán, Honduras. But there are new tours each season, increasingly designed to appeal to general as well as special interests. If your travel agent doesn't know about the variety of current Central American tours, then he hasn't been doing his homework.

WHAT TO WEAR

Don't be misled by the image of "the tropics" as steaming jungles and fail to bring a sweater, a raincoat, and a spring suit. Guatemala City, San José, and Tegucigalpa can be downright chilly on occasion, and even San Salvador and Managua, the capitals with the tropical reputation, can be cool and windy in altitudes above the city.

Central American dress is simple, informal—but never gaudy. That's for parrots. Except in their own patios, women seldom wear slacks, and shorts practically never. Conservative as they are, the smart city women do not wear hats (to church, or any-where else) or gloves. Their hair-dos are the daily pièce de résistance. Make-up is subdued. Heels are high.

A North American woman should plan to bring along exactly the same simple, "versatile" wardrobe that she would take to Europe: a sleeveless dress with a jacket that can be dressed "up" or "down," according to the occasion and the time of day, and drip-dry traveling things, a sweater, and a raincoat.

No need to worry about running short of stockings, under-wear, or shoes; you can buy these anywhere. Attractive store-bought dresses are hard to find, except in Guatemala City or San José. They are imported from Europe and the United States and cost from a quarter to a half more than they would in the United States. For decades Central American women have had their dresses made by local seamstresses; they point to a picture in a fashion magazine and say, "Make me this," and the genie makes it.

Men wear jackets and ties in first-class restaurants and hotels after sundown; before that they can go anywhere in a shirt and slacks. A man can have much more fun than a woman shopping for clothes in Central America; the men's stores are smashing, with well-designed slacks and shirts that never fail to intrigue visitors. And they are very cheap compared to stateside prices.

Mayan temple-pyramid, Tikal, Guatemala (Ramón Osuna)

Giant Mayan stone head, Copán, Honduras (Ramón Osuna)

Grand staircase, Copán, Honduras (Ramón Osuna)

Mayan stela, Copán, Honduras (Ramón Osuna)

Religious procession, Guatemala (Ramón Osuna)

*Pagan rites performed on steps of the church of the Indians at Chichi-
castenango, Guatemala* (Ramón Osuna)

Indians performing rites, Chichicastenango, Guatemala (Ramón Osuna)

Market inside ruined building, Antigua, Guatemala (Ramón Osuna)

Colonial arcade, Antigua, Guatemala (Ramón Osuna)

View of main square, Guatemala City (Ramón Osuna)

Poas volcano, Alajuela, Costa Rica (Instituto Costarricense de Turismo)

Monument to the poet Rubén Darío, Managua, Nicaragua (Ramón Osuna)

Colonial church, León, Nicaragua (Ramón Osuna)

View of main square, Tegucigalpa, Honduras (Ramón Osuna)

High altar of the cathedral, Tegucigalpa, Honduras (Ramón Osuna)

Market day, San Salvador (Ramón Osuna)

Coffee plantation, El Salvador (Ramón Osuna)

Oxen in a canefield, El Salvador (Ramón Osuna)

View of Lake Atitlán, Guatemala (Ramón Osuna)

View of modern amphitheater, Guatemala City (Ramón Osuna)

Courtyard seen through Moorish archway, Antigua, Guatemala (Ramón Osuna)

Hotel El Salvador Inter-Continental, San Salvador (Ramón Osuna)

TIPS

Small tips are the custom in Central America. To tip 10 per cent of the bill is considered madly generous; waiters, bartenders, and the like usually receive less. Samples: tip a bellhop the equivalent of a dime or fifteen cents per suitcase; give a hotel maid the equivalent of twenty-five cents a day, or less, regardless of the quality of her service; tip barbers, beauticians, and shoeshine boys one-third to one-half less than you would in the United States. Hotel maids are frequently not tipped at all; taxi drivers are lucky to get the equivalent of an America quarter for a $5 ride.

This must be said: no matter how bravely, no matter how warmly or merrily they smile, Central Americans in menial positions are far more pinched for funds than most North Americans can realize. They may work in an elegant hotel but they probably live in a shack with a cardboard roof and a dirt floor.

The argument against over-average generous tipping is that the tipees will be spoiled for future tourists, not to mention the local trade. It is also believed that by fulsome tipping a North American will reinforce the international image of the Rich American who isn't simply being generous; he's just spilling over. Tippers, consult your consciences. Knowing what the dismal norm is, feel perfectly free to tip as you choose.

MAIL

Allow five days to a week for a letter to reach Central America from the United States. (The usual elapsed time is four days, but this is not *always* the case.)

If you have an itinerary, mail can be sent to you at hotels and pensions, marked "Please Hold." If not, better have your mail sent care of the American Embassy in the capital cities. General delivery is not a good bet. A gringo, one with a middle name particularly, is apt to lose his mail for this reason: a Central American's middle name is actually his *last* name (his father's name), whereas his last name (his mother's) is his middle name. Thus Juan García Solano is "Señor García," and he is usually listed in telephone directories as Juan García S. If *your* name is Susan Brown Wells, your mail is likely to wind up under "B" for Brown in the post office, and if you inquire for mail for Susan Wells you may be disappointed.

The "wish-you-were-here" crowd at home, especially stamp collectors, will enjoy your postcards and letters all the more for the extraordinarily beautiful stamps of Central America. Hotels and pensions will stamp your mail accurately; if you elect to visit the local post office, go to the air-mail window; the clerk will weigh your letter and sell you stamps. Mail clerks will not moisten and attach the stamps; you must do this yourself. (Better not lick stamps out of respect for unfamiliar germs; use the wet sponge that is always available at a nearby table.)

HEALTH PRECAUTIONS

Well in advance of the trip, ask your doctor what shots he considers necessary protection for south of the border. He may recommend a typhoid series, a tetanus-toxoid booster shot. Ask him to prescribe medicines for diarrhea (the traveler's blight the world over) and for the prevention of amoebic dysentery. Take these pills along. You can buy aspirin (there the product is known as *mejoral*) anywhere in Central America. Isthmian drugstores do not require doctor's prescriptions to sell you drugs (as of now), although they are beginning to turn down requests for sleeping pills or barbiturates. However, without a prescription, you may buy tranquilizers such as Librium or Miltown, and all of the powerful antibiotics.

If you need medical care, better head for a capital or major city, where the doctors are generally excellent; many of them have gone to medical school in the United States and speak English. Medicine in smaller communities is often practiced by medical amateurs. An American we know was once sewn up, after an accident, by a farmer with veterinary skills. In a small town in El Salvador, we met a young pharmacist who owned a drugstore. He was known locally as "the little doctor," being the only person in that city who could ably bandage a wound, give an antibiotic shot, prescribe for whatever the complaint.

By taking reasonable precautions during travels, you can reduce to a minimum the possibility of needing a doctor.

Do not drink water or use ice cubes except in the capital or major cities; do not order salads (although peeled tomatoes are okay). Don't buy refreshments sold hot or cold on highway or city streets. Eschew raw seafood, such as clams and oysters; they may be safe in the top restaurants but it is better to stay with cooked food of all kinds. And don't push yourself in unfamiliar altitudes (such as rushing up the side of an 11,000-foot volcano).

An over-finicky attitude can spoil your trip, however. We have spent years in Central America and have never been ill despite taking chances by eating salads and raw seafood, drinking tapwater, and using ice cubes. We took risks, however, and we cannot recommend such recklessness to others.

SAFEKEEPING OF POSSESSIONS

Robbery is a hazard in Central America as it is in the United States; it is perhaps more difficult to anticipate and forfend because the setting is unfamiliar.

You can leave your belongings in a hotel, motel, or pension without anxiety; to leave them in an unwatched car is dangerous. If you park during a movie, a small boy is sure to materialize and offer to watch your car. He will watch it faithfully. The custom is to reward him with the equivalent of an American dime or quarter; he has no "rates"; he will accept any small change.

In the event of a robbery, you can report it to the police but it will get you nowhere. Stolen goods are seldom recovered.

AFTER DARK

Movies are plentiful in Central American cities and towns; most of them are made in the United States, so English is spoken, with occasional dialogue flashed on the screen in Spanish. The better hotels have installed TV sets in the rooms, but the programs are pretty dreary, running to heavy dramas emoted in Spanish. (This situation is sure to improve.)

There is a national theater or cultural center in each capital where concerts, ballets, and plays are scheduled throughout the year. To add to fine performances by national companies, artists from South America, Mexico, and the United States are increasingly being scheduled. Folk dance and song groups, usually composed of amateurs who do an exciting job, are of special interest.

Concerts of pre-Columbian music, where primitive Indian instruments are played, are fascinating.

Today every Central American nation has a cultural director, heading up a staff of specialists in the arts. They arrange for, and schedule, concerts and exhibits. Often an exchange is involved: Central Americans will swap a collection of precious pre-Columbian art for a special exhibit from the great museums of the world. The presence of a national university in each of the capital cities adds to their cultural resources.

Consult the government tourist bureau for current events in music, painting, sculpture, drama, and ballet.

(For night clubs, see Part II.)

READING

This is very scarce. For the length of the isthmus, the *Miami Herald* is the only newspaper available in English, and there are few paperbacks in English in the bookshops. However, you can find the *New York Times*, current American magazines, and a well-stocked library of books in Cultural Exchange reading rooms in the capitals. These are downtown and easily reached in each city. They are operated by the United States Information Service in cooperation with Central American governments.

MEETING PEOPLE

A great joy in Central America is meeting the people. They are cheerful and friendly. The best way to get acquainted with nationals other than clerks, waiters, or garage attendants is to have a project, pursue a hobby or professional interest; this will put you in touch with congenial counterparts. Most golf clubs will give guest cards to visitors; the membership is international. Ask your hotel manager to arrange this for you, or tell you how to apply.

There is an American Society in each capital with regularly scheduled events, dances, lunches, outings. A directory of the American Society, with addresses and telephone numbers of members, is available at some hotels. It can also be found at the American Embassy and at the Cultural Exchange library.

Each capital has a Peace Corps (Cuerpo de Paz) office to which volunteers report. Peace Corps volunteers are delighted to show visitors around the villages which are their "sites." Ask the regional office where you can visit an outpost within driving distance.

In each capital there are churches of many denominations where services are usually conducted in English. Church organizations, as at home, sponsor get-togethers aimed at good fellowship (suppers, picnics, discussion groups, and the like), and visitors are welcome.

If you do visit a Peace Corps volunteer or an American missionary through your church, be sure to bring food along. They are usually short of rations. A missionary once told us, "We are glad to have company, but they usually don't realize how hard up we are—and finding enough food to go around is a problem."

EMERGENCIES

Your hotel manager should prove a good trouble-shooter, the government-operated tourist bureaus in the capitals are obliging and concerned, and the staff of the American Embassy is familiar with local resources and can advise you in an hour of need.

INFORMATION

For detailed maps of each nation, up-to-date information on sports events, concerts, exhibits, and other current happenings, contact the government tourist bureau in each capital.

Guatemala: Instituto Guatemalteco de Turismo, Guatemala City.

El Salvador: National Tourist Board, San Salvador.

Hondurus: Oficina de Turismo, Tegucigalpa.

Nicaragua: Junta Nacional de Turismo, Managua.

Costa Rica: Instituto Costarricense de Turismo, San José.

3 / Three Miles, Three Seasons

CLIMATE

Central America is interesting geographically because of the variety of its terrain within relatively little space. El Salvador is approximately the size of Maryland, Honduras can be compared to Ohio and Guatemala to Tennessee. Altitudes range from sea level to over 11,000 feet.

In each of the five republics you will find four climates at any time of the year. They are: tropical summer at sea level; temperate summer at 2000 feet; spring at 4000 feet; and fall above 6000.

You can experience a dramatic difference in the 36 miles between the city of Cartago (Costa Rica), which has an early summer climate, and the mountain pass south on the Inter-American Highway, at Cerro de la Muerte, 11,152 feet above sea level, where the climate is like that of late fall in New England. You will roll up the car windows, turn on the heater, and wonder why this part of the world is known as "the tropics."

There are fireplaces in many mountain and lake resorts. At

Antigua and on the shores of Lake Atitlán in Guatemala, pitch-pine fires are lit in the morning and late afternoon.

Even a small area has its own climatic characteristics, depending upon whether it is in a wind corridor or close to the water, in the woods or mountain meadow or rain forest. Sometimes a few steps can make a big difference, as when moving from the sunny to the shady side of a street, or from a sheltered place into the path of the wind.

However, usually only two seasons are attributed to Central America, the dry season (roughly, from November-December to April-May) and the rainy season (April-May through November-December). Actually the rainy season is not the constant dreary deluge that foreigners suppose. The pattern is rain for only a few hours a day, usually at the same time in the late afternoon. It is a roaring tropical rain, not like the desultory pitter-patter or the steady, moderate downpour in other parts of the world.

Of course it rains throughout the year in the jungles and lowlands. While the average annual rainfall for Costa Rica is 100 inches, much of this falls in the tropical sections. In Honduras the average rainfall in the Atlantic watershed is 100 inches a year, while in the mountainous capital, Tegucigalpa, the annual average is 33 inches. On the Miskito Coast of Nicaragua the average is from 100 to 250 inches because of the easterly trade winds from the Caribbean. In the west, however, the average is 45 inches.

There is an advantage to seeing Central America during the rainy season; the green becomes so intense that it seems to reach a point of bursting into green flame like the tongues of fire that flicker over driftwood logs. This is the growing season for the crops and therefore the vital one to the Central American economy, for exports are still 70 per cent agricultural. When the rainy season begins, it has a heart-lifting effect upon the people, the sort of elation, the same sense of life and urgency, that North Americans associate with spring. The important crops that depend upon the coming of the rains are coffee, sugar cane, cotton, and rice. (Those that grow in the tropical lowlands—bananas, cacao, African palm—are always saturated.)

Each country has a legend about the coming of the rains. Everywhere they wait for the crickets to stop singing. The great hush will then be filled with the sound of pouring rain. In El Salvador the *guace* birds announce both the beginning and the end of the rainy season.

Shortly after the rains come and shortly after they end, when the earth is not too soggy, is the best time to dig for pre-Columbian ceramics. When the earth is dry and brick-hard, there is a far greater risk of shattering the ancient and beautiful pottery.

The chief disadvantage of the rainy season is that some roads become impassable with washouts and landslides. But most tourists and business people stay with the main or "all-weather" roads, which are kept in good shape.

The dry season is usually better for travel, and there is, of course, much to recommend it. Midwinter to early spring is the height of the dry season, and it is the gay time of the year for Central Americans, who flock to resorts. The holiday spirit builds up to a climax during Holy Week, shortly before the onset of the rainy season after Easter.

However, the unrelieved beaming of the sun can become tiresome; green fades from the land, which turns a sort of terra cotta, and the dust blows, and the wind blusters. Foraging animals grow scrawny, and buzzards circle in the dazzling sun. The dust makes vividly colorful sunrises and sunsets, though. And the trees and the shrubs and flowers do not stop their incessant blossoming. In Central America, deciduous trees seem to be of many minds about when to drop their leaves and when to put forth new ones. Not in any one stand of trees do they react to a season with unanimity; at any time of the year you will see some trees with absolutely bare branches, others blossoming or putting out new green foliage.

TOPOGRAPHY

Central America is unique because there are many altitudes on the mountain ranges. There are vantage points from which two oceans can be seen. Two popular places for viewing the Atlantic and Pacific are the crater of the volcano Agua, near Antigua (Guatemala), and the crater of the volcano Irazú, near Cartago (Costa Rica). There are magnificent panoramas all along the Inter-American Highway.

In Central America you learn to think differently about the characters of the Atlantic and Pacific Oceans. The Pacific (or west) Coast of the isthmus has the cooler climate, while the Atlantic (east) Coast is the more torrid and humid. The capital cities are ranged along the Pacific Coast: Guatemala City, Guatemala; San Salvador, El Salvador; Tegucigalpa, Honduras; Managua, Nicaragua; and San José, Costa Rica. In the cleared jungles along the Atlantic Coast are the majority of great banana plantations or "divisions."

Because of its two oceans, the little isthmus has twice the coastline of the states of Oregon and California. The beaches are largely undeveloped paradises.

The Pacific Ocean does not seem peaceful when it comes pounding in on unsheltered beaches. On the west coast the sand is often black, due to the content of pulverized volcanic rock from the volcanoes that rise one after the other close to the Pacific. La Libertad, west of San Salvador (El Salvador), is a beautiful black beach where the surf is rough. Deep blue water breaks on black beach, making scallops of white lace, while black sea birds and snowy clouds move overhead.

On the Atlantic, to the east, the beaches are wide and white. The surf rolls in at a slower tempo, as if it were as much affected by the tropics as the people are; the water, at Tela (Honduras) and Puerto Limón (Costa Rica), is a limpid blue-green, and groves of coconut palm trees bend to one another along the shore. Here, in the little lagoons left by the receding tide, you can see the flashing of jewel-like tropical fish.

On the Pacific the most popular beach resorts are La Libertad (El Salvador), Corinto, Poneloya, Masachapa, San Juan del Sur (Nicaragua); and Puntarenas Sámara (Costa Rica); and San José (Guatemala).

On the Atlantic there are heavenly beaches the entire length, but the most accessible are near La Ceiba and Tela (Honduras); Bluefields and San Juan del Norte (Nicaragua); and Puerto Limón (Costa Rica).

Dozens of excellent harbors and ports on each coast are of interest to boating and fishing enthusiasts. Offshore islands are gradually being developed for lovers of skin-diving, spear-fishing, and shell-collecting. The most famous island on the Pacific, but as yet fit to be visited only by those with full camping equipment, is Cocos, 400 miles southwest of Costa Rica. Treasure hunters, a very special and nutty breed of explorer, perennially dig on Cocos for buried pirate treasure. However, as one national wryly remarked, most of the gold is not found by the gringos but is left in Central America by them.

The majority of the islands close to the Pacific shore are situated within the Gulfs of Fonseca, Nicoya, and Dulce. The six beautiful Islas de la Bahía (Bay Islands) are on the Atlantic, or Caribbean, off the cost of Honduras. Roatán, Utila, Guanaja, Barbareta, Eleana, and Morat may not all show up on the map, but they comprise their own "department," or state, within Honduras. They are being developed as vacation places. Green Corn Island, off the coast of Nicaragua, is an increasingly popular weekend and holiday resort.

Central America is blessed with inland waters and crisscrossed by sparkling rivers and streams.

At Tres Ríos, Costa Rica, between the capital, San José, and the little city of Cartago, the waters flowing east empty into the Atlantic, the waters flowing west into the Pacific. As with the Continental Divide in the United States, the land is inclined so as to lead converging waters in opposite directions. Thousands of vividly blue and jade-green crater lakes have formed in extinct volcanoes. Other lakes, products of rivers and springs and rainy season run-off, are situated in valleys and hollows.

Near the ruins of Utatlán, in the highlands of Guatemala, Lake Lemoa and Lake Ilotenango are thought to have been formed by the tears of the last Quiché queens, Icchaom and Zuxit, when their husbands were slain in combat with the Spaniards and Utatlán burned by order of the conquistador Pedro de Alvarado.

To this day Maya-Quiché priests take sinners to the shores and sprinkle their foreheads with water from the sacred lakes. The tears of the queens are thought to purify them.

The largest lakes of the isthmus are Atitlán and Izabal in Guatemala; Ilopango in El Salvador; Yojoa in Honduras (northwest at Tegucigalpa); and Managua and Nicaragua in Nicaragua (linked by the Tipitapa River).

Some of these lakes have freakish behavior problems. Atitlán is visited daily by a strange wind called the Xochimilco; it rises about noon, causing whirlpools and choppy water. Boatmen and swimmers are very leery of the Xochimilco and avoid the lake at this time. Lake Ilopango and Lake Managua are subject to extreme high and low tides now and then. These tides are not governed by the moon but by some force under the earth, probably volcanic. One January day in the 1880s, when the dry season was well under way, Lake Ilopango's waters rose suddenly and inexplicably. The lake overflowed its enormous crater bed and dredged itself a channel. Then the level of the lake was lowered as dramatically as it had risen, almost like dishwater draining from a sink, and there was then revealed a new island in the center of the lake, 150 feet high. Today swimmers in Lake Ilopango report that there is a distinct tug in the water that can be felt; something seems to be trying to waft them from the shore toward the middle. The force is not strong enough to be alarming, but it brings to mind the fact that the bottom of the lake is the crater of an old (but who knows how permanently extinct?) volcano.

Lake Managua, on the western shore of which the capital of Nicaragua is situated, is said to rise and fall dramatically every seven years, sometimes wiping out weekend cottages or the palm-thatched huts of the poor, sometimes revealing the ruins of early colonial settlements or pre-Columbian idols and temples.

Sport fishermen from all over the world come to fish in Lake Nicaragua and its outflow, the San Juan River. Outlandishly inappropriate denizens inhabit the lake: salt-water species such as sharks, tarpons, and swordfish. How the salt-water fish accustomed themselves to fresh water is still a mystery; the popular guess is that in the beginning of time, when the earth was heaving, land rose between the lake and the ocean. Lake Nicaragua was landlocked, and the salt-water fish were trapped there. Over the ages, one rainy season following another, the salt water of the lake was very gradually diluted. The generations of salt-water species learned to tolerate fresh water, to be at home in it. More recently it is believed that there is a constant movement of sharks from the Caribbean up the San Juan River and into the lake.

There are interesting islands in Central America's big lakes. Tropical Flores Island in Lake Izabal (Guatemala) has partly revealed Mayan ruins in its jungle and is the world's chewing-gum capital. The sapodilla trees that thrive there provide chicle, the basic ingredient of chewing gum. There *chicleros*, masters of the special skill of drawing off the sap, live with their families.

Isla Zapatera, near the western shore of Lake Nicaragua, is an apparently inexhaustible treasure trove of pre-Columbian artifacts, which are constantly being unearthed by both professionals and amateurs. Isla de Ometepe, also in Lake Nicaragua, has two huge, decorative volcanoes: Concepción and Madera. The fabulous *isletas* of this great lake—almost six hundred of them— were produced by the eruptions of a single nearby volcano, Mombacho. The *isletas* are now much-visited picnic, weekend, and holiday retreats. Many airy, modern summer homes have been built on the islands; hotels or hotel-marinas for tourists are now in the drawing-board stage.

Central America has important navigable rivers. Vital to transportation and trade are the Motagua in Guatemala, which empties into the Gulf of Honduras at Puerto Barrios; the Lempa in El Salvador, which flows into the Pacific south of La Libertad; the Coco (also called the Segovia), which flows into the Caribbean at Cabo (Cape) Gracias a Dios and serves for the greater part of its way as the boundary between Honduras and Nicaragua; the Escondido, which conveys ocean-going craft from Bluefields to Rama in Nicaragua; and the San Juan, whose mouth is on the Caribbean, exactly on the border of Costa Rica and Nicaragua. Historically the San Juan is the most important river in Central America.

To topographical attractions must be added the hundreds of thermal and medicinal springs in all of the countries, and the caverns and caves that are fun to explore. Some have pre-Columbian murals, some were used as hideouts for pirates.

FLORA AND FAUNA

Taking a broad look at a map of the Central American republics, one is struck by the prevalence of wide-open spaces. Naturalists, hunters, and explorers can find hundreds and hundreds of miles of untouched wilderness. Perhaps one reason for this is that northeast of the Inter-American Highway, most traveling is done on foot or on burros or horses, using ancient Indian trading trails that have existed since pre-Columbian days. The Inter-American Highway itself, from Cartago in Costa Rica, south over the mountain pass that leads to San Isidro, Palmar Sur, and eventually to David in Panama, has evolved from just such a trail. Pack animals are still preferable to machine-powered vehicles because they have wary and nimble hoofs and are imbued with a desire to survive. Sometimes these outlands can be reached by dugout canoe, or by Jeep proceeding over beaches or through clearings. But many Indian villages are still lonely autonomous units, out of touch with the mainstreams of society.

The great wilderness areas and the varieties in climate have given Central America a veritable Garden of Eden of flora and a Noah's Ark of fauna. Plants and creatures long familiar to North Americans inhabit the isthmus, plus those that can only be found in tropical jungles and on mountain heights unknown to residents of the United States. You will find the robin as well as the quetzal, the skunk along with the tapir or armadillo, and the familiar plant impatiens grows in the same acre with the exotic orchid.

Central America is heaven for the botanist; many journey to

certain areas to study intensively a certain plant family, such as the avocado family. According to Dr. Malvina Trussell of Florida State University: "You can spend a lifetime studying the flora along 500 feet of road leading to the top of Irazú volcano. . . . Plants vary in size, from the giant leaves of the *Gunnera insignus,* measuring six feet across, to the one-eighth-inch leaves of the lovely *Gomozia granadensis* with its clear red fruits and almost microscopic white flowers. . . . Days may be spent studying the six-inch fruticose lichens covering each fence post or the six-foot fronds of the large ferns. . . ."

Central America is one of the world's most productive locations for medicinal herbs, which is why many international drug companies have established businesses there. A brief sampling from El Salvador alone:

Ishacaca: Indians used the root for dysentery.

Sanguineria: mashed leaves were applied to snake bite.

Verbena azul: boiled leaves were effective as a vermifuge.

Manzanita: soothing to a sore throat.

Floripundia: when inhaled as a cigarette, relieves asthma.

Ornithologists and amateur bird-watchers have a literal field day from one end of Central America to the other. Thousands of birds are migratory or full-time inhabitants, and there are more undisturbed areas for observing water fowl and shore birds than elsewhere in the world. There are dozens of kinds of every species: 38 kinds of hummingbirds, 32 kinds of parrots, 47 kinds of grackles, for instance.

Among the species that either visit or inhabit Central America are grebes, herons, egrets, falcons, hawks, curlews, sandpipers, macaws, parrots, parakeets, owls, hummingbirds, quetzals, woodpeckers, flycatchers, martins, swallows, ravens, wrens, thrushes, robins, mockingbirds, thrashers, vireos, warblers, grackles, orioles, finches, tanagers, grosbeaks, buntings.

Many of the birds familiar to North Americans were also favorites of the Mayas. Mayas called the bobwhite *bech ha;* the hummingbird *tzunuum;* the red-winged blackbird *chuleb;* the cardinal *co-pol-che;* the whippoorwill *chak-puhuy.* To the Mayas, that gentle, beautiful bird the quetzal, which still can be seen in the highlands, on the upper reaches of volcanoes, and in the rain forests, was "God of the Air." The male's brilliantly colored tail-feathers were used for ceremonial headdresses. The bird would be trapped, its two-foot plumes removed, and then it would be released.

Game birds abound in Central America—duck, guinea hen, wild turkey, snipe, doves.

Animals are as various as the terrain and the altitudes. They include species of monkey, tapir, puma, jaguar, ocelot, coyote, deer, fox, manatee, anteater, armadillo, sloth, rabbit, beaver, weasel, bear, badger, guatusa, porcupine, skunk, peccary, wild boar, agouti, opossum, coati, raccoon, kinkajou, and many more.

The reptiles of Central America, however, would not fit into an old-home-week reunion with North American species, except for the rattlesnake and the moccasin. They are zoo celebrities mostly and include the horned viper, whip snake, boa constrictor, fer-de-lance, bushmaster, and coral snake. Though it is not a good idea to be recklessly unobservant when walking, the only reptile we saw in all of our trips was a worm-sized baby. Reptiles seem to be exactly as interested in not being stepped on as you are in not stepping on them. Lizards of all sizes are common, green and brown iguanas especially; so are crocodiles and alligators.

The Central American insects in their various incarnations are of particular interest to entomologists. Even familiar ones come in different colors from those we know in North America: ruby-red dragonflies swoop over water; grasshoppers with red jackets and antennas have an armored look and are the orange-red color of ancient Chinese chests. There are huge, gorgeous, unbelievable butterflies and moths.

There are untold species or flora and fauna in Central America that cannot be found elsewhere. We know this because of the examples of uniqueness that already exist, and because so many hundreds of miles have not been explored by naturalists. The only place in the world where the scops owl lives is in the region of the San Miguel volcano, near San Miguel in El Salvador. Lake Atitlán is the sole habitat of a species of duck, the *Polidymus cigas*. And 50 miles north of Puerto Limón in Costa Rica there is a 20-mile stretch of beach which is the breeding ground of the green turtle.

Gourmets know the Caribbean green turtle as a delicacy, but few have ever visited its paradisiacal breeding grounds. To be one of the few, you must rent a seaplane, launch, or burro—and probably a guide. You might agree with Ogden Nash who, observing that the creature lives in a chastity belt, wrote:

> I think it clever of the turtle
> In such a fix to be so fertile.

4 / Living, Breathing Mountains

So far as we know, nobody has ever bothered to count the volcanoes in Central America, but there are more concentrated on that narrow little isthmus between the borders of Mexico and Panama than in any other comparable area in the world. Recently geologist Otto Bohnenberger counted noses, found 324 in Guatemala, 187 in El Salvador, 16 in Honduras, 111 in Nicaragua, and 50 in Costa Rica. But even this most exhaustive census in post-Columbian times could not take into account the small volcanoes in the roadless wilderness, the hundreds of cinder cones and crater lakes any one of which may, at any moment, turn itself into a mountain. You can never be sure when some small volcano will blow its stack, grow with deposits of lava and ash, and upstage all the others with its brilliant pyrotechnics.

Most of the giants, some two miles tall, are close to the Inter-American Highway along the Pacific Coast. Their sooty blue shapes are silhouetted like witches' hats; the active ones puff cloudy exhalations.

Volcanoes loftily preside over the capital cities of Central America, loom over lake shores and ocean lagoons. Often you see them backed up against a sunset, with coffee plantations on their cool, shady slopes, and green fields of cotton or sugar cane or rice at their feet.

One's first volcano can be a shock, like seeing a purple cow. When I first arrived in Guatemala City to explore Central America it was night. Next morning I looked out the window, and there, sharp in the light, was a stunning apparition, making into molehills any mountains I had ever seen. This was Agua.

The best way to get a perspective on the incidence and stature of Central American volcanoes is to visit Minerva Park in Guatemala City. There you'll find a huge relief map of Guatemala sculptured to scale in khaki-green concrete. From observation towers you can look down on the convolutions or you can walk around the periphery of the park to get an impression of the elevations. The thirty-three ranking volcanoes appear steeply upthrusting, like stalagmites.

Once you have spent some time in Central America, driving from country to country, you get to know the volcanoes individually, by sight and by name. You recognize the tapering shape and conical peak of Momotombo, on the shores of Lake Managua in Nicaragua; the jagged, wide crater of San Miguel, near the little city of that name in El Salvador; the deceptively supine form of Irazú, above Cartago in Costa Rica. You learn their astonishing stories. You come to feel that each volcano is more than a mountain; it is a personality with definite idiosyncrasies. Even their names have an eventful sound: Mombacho, Cerro Negro, Fuego, Telica, Turrialba.

Volcanoes are so much a part of the adventure of Central American life that it is important to know a volcano at first hand. You must get close to it to feel its impact. Even an utterly quiescent volcano can be awesome, can bring your heart up to your throat.

A bewildering characteristic of the volcano, which is invariably the biggest thing in sight, is its apparent mobility; it seems not to stand still. First it pops up on the right side of the highway, now blocking your way, now ducking behind a shoulder of the immediate curve; then it turns up on the left. One day we visited Irazú in Costa Rica, taking a steep but excellent paved road up from Cartago in the valley. As we came closer, the volcano seemed to sneak away from us, step by stealthy step. I thought we would never catch up with it, but we went zipping through old drifts of ash and finally surprised it.

Before making a trip to the crater of a volcano, you should be sure that it does not have its head in the clouds, although, even when there is no vapor in sight, there is no guarantee that clouds will not come sailing in on the wind and fondly anchor themselves to the volcano. Clouds are attracted to volcanoes like moths to a lamp; they come nosing up to them and hang there, magnetized.

Once, on a flawlessly clear Sunday, we climbed San Salvador's volcano, El Boquerón. There is a steep, somewhat gravelly dirt road on which one can drive to the crater, but our car boiled over halfway up, so we trudged to the top. There was foliage hedging us in so we couldn't see where we were, but it made our final emergence and outlook all the more breathtaking. Suddenly we were at the very top of the world with nothing above us or around us. We were dazzled by the bright blueness and the sharp sun, greeted by the wind, which rushed at us almost too effusively. Far below us was a broad panorama; we could see all of distant Lake Ilopango.

Any mountain can give you a grand view of the valley places. But a volcano gives you another, rarer, downward look—into its crater. It's enough to make you gasp, though you might be already gasping from the exertion of the hike and the altitude.

Looking into El Boquerón (which means "large hole"), I felt that I had to hold onto something; I kept my hand tight around the railing of the lookout. My eyes followed the precipitous sides of the crater down and down to a perfect dark gray cinder cone rising from bottom center. It looked molded, like a wasps' nest. This cone, Boqueroncito (Little Boquerón), had come thrusting up during an eruption in 1917. The intense heat had evaporated a lake that had filled the mile-wide old crater. But now Boqueroncito is as cold as a rock in a New England cove, and the steep sides of the crater are covered with foliage. Indians live down there, but we could not see their shelters, only trails. Far below us a big hawk hovered, planing on the air currents.

There was a pine tree on the edge of the crater. We lay down in its shade, listened to the rushing wind, and recovered from the dizziness of looking down at Boqueroncito.

The interesting question about a volcano is whether it is active or quiescent. But of course this can never be answered for sure for more than a minute at a time. A volcano can be absolutely quiet for decades, for centuries, then suddenly and awesomely blow its stack. Pacaya, near Lake Amatitlán (Guatemala), was as quiet as any ordinary mountain when I was there one March; in December it was erupting briskly, pulsing out red-hot lava, chuffing mushroom clouds of steam and ash. In July 1968, Arenal, a quiet green mountain in pastoral Costa Rica, astonished the world by a horrendous outburst. It threw enormous bolders for 30 miles, buried villages under ash, belched a cloud of fire that incinerated a station wagon and its passengers—officials who had come to estimate its effect upon the countryside. Arenal had not been thought to be a volcano; it had not shown signs of life since Columbus. Volcanologists believe that Arenal's eruption may herald the formation of a new volcanic range, farther inland than the presently active one that is close to the Pacific.

In the fall of 1968, Cerro Negro, near León (Nicaragua), was in full eruption, making hammering sounds as if from a smithy of giants, exhaling with such force that it could be heard for miles, spouting fountains of fire that spilled down its sides in gleaming golden rivers. Even the old large crater at its peak could not absorb its inexplicably sudden tensions; a new crater blasted forth at its foot, gnashing rocks together, emerging with awesome vigor.

Visitors are reminded that the seemingly solid, generally amiable surface of the earth can be tossed about like the sea in a gale; land heaves and, after the cataclysm, is fixed in new attitudes. Anybody who thinks that God finished the job of creation in less than a week in the days of the Old Testament has another think coming with a volcano. Since man does *not* like to conclude that he knows it all (because, if he does, what he knows is still somehow disappointing), such a mystery as that of Cerro Negro's beautiful declaration of wonders makes him more happy than frightened. It lifts his heart, and he comes for miles to watch it.

Cerro Negro stopped erupting on December 8, the first day of Nicaragua's most important religious holiday, the *Purísima*. Nicaraguans felt that it had ceased out of respect.

There is at least one instance in Central America of the capricious quitting of volcanic shenanigans being regarded as a disaster. Take Izalco, one of El Salvador's famous volcanoes. From records we know that Izalco was born in 1770. Present-day residents of the ancient Indian village of Izalco, descendants of families who have lived there for centuries, say that a farmer noticed a log mysteriously smoldering in his field. Then the log was tossed into the air by an explosion and a fountain of red-hot lava. Izalco grew tall from its own spewing of lava and ash until, in eighty-six years, it stood more than 650 meters above sea level. It was known to sailors as "the lighthouse of the Pacific"; for years it was a reliable landmark, erupting regularly with great fountains of light every three minutes. In the 1950s, to give visitors a ringside view, the Hotel Montana was built overlooking this dramatically *active* volcano, on the slope of Cerro Verde. The plumbing was installed and the first guests expected when Izalco withdrew deep into itself, leaving a scorched crater, silence, and an embarrassed hotel management. The hotel has never been used and is falling into increasingly hopeless disrepair.

Izalco's big, misty hulk backdrops the tiny old Indian village for which it was named. We once visited that quiet pueblo. The blunted tolling of the old church bell was the only sound. The chalky-white bell tower rose against the dark flank of the volcano. We looked up and beyond the tower of Izalco's shadowy vastness in the sky. Here these pueblo people lived, close to the volcano's feet, never truly safe from volcanic mayhem. We heard a faint shuffling and turned to see a funeral procession wavering down the cobbled street toward the church. The people were walking carefully, with steadfast steps, as you do when you are carrying something heavy in your hands or in your heart. And Izalco waited, almost like a priest at an altar at the end of the aisle, stating in silence, with a long, steady look, the unpredictable cycles of life and death.

Nicaraguans say that the devil lives in Cosegüina, whose lordly form occupies an entire long peninsula in the Pacific Gulf of Fonseca. If only the devil were as unobtrusive, these days, as that volcano! Cosegüina has an impressive past because it made the second loudest noise in the history of the world when it exploded on January 22, 1835. (The ranking loudest noise was made by Krakatoa, the famous volcano located on an island between Java and Sumatra.) When Cosegüina had that cataclysmic eruption, ash and pumice fell for hundreds of miles, seething black clouds darkened the skies as far north as Mexico, as far south as Colombia. Wild animals were frightened and mingled with domesticated animals without molesting them.

Adventurers are always exploring Cosegüina. They have calculated that it takes ten hours on horseback to ride around the rim of the crater. Fliers who have spiraled small planes down into the crater have declared that the crater lake deep inside the volcano is 800 feet above sea level and that the surface of the lake is more than 7625 feet, probably closer to 9000 feet, down from the rim.

Once Lex hitched a ride from Managua to Guatemala City with a pilot friend. They flew directly over Cosegüina, and Lex could not believe the size, the vast maw, of this primordial presence. On our trip, when we approached Honduras on a stretch of highway that overlooks the Gulf of Fonseca, he pointed to the incredibly big bulk on the long peninsula and said, in a voice that was almost comically awestruck, "Cosegüina."

The substantial presence of the so-called "extinct" volcano, Agua, breathes down the neck of Antigua (Guatemala), the original capital of colonial Central America. Looking up beyond the thickly blossoming bougainvillaea that cascades over rose tile roofs, you can see its immense bulk etched against the bright blue sky. It is possible to follow a trail up the flank of the volcano to the crater's edge, 10,000 feet above Antigua; from here you can see both oceans. A friend of ours, Carlos Ortiz, made that ascent on foot; the trip took him from four in the afternoon to six the next morning. He and his friends walked from late afternoon through the night, to avoid the blazing hot sun. Carlos and his party slept inside the crater for protection against the wind. (When climbing a volcano, bring something warm for the chill at the top.) He said the sunrise and the magnificent view were well worth the effort of the climb.

The Indians grow flowers for Guatemalan markets on the volcano's fertile slopes, lilies and daisies and carnations and all sorts of lovely and fantastic tropical blossoms. But this gaiety is lost in the general foliage and the solemn darkness of Agua, which has been said to create an atmosphere that is *triste*.

Many of the volcanoes that we visited were showing signs of life, though they well may not be now. The Guatemalan volcano Fuego is linked, by proximity, to Agua (Fire and Water, they are called in English). Fuego has been unceasingly *activo* since the days of the conquistadores; you can see its breath by day, sometimes its glow at night. Now and then, every decade or so, lava wells up and flows over the crater.

You meet the formidable, still tricky Santiago, sometimes called Masaya, when you drive south from Managua in Nicaragua toward the Costa Rican border. You will see Santiago close to the highway on your right. It may take you by surprise, for, despite its long and dramatic history, it does not look to be very important. It is broad rather than tall; it is so low that you can see its gaping, scorched crater surrounded by bald, khaki-colored, ravaged-looking shoulders. There is no vegetation, always a sign of an unsettled, recently active volcano. Pure lava rock covers its slopes and its valley. Nicaraguans are very leery of Santiago.

One of the earliest travelers to this area was the Spaniard Gonzales Fernandez Oviedo. On July 26, 1529, he recorded that in the darkness of the night the light from Santiago's crater "shown with such force" that it was possible to read and write at "*tres leguas*" (three leagues). Colonial historian Francisco de Bobadilla, who observed it in action, wrote: "During certain times of the year, on calm days, one can hear the frightful roars [*espantosos rugidos*]; it sounds as if gigantic lions and tigers from another world were caged on that mountain."

A Nicaraguan legend relates that a wise old woman lived in Santiago's crater. To the Indian leaders, or *caciques*, she was as the Oracle at Delphi had been to the Greeks. In times of decision, the chiefs would hike up to Santiago's crater and wait for their soothsayer. She would appear, snaggle-toothed, through the mists associated with craters. She would tell them important things, such as when to expect the rainy season, when to plant, when to harvest. She would warn them about disasters, predict the fortunate times.

Then the conquistadores came. They were different from any pestilence the Indians had known. These strangers, sometimes blond and blue-eyed, were unlike any human beings in their experience. Nobody knew what should be done about them, or how dangerous they might be. They perplexed the Indians as no doubt men from Mars might baffle us.

The chiefs went to visit the old soothsayer of Santiago. Out she came with a grave look. She said that the newcomers were *malo* (bad). Sternly she added that until the white men had been ousted from these lands the *caciques* would not see her again. She then went back to her home in the crater and has never emerged.

Under the dominion of the Spanish conquistadores, the Indians near Santiago lost much that they had once relied upon. They did, however, acquire something new; they were given their own saint, San Gerónimo. San Gerónimo lived, in effigy, in the church that was built by the missionaries. He was carried, like all saints in Central America to this day, at the head of processions during fiestas.

Then one day, they say, that pueblo shook with a mighty explosion; columns of black smoke and fire came out of Santiago, and the people could see a thick river of lava starting down the mountain. They had never asked San Gerónimo for anything, but they had been told that he was powerful and would intercede for them in heaven. They hurried to the church, held the saint up in front of them and, as in a holy day procession, advanced toward the murderous lava. As San Gerónimo came up to the lava, it stopped flowing. It broke off with a great crack and fell into a lake, presently known as the Laguna de Masaya, which can be seen just past the volcano.

After this narrow escape the people began to speak of moving *más allá*, which means, literally, "more far," "farther away." They soon built a new pueblo that was *más allá* from Santiago. And that is how the present city of Masaya got its name. Many of the old adobe houses date from the time the pueblo was rebuilt. The families that live there today are famous for their hand-woven and crocheted *hamacas* and their beautifully designed and colored woven handbags, straw hats, and baskets.

We recently climbed Santiago, taking a steep trail of crumbled volcanic cinders that led between tumbled boulders of porous lava. In its crevices exquisite little alpine plants had taken hold and were blossoming, tiny stars and trumpets of reds, blues, yellows, and purples. Halfway up to the summit, we paused to rest and saw the most amazing panorama. Entirely circling the miles of valley below us was the rim of an ancient crater, of which old Santiago itself was a relatively recent cone. The highway on which we had driven ran right through it; the people who lived and farmed in the valley probably did not realize that their earth was a crater. We could see small cinder cones rising here and there in the broad plain—cones that were probably thought to be grassy little hills.

At last we reached the summit and smelled sulphur in the clouds of steam from the crater. We gazed fearfully into the gaping hole, as deep as several football fields are long. The steam clouds were churning out of a fissure in the pools of congealed lava at the bottom. There was absolute silence as Santiago breathed and the wind blew its breath away. Heading down the slope afterward, we were in a strangely giddy and silly mood, laughing for no reason, like children who have gone too far and somehow gotten away with it.

Driving through El Salvador toward Honduras, nearing the city of San Miguel, you will first see the huge form of the San

Miguel volcano ahead of you; eventually it will lie in full view to your right. Its crater is wide and jagged, and, if there are no obscuring clouds, you will see it smoking. San Miguel's peaked top was blown off in 1586, a fact somehow recorded when there were few within sight of that dramatic beheading who knew how to write.

San Miguel, like all volcanoes, has its legends. During an eruption in 1655, red-hot lava overflowed its crater and moved into the city. Buildings burst into flame and were destroyed. Everything was desolation and dismal ashes. But two objects in all of San Miguel remained untouched, not even smudged by smoke. One was a sculptured wood effigy of the fallen angel Lucifer (and we all know that a roaring fire is old home week to him). The other was a wooden likeness of St. Francis of Assisi, which was found intact in the ruined church of San Francisco. Today one can drive through the city of San Miguel and take the road that winds up through the coffee trees which thrive on the volcano's lower slopes, to the lava line. From there you can see miles of black lava: a devastated area of tumbled, porous, cindery rock.

The highway crosses over a big tongue of lava that once flowed into the valley from San Miguel's crater—though it is hard to imagine such tumbled rocklike masses as ever having been capable of motion. Built on this lava flow is an interesting new village, which the upwards of six hundred residents call La Burbuja (The Bubble). Poor Salvadorans who could not afford to buy land have moved here, applying for official permission to the mayor of the nearby town of El Tránsito. Their homes and fences are built entirely of lava stone, and the Peace Corps is helping to construct a school there, also of lava. Nearby there is a large lake fed by underground streams that course below the surface of San Miguel's stony flank; during the rainy season the porous lava absorbs the water and slowly feeds it to the lake. The people of Burbuja make their living by fishing that lake, and selling their catch in the markets of El Tránsito.

One of our most dangerous trips, although we did not realize it at the time, was to a fumarole at the foot of the volcano

Telica, on the outskirts of the little pueblo of San Jacinto in Nicaragua. At the end of the one and only street there was an ancient stone arch, perhaps a vestige of a colonial church. We parked the car short of the arch; we walked through it and saw a large, flat, steaming, roundish area just ahead of us. We could hear it; it sounded like an old choo-choo train—*shhhhhh . . . choooooo . . . whoof . . . sssssssssss.* The crust seemed hard; we walked over it between the steaming and bubbling places, getting a sort of hot foot but feeling elated at its life and our closeness to it. There were places where a mudlike substance bubbled, making funny-paper sounds like *glub-glub;* and places where the rusty, stippled rock sizzled as at a clambake. Lilliputians tiptoeing over Gulliver must have felt very much as we did.

A young Indian woman came down the wooded slope beyond the fumarolic crater. On her head she carried an enamel basin full of corn that she had just ground for tortillas at a small community mill up on the side of the volcano. She told us that it was dangerous to walk where we had walked. Sometimes cows or horses fell through places where the crust was thin. Once someone had been walking across the crater and one leg had plunged through. When he pulled it out there was no flesh. Later, a geologist shook his head at us and quoted, "Fools walk in where angels fear to tread."

Irazú, near Cartago in Costa Rica, is another example of volcanic unpredictability, though it has been watched and visited since the days of the conquistadores. Its crater is approximately 11,325 feet above sea level. For decades volcanologists dismissed Irazú as "quiescent, with weak fumarolic activity." The volcano's potential for producing instant doomsday was forgotten.

On March 13, 1963, when President John F. Kennedy arrived in nearby San José, the capital of Costa Rica, to confer with Central American presidents, his welcome was indeed *fuerte.* Irazú apparently caught the shoot-the-works spirit. Voom! Black clouds rose 10,000 feet, mushrooming like the dark vaporous blossoms of atomic explosions.

Lex drove to see Irazú shortly after this outburst. He was

struck by its beauty at night: "It threw out burning rock, all colors—red and green and blue. They shot up and came down like meteors." Irazú was just the opposite in the daytime; not beautiful but weird—"a gray haze, dead trees." It was cold and clammy and so murky near the crater that one could not watch an eruption, but could hear rocks falling. Some rash visitors were killed at that time, venturing too close to the edge of the crater. "Bombs," which had been spurted up as liquid lava, congealed into elliptical streamlined rocks as they fell.

The residents of Cartago, San José, and other adjacent Costa Rican communities lived patiently with the rain of Irazú's volcanic ash for two years. Ash fell profusely as far away as Puntarenas, the lovely seaport resort that is a hundred miles from the capital. Women wore veils and hats, as if they were beekeepers, and constantly coped with the accumulation in their homes. Some forty thousand tons of ash were shoveled and swept from the streets of San José when at last Irazú stopped huffing and puffing.

There was a terrible aftermath to the accumulation of ash, however. During the rainy season of 1964 the thick mantle of ash around the shoulders of Irazú turned into an oozy sludge and began to slide down the slopes. The avalanche made a horrible sound. It fell into rivers and changed their courses or dammed them up; it pushed big boulders around as if they were pebbles. Mercifully the avalanche moved slowly and so people and animals in its path generally escaped, but it covered villages, destroyed hundreds of acres of crops and grazing lands for cattle.

Anyone visiting Irazú today should first drive through Cartago and view the miles of halted avalanche; still as a glacier, it stands in thick, khaki-colored mesas with clifflike sides, sometimes 75 to 100 feet thick. It is unbelievable that such a quantity of material could have come out of one single volcano; suddenly you understand the phrase "bottomless pit." Yet nature mends fast, and it is easy to forget a scorched past in the present verdure.

As we drove up to the crater, there was no sign of past afflic-

tion; there were herds of cattle in the emerald mountain meadows, carpets of blue alpine flowers. The air was beautiful, dry
and sweet. Every advance upward gave us a more generous
view of the valley below and the heights beyond, intensities of
gold, the fleeting shadows of clouds, the burning green and saf-
fron of fields and slopes. You couldn't look hard enough or long
enough to memorize the view because it wasn't the same from
one minute to another. It was like a progression of quickly
played chords.

Irazú had somewhat withdrawn into itself again, but there
were peripheral signs of recent activity and restlessness. You
could see drifts of ash that had been pushed off, like snow, to
the sides of the road, and dead trees. When we had started,
there had been not a hint of haze around Irazú, but now there
was a chilly mist and we could see nothing below us.

The Costa Rican government has built a large cement lookout
balcony back from the crater. A sign warns visitors not to advance any closer without a guide. A young man in khaki, who
belonged to Costa Rica's National Guard, was on duty to
protect visitors from Irazú; he offered to take us to the active
crater.

We followed him down to a plateau of ash below the lookout.
The wisps of sulphurous steam that we smelled seemed to be
coming through the smooth, springy surface of gray ash. I put
my hand on the damp, grainy ash; it felt warm. As we walked
I heard the volcano. "Shhhhhhh!" it said, right in our ears.

It was a long walk across the plateau of ashes, through the
sulphurous, blowing, cold mist, to the edge of the crater. "This
is where the people were killed during the eruptions," we were
told. And our guide warned us to be careful about breathing the
sulphur. I wondered how to be careful.

From the edge of the crater we could see only a few precipitous feet down; the maw was filled with clouds. The guide
crouched by the abyss, listening. Lex crouched, and I finally
crouched too. Lex and the guide spoke to each other in low,
discreet voices, aware, apparently, of a presence. The guide

murmured to Lex, like one pallbearer to another. I wished that I had brought a sweater.

Suddenly, exactly as if a magician had whisked away his cape to reveal the surprise, the clouds lifted, perhaps dispelled by the deep-down activity of the volcano, and we could see down the scorched, rough sides down to the very bottom, incredibly far away. There, from a chimney-like aperture (a new cone, perhaps), came two distinct, churning clouds, one white, one gray, and they climbed up fast, boiling, energetically activated. Fascinated, we watched the center of activity, saw the emanation climb up into the sky over our heads.

Then, as quickly as the mist had been whisked away, it again completely obscured the crater. We stood numbly, uncertainly, at the edge. It was over. Resignedly, without trying to say what we couldn't say, we started back.

5 / The Mayas'
_Thirteenth Heaven

Hundreds of visitors annually are attracted to Central America by the pre-Columbian ruins and artifacts that can be found throughout the five republics. It is more interesting and rewarding to visit these sites if you know at least a little something about the history and culture of the ancient Mayas.

Actually, there is a great deal more involved than understanding the past. Mayan influence can be strongly felt in Central American culture today. The ancient Mayas were corn farmers during the growing season, craftsmen for the rest of the year. This is still the pattern of the rural Central American. And to this day women grind corn on the traditional Mayan *metate* and bake tortillas.

Often a custom thought to have been introduced by the Spanish was part of isthmian culture for centuries before the coming of colonists. The central plaza is a feature of all the old colonial cities, Antigua (Guatemala), Granada (Nicaragua), San Miguel (El Salvador). But ancient Mayan cities all had great plazas of limestone; they can be walked on today at Copán (Honduras) and Tikal (Guatemala), and other ancient ceremonial centers. It is indeed Spanish for a person to incorporate both parents' names—his father's name in the middle, his mother's name last—but it was also a Mayan custom long before the arrival of the first conquistador.

Carrying the effigies of patron Beings in processions was known long before Catholicism was introduced here. The Mayan gods were always being taken on strategic trips. For instance, presiding gods changed office every new year. As the old year ended, the god who had been its patron was carried to the exit of the town (usually the southern end) and the incoming god was carried to the entrance at the north and brought into the city. There were feasting and dancing and music before the word "fiesta" was heard in that land.

Market day, which is still observed in all the pueblos and cities of Central America, was also a Mayan custom. In fact, you see Indians walking along roadsides with market goods in baskets on their heads—chickens, fruit, little pigs—and frequently that road began as a Mayan trade route. Mayas who lived near lakes or rivers or ocean shores brought goods to market in giant dugout canoes, the same type that are in use today—though now sometimes equipped with outboard motors.

During the annual celebration of the Feast of the Immaculate Conception in Granada (Nicaragua), a woman figure on stilts strides down the street as a tradition of the fiesta. Elderly Mayan ladies danced on stilts to avert bad luck as their new year approached.

There is even a lingering vestige of the Mayan custom of a sacrificial offering to propitiate the gods. The "Dance of the Mountain Pig," which is still performed in El Salvador, has come down through the ages. The chief dancer wears a garment of pigskin. At the height of the ceremonial dance a pig is sacrificed, and pieces of his flesh are handed around to celebrants, much as small portions of the victim were distributed in the latter days of the Mayan New Empire.

For purposes of understanding contemporary Central America as well as its historical ruins, here is a quick look at Mayan life and times, at what was literally their Heaven on earth.

Over the past century we have learned enough about the

priest-prince of Mayan times to visualize him. He walks across a limestone-white plaza toward a pyramid, a skyward temple with a steep flight of steps. It is a stairway to Heaven.

He is wearing a magnificent helmet of red macaw feathers; sprouting from it are the three-foot-long, iridescent tail-feathers of the quetzal; he wears a necklace of jaguar's teeth; a golden fur cape of spotted ocelot is fastened over his naked chest with a jade clasp. His breech cloth has hummingbird feathers woven into the fabric; his sandals are elegant, high at the heel. His front teeth are mosaics, inlaid with bits of jade. He is a *halech uinic*, a priest-ruler. It is two centuries after the birth of Christ, and the place is Tikal, in the Petén region of Guatemala.

He does not think of himself as exactly mortal. He believes that the earth itself is the lowest of Thirteen Heavens, but Heaven still. His life and his religion are one; it is not a "Sunday religion" as in latter-day Western society. It is a man's religion, and the worshipers are not preponderantly women, as so often they are in Christian churches.

The heart of his city is not a market place but a religious ceremonial center. Even the ball games are played as a religious ritual. The gods watch over every precious minute of every day; each profession and craft is as consecrated as a religious order; each has a designated time to commune with the gods. In the fourth month, called *Tzec*, there are religious ceremonies for beekeepers; a special wine made of honey and bark is drunk. Even war captains, elected for a term of three years, are consecrated. While they serve, they are bound to celibacy, are carried around on palanquins, and are fed a special diet of fish and iguana. Every part of life is lived ceremoniously. On the first day (*Imix*) of the first month (*Pop*) of each new year, Mayans discard on a community dump all their household goods, their mats and bowls and implements, and start anew.

Little was known about the Mayas and their Thirteenth Heaven until archaeologists began slowly to reclaim their cities from the jungle less than a century ago. Even today the surface has just been scratched. Sites of old cities are constantly being discovered throughout Central America. At first, because of the similarities of the culture of the Mayas and that of other great civilizations—the Egyptian, the Greek—it was thought that there must somehow be a connection. Today most archaeologists believe that the Indian genius developed independently. Ancestors of the Mayas probably crossed from Asia to North America over a narrow isthmus that once spanned the Bering Strait, as the isthmus of Central America now bridges two oceans between the continents of North and South America. Migratory instincts evidently led Mayan progenitors to their particular promised land, to what is now Mexico's Yucatán peninsula, the Petén region of Guatemala, and the nearby jungle rain forests of Honduras.

None of the other tribes of Indians—the Incas, the Aztecs— approached the genius of the Mayas. The important turning point in Mayan development was evidently the discovery of how to cultivate the still-beloved *maíz,* or corn. This changed them from nomads, desperate hunters, into a community-minded society.

As the vines have been cut away and the humus of centuries shoveled off ancient temple and palace steps and platforms, archaeologists have found architecturally wondrous limestone cities. They have uncovered temples, palaces, ball courts, sweat baths, colonnades, platforms, reviewing stands, stadiums, walls, causeways, bridges, aqueducts, observatories for astronomers, reservoirs, market buildings. They have found sculptured tablets, high shafts of limestone covered with intricate hieroglyphics. These stelae can be seen in the ruins of all Mayan cities, and archaeologists have begun to unravel their mysteries. The mathematical symbols of the Mayans have been figured out, so that the dates on which the stelae were dedicated have been established. A stelae was usually raised to commemorate the ending of a *Katun,* or their twenty-year period, though sometimes, as at Quiriguá, stelae were also raised at the end of a *Hotun* (or five-year period) and, more occasionally, at the end of a *Lahuntun* (or ten-year interval). There are stone monuments recording nearly twelve hundred years.

The sculpture in high and low relief on inner and outer surfaces of temples and palaces described how the Mayas lived. The homes of the ordinary folk were exactly like those still used today throughout Central America. The roof was of steep-pitched palm thatch, to allow the rain to run off; the flimsy walls were of cane; and the house was held together by vines and fiber strands rather than by nails or dowels.

By the numbers of house mounds on the circumference of cities, where once the ordinary people lived in their thatched homes, archaeologists have figured out that the population was dense. In Uaxactún (Guatemala), which was not one of the biggest of the Old Empire cities, the population exceeded fifty thousand.

The Mayas had much in common with other great and colorful societies of the Old World. They would have been at home at King Arthur's court. Sculptured standard bearers positioned around their ceremonial sites once held the staffs of tournament-like flags or banners, bright with featherwork and streaming in the wind. The ruler-priests presided on thrones. There were jesters and dancers on stilts.

The Mayas were in many ways like the Greeks. (Archaeologists have called a large plaza surrounded by temples at Tikal the Acropolis.) They loved sports; ceremonial tournaments were played on their ball courts. All ball games are thought to be extensions of this Mayan invention. Players wore masks (as in baseball, football); they used their bodies as bats (as in soccer); the object was to propel a crude rubber ball through a high stone ring (as in basketball).

And, like the Greeks, Mayans were on speaking terms with the gods. They were half gods themselves anyway, living as they did in their Thirteenth Heaven. Their supreme deity was Itzamna, whose consort was Ixchel, the "rainbow lady," goddess of weaving, medicine, and childbirth. All the other gods were the progeny of these.

Because agriculture was basic to their civilization, they perhaps felt closest to Chac, the rain god. Actually Chac was four spirits, four idols, who lived at the four corners of the world. Chac Xib Chac was the rain god of the east, and his color was red; Sac

Xib Chac of the north was white; Ek Xib Chac of the west was black; and Kan Xib Chac of the south was yellow.

When sacrifices were made to the gods, the four assistants to the officiating priest were called *chacs*. Most archaeologists believe that during the peak of Mayan civilization, in the centuries of the Old Empire, which coincided with the first years of Christianity, human sacrifice was not customary, but animals were sacrificed as in our Old Testament. Mayan ladies and gentlemen sometimes drew blood from their ears, tongues, noses, or lips to anoint an idol sacrificially. Later, in the far less happy New Empire, humans were sacrificed, sometimes to gods, sometimes to accompany an important person into the hereafter. Before a temple or an idol the victim was stripped, bent backward, arched over the sacrificial stone, while his arms were held by four *chacs*. The *nacom*, priest-executioner, made an incision in the chest with an obsidian knife and removed the beating heart. Blood was smeared over the idol of the god being honored or propitiated.

Like the ancient Egyptians, the Mayas built pyramids over funerary crypts and left objects with the dead that would be useful in the life to come. And, like the Egyptians and others, they wrote in hieroglyphics; the Mayas used infinitely resourceful carved designs for glyph symbols.

Today we still marvel over the "Renaissance man," that many-faceted European genius. The Maya was a farmer for a few months and a great artist for the rest of the time, building the steep temples, sculpting the panels and the statues and the stelae. He never did learn to domesticate beasts of burden, but he learned how to quarry and move limestone shafts that weighed up to sixty-five tons, using strong fibers and hardwood logs. He never had metal tools, but limestone, from which he constructed temples and palaces, was soft when quarried, hardening later, so obsidian and flint tools were equal to the tasks of slab-cutting and sculpture.

A characteristic of Mayan architecture is that individual buildings or groups of buildings do not conform to the natural ups and downs of the land; they are invariably erected on multi-

leveled raised platforms, courts, and terraces connected by
stairways. A single stone platform at Tikal contains more than
five acres of buildings (Group E). All Mayan temples and palaces
are pyramidal, rising terrace by terrace from a broad base to a
small, chimney-like top. The highest temple at Tikal (Temple
Four) measures 210 feet from base to roof comb and is composed of five stories. The chambers within Mayan structures are
vaulted, supported by means of sapodilla wood; many of the
beams are carved murals; they are among the most important
surviving records of the costumes and customs of the time. They
show processions, priests and warriors and ladies in full regalia.
The sapodilla wood has withstood centuries of jungle dampness
and overgrowth to show exactly what a fancy Mayan sandal
looked like, or a plumed helmet, or a round shield of tapir skin,
or a peaked hat traditionally worn by a human victim to be
sacrificed.

The style of Mayan buildings is stunning; white buildings
reach up beyond the trees to be seen in light and shadow against
a blue sky; there are the dramatic flights of stairs; there is the
spaciousness of courts and platforms, the sense of an uncluttered,
orderly world controlled by a unique concept of beauty, con-
ceived in reverence. And yet, despite the brave style that moves
contemporary visitors from skyscraper cities, these builders were
naïve architecturally. The contrast between the floor space of
an inner chamber and the thickness of the walls is striking. In
Temple Five at Tikal, the tiniest room atop the pyramid has a
wall 15-feet thick, while the actual width of the chamber is 2½
feet. In Temple Four, the highest structure known to have been
built, the walls are up to 40 feet thick. Shelter does not appear
to have been as important as shape; inner coziness and comfort
must have been secondary to a design that reached for the sky.

Stairways are always outside, ascending the steep temples and
palaces. Outside, too, on the façades of the buildings, are the
magnificent sculpture and hieroglyphic panels, whose texts are
only beginning to be understood. Fun or fantasy, as we understand it today, is rarely expressed. One vaulted tunnel that
leads through the bottom floor of the palace in Group G at Tikal

is entered through a fantastic stone mask, but the Mayas did not seem to need or want whimsy; they were seldom, if ever, cute. Their old cities suggest simplicity, severity, an intentness of purpose. And those who visit them today sometimes wonder whether the Mayas were ahead of, or behind, modern society.

But they were human. Many of the things they experienced are still experienced by present-day flesh and blood. Social patterns are often familiar; the eldest son was first to inherit the family property and the family responsibilities, for instance.

The Mayas made flutes out of reeds (*chirimías*), whistles from clay, horns out of conch shells, war trumpets from wood (deep-toned as oboes). They discovered that there was a beautiful sound when a turtle shell was struck by a deer antler; they made drums out of hollow trees and carved them with intricate bas-relief designs. They clacked animals' jawbones in their rhythm bands and shook gourds. Their scale was five-tone, pentatonic; a portable marimba was one of the first scale ascending-descending instruments.

The Mayas ate very well; they raised turkeys and bees. They grew corn, tomatoes, yucca, beans, squash, peppers, and fruit. Hunters brought home deer and peccary, duck, pigeon, partridge. Fishermen in their dugout canoes (often fashioned out of the sacred trees, and the ceiba) ferried back oysters, lobsters, clams, conch, and all manner of salt- and fresh-water fish that they had caught in their nets or stunned with their poison.

The women spun cotton and fiber, using a spindle, and made jewel-like colors from vegetable and animal dyes (indigo, cochineal). Each color meant something: the color of war was black (prompted by black obsidian weapons); yellow meant food (derived from golden corn); red stood for blood or sacrifice; blue for religion (the cakes of *pom* incense, made from the sap of the copal tree, were always painted blue); green was the color of royalty (no doubt because the quetzal feathers used in the helmets of the great priest-princes were prismatically green).

The looms on which they wove their tapestry-like fabrics, incorporating seemingly inexhaustible original designs, were exactly like those used by their descendants today. The simple looms were hung on a tree or a wall; the looms slanted into the women's laps as they knelt and wielded the shuttle of bright cotton or wool.

Mayan money literally grew on trees; their currency was cocoa beans.

One of the most interesting characteristics of that culture was the reverence for time. Their arithmetic was evidently evolved for calendrical, not for the usual mercenary, reasons. They were mathematical geniuses; they applied the cipher zero before the Hindus; they added and subtracted simple symbols: a dot for one, a bar for five, and an elliptical zero for units beginning with 20.

They measured their solar year by naming eighteen months of twenty days (*Pop, Uo, Zip, Zotz,* etc.), and the nineteenth month (*Uayeb*), had five days. Of the twenty Mayan days— *Imix, Ik, Akbal, Kan,* etc.—*Ahau* was the most important. Its patron was Itzamna.

They also had another calendar, the Long Count, closer to their hearts, in which they thought in larger units of time, centuries ahead of them, centuries behind them. Their Long Count:

> *Kin*—1 day
> *Uinal*—20 Kins
> *Tun*—18 Uinals
> *Katun*—20 Tuns
> *Baktun*—20 Katuns

On Stela 3 at Tikal, the Long Count date has been deciphered as 9.2.13.0.0—9 *Baktuns,* 2 *Katuns,* 13 *Tuns,* no *Uinals,* no *Kins* —or 1,315,080 days.

Mayans thought in large time cycles. It was as if they were on the open bow of a moving ship at sea, able to look both forward and backward. Over the centuries they perceived certain patterns repeating themselves; priests and sages felt that there were predictable cycles of fortune or misfortune.

The archaeologist Sylvanus G. Morley has pointed out that the base date from which the Mayan Long Count was always calculated was 9.0.0.0.0 *Baktuns,* which ended on the day *8 Ahau.* A date called *Katun 8 Ahau* repeated itself every 256¼ years. (You can see *8 Ahau* written at Tikal, on Altar 14, Structure 3 D-99.) In Mayan history, all *Katun 8 Ahau* marked times of change. The last Mayan stronghold in the Petén rain forest region of Guatemala was that of the Itzá on Lake Petén Itzá. Morley believes that the Itzá felt doomed because of the approach of *Katun 8 Ahau* and they fled when the Spanish attacked—in the Christian calendar year 1697.

But, long before that, many of the old Mayan cities that had risen in the jungles had been abandoned. Cortés in 1524–25 stumbled upon towering temples and palaces that were desolate and overgrown with rampant foliage. Earlier, in 1502, Columbus came across Mayas in their dugout canoes off the coast of Honduras and said that their craft reminded him of Venetian gondolas. So some still lingered in the area. But where had the hundreds of thousands of Mayas that had lived for centuries in the inland rain forests moved to? And why?

We know that many moved to the highlands of Guatemala, to places they named Quezaltenango, Chichicastenango, Momostenango, Chimaltenango, where their descendants still live, wearing colorful clothing that has remained unchanged in style for centuries. The aquiline, full-mouthed profile of today's highland Indian of Mayan stock is often an exact mirror image of the profiles found in the sculpture and friezes in the museum cities of Tikal (Guatemala), Copán (Honduras), and other ancient ceremonial sites.

But why did the Mayas abandon their great cities? Archaeologists are still guessing. Did a plague or some similar tragedy kill off all but a few, who fled from sites of pestilence? Had there been a population explosion that led to the exhaustion of the land and forced them to seek new acres that could support their staple crop, *maíz?* Had the infiltration of the Toltecs from what is now Mexico and the influence of their bloodthirsty god, Quetzalcoatl, broken the once-noble Mayan spirit? Nobody knows for sure the reason for the fateful exodus.

And why, when they left their Thirteenth Heaven, did they

also leave behind their cultural greatness? Why in future
generations did they become merely primitives with some inherited skills, such as weaving and growing corn—primitives
who still worshiped the old gods but had no will to build
temples or palaces or any structures more sophisticated than
the hut with cane walls and thatched roof? Today the direct
descendants of the Mayas are the most uneducated citizens in
the Central American nations and most loath to adjust to the
world as it evolves and "progresses" in the age of moon shots.
Many leaders on the isthmus today think of the Indian population as an incorrigible drag on an ongoing society.

The last commemorative stela of the Mayan Old Empire was
dated 10.3.0.0.0 (corresponding to A.D. 889 on the Christian
calendar); the New Empire, in which a cultural recession gradually took place, lasted from the tenth century to the sixteenth
century. Some archaeologists classify the rise and fall of the Mayan
civilization differently. They begin with a Preclassic Period,
which dates from 600 B.C., perhaps earlier. This was the forma-
tive period, the prelude to the Classic Period during which the
most magnificent accomplishments were realized, beginning
about A.D. 250 and reaching a peak shortly before the collapse
of Tikal in about A.D. 900. All in Mayan life that occurred after
that is characterized as Postclassic. The years since A.D. 900
have shown a steady deterioration in Mayan vigor; they have
been years of a lost heritage.

Vines began to crawl up the steps of limestone temples; roots
cracked causeway pavements and courts; hummingbirds and
macaws flew over silent plazas; and howler monkeys (hoo, hoo,
hoo) swung from the trees and spider monkeys sat big-eyed on
temple steps. There was a terrible silence; growing things don't
make a sound. Somehow a tide had gone out.

There is no allotted time span for the life of a civilization, such
as the comfortingly predictable nine months to carry a baby
from conception to birth. The exact hours from the birth to the
death of a great society remain a mystery.

6 / Since Columbus

Through the centuries since Mayan times, each Central American country has developed individually; in every case, the story is unique. But there are certain events that bind them together and make them the family of nations that they actually are, though they have been historically edgy about their autonomy.

The broad sweep of history in these five republics makes an ironic chronicle. Here was the center of the great Mayan civilization which, soon after the birth of Christ, was one of the most advanced in the world. Early in the sixteenth century, long before the colonization of North America, there was an outpost of the European Renaissance in Antigua (Guatemala). Yet today much of Central America must be classified as "backward" and "underdeveloped," lacking the skills of modern society.

Aside from the pre-Columbian epoch, the historically significant periods for Central Americans are those dating from discovery, seizure, and colonization by Spaniards in the sixteenth century, and from the declaration of independence from Spain and subsequent efforts to unite and work for the common good in the nineteenth century.

We begin with the year 1502 when Christopher Columbus, on his fourth and last voyage to the New World, sailed into the Caribbean looking for a short cut to Cathay and the East with its riches. His square-rigged caravels survived a storm off a point of land that he called Cabo Gracias a Dios (thanks to God), which is situated at the mouth of the Río Coco, on the border of Honduras and Nicaragua. He also anchored off the Islas de la Bahía, northeast of the port of La Ceiba, Honduras. Island dwellers today are descendants of pirates who once waited in the coves to ambush vessels that sailed "The Spanish Main," bringing treasures from the New World to the Old.

Seabirds were the only residents or visitors when Columbus anchored off the island of Guanaja late in the summer. Every half hour the seamen on watch turned the hour glass, the ship's clock of the day, and sang out at daybreak:

> Blessed be the immortal soul
> And the Lord who keeps it whole,
> Blessed be the light of day
> And He who sends the night away.

From Guanaja, Columbus proceeded to the mainland, to what is now called Puerto Castilla, the first peninsula east of La Ceiba. The ship's log relates that Columbus was indisposed on August 17, 1502, and so he sent his brother, Don Bartolomé, ashore to claim the territory for Spain. Columbus named the land Honduras from the Spanish word *hondura,* which means "depth" or "profundity."

On this voyage also, Columbus found shelter leeward of a tiny island off Puerto Limón, Costa Rica. He called it "Little Orchard," and today it is known as Uvito (little grape). He named this land, characterized by a lovely shore of palm trees and white beaches and crystal waters, Costa Rica (rich coast). He was impressed by the gold ornaments worn by the Carib Indians and did not realize that gold was actually hard to come by. There was the earth and its riches, but it was the metal gold, and specifically gold, that made men's eyes light up then.

There were other explorers who vied with Columbus in claiming the new world for Spain. Francisco Pizarro found Peru and Inca gold; Alonso de Ojeda, Diego de Nicuesa, and Martín Fernández de Enciso concentrated their efforts south of what is Central America. Vasco Núñez de Balboa, on a height in Panama, was the first to behold the Pacific. But none was so directly associated with Central America as the Genoese who sailed for the Spanish crown. Central American history pivots around his visit; all that has ever happened there is characterized as pre-Columbian or post-Columbian.

On the heels of the explorers came the conquistadores; some traveled south from Mexico, others north from Panama and Colombia. Among the most famous of these were Francisco Fernández de Córdoba, Gil González Dávila, Pedro Arias de Ávila, who in bitter rivalry operated in the areas that are now Costa Rica and Nicaragua; and Martín Estete, known for his cruelty to the Chaparrestique Indians in the land now called El Salvador. In their thirst for gold the conquistadores were almost as busy fighting one another as the Indians.

A typical case involved two officers of Cortés, Mexico's conqueror. Cristóbal de Olid was dispatched southward from Mexico by Cortés to take over Honduras. Instead, he claimed it for himself. Cortés then sent Francisco de las Casas to deal with Olid. Olid took las Casas prisoner and also captured another rival in that earlier Mafia-like fraternity, Dávila. The two prisoners plotted, arranged to spend an evening with Olid, and killed him. In another case, Francisco Fernández de Córdoba was beheaded in the plaza at León, Nicaragua, by *his* insupportable rival, Pedro Arias de Ávila, whose name was contracted to Pedrarias.

As there was only one explorer of unique significance to Central America, so there was one conquistador whose triumphant exploits were most fateful in Central American history. The name that really counts is that of Pedro de Alvarado who, in 1523, was dispatched south from Mexico by Cortés.

First he concentrated on subduing the proud Mayas in Guatemala. Near Quezaltenango, at Olintepeque, on February 24, 1524, Alvarado was confronted by the warriors of the Maya-

Quiché prince, Tecúm Umán. The Indians were almost naked; they were armed with stone-tipped spears and carried small round shields of tapir skin. Alvarado and his men were mounted on horses; they wore armor and carried sharp metal spears. The Mayas had never before seen horses; they thought that the horse and the man were one creature—just as the Greeks imagined centaurs in their mythological legends. These did not seem to be men they were facing but gods or emissaries of the gods.

The Mayan warriors were easily slaughtered by the towering Spanish. Prince Tecúm Umán, gallantly concerned for the lives of his men, went forward alone to meet Alvarado and duel with him. It didn't take long. Legend, in its delicate merger with history, records that a quetzal, the gentle bird of bright plumage and long tail-feathers that flies high near the peaks of volcanoes, mates in the rain forests, and is known as the bird of freedom, came to the grievously wounded prince, fluttered down beside him, and died with him. Alxit, Tecúm Umán's princess (María Tecúm as the Spanish called her), heard of his death from runners, who had picked up the news from drummers. She committed suicide by driving poison into her breast with a sharp stone.

Southward, Alvarado met fierce resistance from the Pipiles, a tribe of mixed Mayan and Indians who had emigrated from Mexico. In a battle near what is now San Salvador, he was pinned to his saddle by an Indian arrow but fought on to victory. In 1536 in Honduras (where Alvarado founded the city that he named for himself, San Pedro Sula), Indian opposition was led by Chief Lempira, who confronted the Spanish with thirty thousand warriors. Shrewdly deciding that a battle would mean defeat, Alvarado invited Lempira to a peace conference and had him assassinated. Without their leader, the Indians offered no further resistance.

Often the pattern of conquest was one of treachery. Indians who had never met Spaniards were usually friendly and cooperative. In 1521, when Gil González Dávila crossed the Gulf of Nicoya to what is now the peninsula of Nicoya in Costa Rica, Chief Nicoya greeted him cordially and lent him guides to lead him into Nicaragua. There Chief Nicarao (for whom Nicaragua is named), a peace-loving man, agreed to have his people converted to Catholicism and promised allegiance to the Spanish crown. However, when his people were driven from their communities and hundreds were killed, he fought bitterly and died in combat. The Indians withdrew into the most inaccessible parts of the Nicaraguan wilderness. Back on the peninsula of Nicoya, in Costa Rica, González was followed by Spanish occupation forces led by Córdoba, whose treatment of the originally friendly Chief Nicoya and his people is a horrifying episode in the history of Costa Rica; children are said to have been fed to war dogs and maidens raped.

Native contempt for Spanish avarice was reflected in an incident on the southern end of the isthmus. Indians captured several of the hated Pedrarias's soldiers and poured molten gold down their throats, saying, "Eat, Christians! Take your fill of gold!" As late as 1833, an Indian leader, Anastasio Aquino, fought his way into the town of San Vicente in El Salvador, sacked it, seized all valuables, placed on his head the gold and emerald crown of Nuestra Señora del Pilar, in the church of that name, and carried off a number of Spanish ladies as hostages. He was pursued and finally captured and hanged.

In Antigua, Guatemala, where the climate was cool and the steep ascent made attacks from enemies difficult, Pedro de Alvarado founded the colonies' capital city. By coach he brought from the coast books, furniture, and fabrics shipped from the Old World. From here he governed the far-flung empire in the name of the Captaincy-General, the Spanish crown's delegated authority.

In July 1541 Alvarado died of injuries incurred when a riderless horse shied and fell on him. His twenty-two-year-old widow, Doña Beatriz de la Cueva, ordered the palace and public buildings painted black and draped in black. The city was still in deep mourning on September 10, the day Doña Beatriz signed a decree proclaiming herself governor. *La Sin Ventura,* she characterized herself on the document—"the hapless one."

That midnight there was a severe earthquake in the midst

of a thundershower with roaring tropical rains. No one is sure whether or not the earthquake originated in the depths of the volcano Agua, perhaps in the root system, but it rocked the crater lake on the summit. In the cataclysm the water in the lake slopped over and sent a sudden torrent rushing down upon Antigua. Of the 1400 residents, 1300 perished in the flood or were buried in the silt. Doña Beatriz carried her five-year-old daughter Anica to the palace chapel; there they and eleven ladies of the court died when the roof and walls collapsed.

Thus was the original Antigua destroyed, but it was immediately rebuilt a little farther away from the foot of Agua, and Antigua remained the hub of Central American government until 1773, when an earthquake was followed by a plague and the capital was moved to the valley, to what is now Guatemala City.

Early colonialism was characterized by a bewildering diversity of policy. Ruthless conquistadores were often accompanied or closely followed by missionary priests, Jesuits and Franciscans and Dominicans, whose purpose was to convert the Indians. They often founded schools and orphanages and used imaginative and loving methods to win over the "savages." The wisest did not insist on strict adherence to traditional Catholic ritual but permitted a blending of ancient pagan customs. Remnants of this compromise persist in Central American Indian communities to this day. On the steps of the church at Chichicastenango (Guatemala), Indians burn blue cakes of *pom*, an incense that dates from ceremonies of the Mayan Old Empire, as an offering to the gods of their ancestors, before they enter the church and approach the Catholic altar.

A sympathetic colonial missionary was a Dominican, Bartolomé de las Casas, who kept a sharp eye out for abuses of Indians and promptly reported them to the crown. He insisted that the Indians be converted by persuasion rather than by decree or force, and he was very successful with the proud and aloof Mayas of the Guatemalan highlands. Father Bartolomé learned the Mayan language and composed ballads that told the story of Christ and his philosophy. He taught his ballads to groups of

Christian Indians, who sang them in remote villages and drew the curious Mayas to mission churches. Another much-beloved priest was Brother Pedro Betancourt of Antigua, whose grave the Indians still decorate with flowers. He founded a hospital for Indians and literally died of overwork, trying to minister to hordes of patients.

At the outset of colonialism, Queen Isabella had decreed that it was illegal to enslave the Indians. A number of Negro slaves were imported to serve Central American landholders; apparently the *idea* of slavery was not abhorrent. Isabella's concern for Indian freedom was a monarchical indulgence. An *encomienda* system was instituted instead, but it put the Indians under the thumbs of Spanish overlords anyway. Under this system, the crown entrusted the Indians to Spanish aristocrats, who were supposed to be responsible for their welfare, their education, health, and religious training, *in return for their labor*. Some *encomienda* holders were more compassionate and conscientious than others, but in general the Indians were not benefited by this hopefully high-minded attitude of their conquerors.

There was a rigid definition of classes, and of class privileges and restrictions, in colonial times, which to this day continues to make upward mobility in society difficult. *Peninsulares*—those who had been born in Spain—were the nobility. *Criollos* (Creoles), who were of pure Spanish blood but had been born in Central America, were not eligible for important administrative jobs. The *mestizos*, of mixed Spanish and Indian blood, were at the bottom of the ladder. Indians or Negroes did not count at all in colonial society.

What eventually led to the wish for independence from Spain was that the conquerors themselves became increasingly attached to the New World; as Central Americans they began to resent the greedy outreach of Spain. There was increasing intermarriage between Indians and Spaniards; the number of Central American residents who had been born in Spain dwindled; *mestizos* became more numerous than *criollos*. A mingling of Old and New World customs resulted in a unique life style. While the first colonial cities were patterned after those in the mother country, with a central plaza and cobblestone streets angling off to the edges of town, roads were usually Indian trade routes. Those of part-Spanish heritage learned to play the marimba, a Mayan instrument, and Indians added Spanish guitars to their processional bands. During the fiestas of Catholic saints, ancient Indian dances were incorporated and performed to *chirimía* and drum. Though Central Americans shared the same faith—to this day over 95 per cent are Catholic—and the common language was Spanish, very few had ever laid eyes on Barcelona, Seville, or Madrid. Isthmians began to resent Spain's draining of their riches.

The first voice publicly to urge independence from Spain was that of a priest, Father José Matías Delgado, who spoke from the bell tower of his church, Nuestra Señora de la Merced, in San Salvador on November 5, 1811. But this dream was already being expressed by individuals and groups from one end of the isthmus to the other. Ten years later, at Guatemala City, the five Central American colonies, united in a federation, declared their independence from Spain, specifically from the Captaincy-General and the Royal Audiencia (the official court of justice), thus ending the colonial period which had begun in 1502.

Spain sent no army to quell this particular American revolution. Geography and the difficulties of equipping and shipping a sufficient striking force appear to have discouraged Spain. The troubles that beset the Central Americans in the first century and a half of independence came not from without but from within.

Central Americans had had absolutely no experience at self-government; the handful in administrative positions had always been appointed, not elected. Most of the people were illiterate and had a chronic attitude of helplessness toward the powerful. In each country the landholding oligarchy was fearful of change. From one end of the isthmus to the other, liberal and conservative forces were at odds. Within each state there was political chaos. A president was more likely to take office or be deposed through military coup than by election. Nicaragua alone had fifteen presidents in six years. When the Honduran army in 1963 ousted progressive president Ramón Morales, it was the 136th revolution in the 142 years of Honduran independence.

Too often those who longed for "stability" found themselves grateful for firmly ensconced dictators, whose policies were likely to be more long-lasting than those of elected presidents. But dictators do not encourage self-government, and when self-government within the states repeatedly failed, the federation itself was doomed.

In the 1830s Ambassador John Lloyd Stephens was dispatched to Central America to convey United States goals and philosophies to the federation. He arrived to find that there was no federation (which was dissolved for the third time in 1838). He spent two years hopelessly searching for a government to which he could be accredited. Stephens traveled extensively, talked to leaders of the day, and in the end gave up and came home.

The states were also constantly feuding with each other, over borders, over national policies considered unfavorable by their neighbors. Guatemala and El Salvador were at war between 1826 and 1840. As recently as 1955 there was hostility between Nicaragua and its neighbor to the south, Costa Rica. Some four hundred Nicaraguans invaded Costa Rica, apparently intending to capture valuable road-building machinery at Liberia. A contemporary Latin Paul Revere warned the Costa Ricans, and the construction equipment was driven away before the invaders arrived. There was successful intervention by the Organization of American States and the attackers went home. And in the summer of 1969 the OAS succeeded in cooling off a shooting war, the so-called "futbol war," triggered by a soccer game between Honduras and El Salvador.

To add to the disruptiveness of these Central American family fights, there were outsiders on the scene whose rivalries compounded the confusion and increased the distracting agitations during the colonial era and after. The British repeatedly quarreled with the Nicaraguans, allying themselves with the Miskito Indians of the Caribbean Coast. In 1740 Nicaraguan history reports a British "plot" to take over the province. They did penetrate inland Nicaragua via the Coco River and sacked the city of Jinotega. Later, troops commanded by Alejandro McDonald, administrator of British Honduras, seized the vital port of San Juan del Norte.

In the mid-nineteenth century the dissolution of the Federation of Central American States was cause for rumbles between England and El Salvador. England had loaned money to the federation. When it fell apart, each state was assigned a share of the debt. El Salvador felt that an unfair burden had been placed upon it, smallest of all the Central American republics, and objected to paying the debt. British gunboats blocked the lifeline ports of Acajutla and La Unión and occupied the island of El Tigre, in the Bay of Fonseca. Ironically the United States, Britain's chief rival, served as intermediary in the squabble and negotiated a compromise. The British men-of-war withdrew.

Individual opportunists in this land of opportunity were rarely native Central Americans, whose fixed status at birth discouraged the incidence of "self-made men." Fortunes were made by foreign dreamers and activists like gringo Minor Keith, who stubbornly built the first railroad in Costa Rica, linking San José with Puerto Limón; took to raising bananas to finance the operation; and, with fellow-Americans Lorenzo Dow Baker and Andrew Preston, founded the United Fruit Company. In the 1920s Lowell Yerex, a New Zealander, flew into Honduras, was struck by the lack of roads and transportation facilities, and initiated a freight and passenger-carrying service by air which became TACA—Transportes Aéreos Centro Americanos—now one of the most prosperous airlines in Latin America.

The Spanish may have been the first and most fateful invaders of Central America, but they were not the last. Pirates, mostly Dutch and English, hid out in the coves of the Bay Islands on the Atlantic and in the Gulf of Fonseca on the Pacific. In those days it was as respectable to be a pirate as it is to be an astronaut today, and their homelands were usually very grateful to them. One of the most famous pirates, Henry Morgan, was knighted by the English crown and became Sir Henry Morgan. It is said that Morgan bought a pirate ship and a "pirate's outfit" (probably including the skull and crossbones insignia, a "cutlass" for his belt, and a patch for his eye) second hand. This second-hand pirate was much dreaded on land and sea.

The British Commonwealth has such pirates to thank for that strip of land adjacent to Guatemala now known as British Honduras. In the seventeenth century a number of buccaneers turned landlubbers, built homes ashore, and became loggers, shipping out profitable loads of mahogany, rosewood, pine, and cedar, which were much in demand in Europe. England and Spain were constantly quarreling over which had the right to "British" Honduras. When Guatemala declared its independence from Spain, England took a tighter bulldog hold on Honduras. Guatemala still has an eye on it, however, and feels that it should rightfully be annexed to Guatemala. It is now the only English-speaking country on the isthmus, although the inhabitants are a melting-pot mixture of the first pirate families, Caribs, Africans, and other strains.

The present fast-developing port of Bluefields, on the Caribbean coast of Nicaragua, was named for a Dutch pirate, Mynheer Blewfeldt. He and other seafaring predators were constantly sneaking up the San Juan River, crossing Lake Nicaragua, and sacking the lovely colonial city of Granada that had been founded by Córdoba in 1524.

The Nicaraguan port of San Juan del Norte, at the mouth of the San Juan River, was stage center for some of the dramatic incidents in isthmian history. It was on the upper reaches of the San Juan River that a nineteen-year-old, Rafaela Herrera, became a Nicaraguan national heroine. She was the daughter of the commander of the fort at San Carlos, which guarded the entry to Lake Nicaragua. That Rafaela did something heroic seems certain, as she was gratefully granted a pension by the Spanish crown. But history books are either conflicting or vague about her actions. There is some confusion over whether her alarm was "The British are coming!" or "The pirates are coming!" (The answer may be that they were British pirates.) In a recent official history of Nicaragua, *Tierra de Maravillas* (wondrous land), a section in English reads: "In 1762 Rafaela Herrera . . . performed one of the greatest feats in our history by beating off the

attacking British. . . ." How Rafaela "beat them off" single-handed
is not satisfactorily explained. One source relates that she "soaked
clothing in alcohol and sent the blazing garments down the river,
repelling the invaders." However, there are very few acknowl-
edged heroines in ancient or contemporary history of Central
America, and we must be sufficiently thankful for Rafaela.

A strip of the isthmus between the oceans—San Juan del
Norte on the Atlantic and San Juan del Sur, a Pacific port—
made a fortune for "Commodore" Cornelius Vanderbilt in the
mid-nineteenth century. During the California Gold Rush, there
were only two ways, both long and dangerous, for Forty-Niners
to travel to the west coast of North America—overland, with
war-whooping Indians and desperadoes on the attack, or around
treacherous Cape Horn, at the southernmost extremity of South
America. Vanderbilt shrewdly saw the short cut in Central
America, via the San Juan River and Lake Nicaragua to San
Juan del Sur. He founded the Accessory Transit Company and
transported Forty-Niners by the hundreds, taking them by ship
to San Juan del Norte, by river boat to Peñas Blancas on the
shore of Lake Nicaragua, and by stagecoach to San Juan del Sur,
where they boarded another vessel for California. The route between the two oceans became known as "the Vanderbilt Road."

This relatively swift passage gave fresh impetus to the idea
of a transisthmian canal. It was not a new thought. As early as
1520 Diego de Mercado had demonstrated the feasibility of such
a canal. The river and the lake offered a sea-level waterway, with
only thirty miles of land between the lake and the Pacific Ocean.
Vanderbilt interested the United States Government in obtain-
ing permission to construct the canal. Of course he wished to
oversee its construction and be handsomely rewarded for it.

England naturally took a dim view of an American-operated
canal; it posed a threat to British commerce. They vied with the
United States to become the authorized constructors of the canal.
In order to reinforce their strategic position on the Caribbean,
they chose an Indian *cacique*, or chief, and crowned him King
of Miskitia; in previous skirmishes the Miskito Indians had proved
to be effective allies.

To avoid a conflict, England's Sir Henry Bulwer and America's Secretary of State John M. Clayton signed a treaty in 1850, the substance of which was that neither country would ever construct a canal over which either would exercise exclusive control. However, in the next decades, American influence in Central America, particularly in Nicaragua, became steadily stronger and British influence waned.

That the canal was finally located in Panama is rumored to have been due to a Nicaraguan postal stamp that pictured volcanoes. It is said that an official letter thus stamped was received in Washington, D.C., and led the Congress of the United States to conclude that Nicaragua was risky. (To this day a number of American citizens, despite violence of all kinds at home, which they either overlook or project elsewhere, fear that Central America is "risky" to visit.) However, one day there may be a second canal, one from San Juan del Norte to San Juan del Sur. It is a perennial idea and still a prerogative of the United States Government to construct; in 1916 the United States and Nicaragua signed a treaty in which the United States was given exclusive rights into perpetuity to construct a canal across the country. For this the Nicaraguans received three million dollars.

During the chaotic years of vendettas between factions within and among the Central American states, of struggles between England and the United States to achieve supremacy on the isthmus, and of the machinations of finagling fortune-hunters who were not native Central Americans, there appeared on the already dizzying scene a Tennessee gringo, "General" William Walker. The plots within plots that were generated by his conquests make one think of a stageful of baritone soloists, each trying to sing "Ol' Man River" louder than the other and behaving as if he were alone on the stage in the spotlight.

Walker himself was the very embodiment of confusion. Ex-journalist and medical student, he had been a liberal in his extreme youth—opposed to slavery and for women's rights, for instance. Somehow, during his exploits in Central America, he became an arrogant opponent of independence. To compound the confusion, the United States wavered in its opinion of

Walker; officially the government disowned Walker, whose actions were never sanctioned. He was a self-appointed "liberator,"
operating with troops of mercenaries armed by privately raised
funds. Nonetheless the United States had reason to be secretly
grateful to him. In 1853 Walker set forth to free Sonora, Mexico,
with the avowed purpose of making it an independent state.
Though he never conclusively conquered the area, Mexico pan-
icked and sold 45,000 square miles of Sonora to the United States
(the Gadsden Purchase); this territory was added to Arizona
and New Mexico.

Walker's efforts to free Sonora made him a hero in Central
America, and it was a Nicaraguan family quarrel that led to his
being invited to join the fray. Nicaraguan liberals, who opposed
the influence of the Catholic Church, and the conservatives, who
supported it, had been feuding for years. The stronghold of the
conservatives was Granada; that of the liberals was León. The
liberals contacted Walker and arranged for him to lead an in-
vasion of Granada. Certain wealthy Americans, who were rivals
of Cornelius Vanderbilt, supplied arms and ammunition, realiz-
ing that if Walker were triumphant he could cramp the Commodore's style in Central America. Walker and his filibusters
(from the Spanish *filibustero,* which means freebooter, bucca-
neer) attacked and captured Granada. Instead of turning over
the government to the liberals whom he represented, Walker
grandiosely had himself elected president of Nicaragua in June
1856.

The opposition to Walker drew the whole cast of characters
on the Central American scene into a grand finale of cross-
purposes. President Juan Rafael Mora of Costa Rica allied all of
Central America against the gringo impostor and implored fellow-
isthmians to march against the horde of "bandits." From San
José, on February 29, 1856, he issued a passionate proclamation:
"Arise! Annihilate your oppressors. . . . Bury your internal differences forever. . . . God will give us liberty and with it peace,
concord, liberty, and union in the great Central American
family." And, because it is Central American to be flowery, he
added, "Your mothers, wives and sisters animate you . . . their

patriotic virtues will make us invincible." Mora's troops were supported and armed by the British, who opposed American triumphs of any kind, and by Cornelius Vanderbilt, who knew that his rivals had financed Walker.

Mora led an army of 300, mostly Costa Ricans, into the Nicaraguan city of Rivas and occupied buildings around the Central Square. Walker, with 550 followers, including some Indians whom he had conned into the cause, set forth to storm Rivas and capture Mora. As Walker and his filibusters moved into the Central Square, Mora and his men opened fire. Walker and his troops took cover in a large building. Mora asked for a volunteer to set fire to the building, in order to flush out Walker. The volunteer became a Costa Rican national hero; his name was Juan Santamaría and he hailed from Alajuela, Costa Rica. Juan ran around the building where Walker was holed up, tossing firebrands through the windows. During this one-man raid Santamaría was shot and killed. (Cannon from the battle of Rivas may be seen today in Parque Santamaría at Alajuela.)

The deaths from the battle were as nothing to those that followed, from cholera. Corpses of slain filibusters and Costa Ricans, fallen or shoved into wells, were thought to have triggered the outbreak. Hundreds of cholera victims were buried in the sands near San Juan del Sur.

Walker's decisive defeat occurred in 1857, when Mora crossed Lake Nicaragua and took Virgin Bay, where Walker and his men were encamped. One column of Mora's army was commanded by a British army captain, another by a Vanderbilt agent. Walker was rescued by an American warship and taken home to the United States. However, he did not have the good sense to stay there. In 1860 he returned to Central America, going ashore at the port of Trujillo, Honduras. There the British, who were patrolling the Miskito Coast, seized him and turned him over to Honduran officials. Next morning he was shot by a firing squad of "barefooted Hondurans." Their aim was not too good and the squad commander had to fire a *coup de grâce*.

A sad reminder of the confusions and power struggles of the years following independence is that most of Central America's heroes and patriots, to whom statues have been tardily erected, were assassinated. Juan Rafael Mora, Costa Rica's heroic president, was eventually deposed by his military leaders, stood up against a tree in Puntarenas, and shot. General Francisco Morazán, who probably fought harder for Central American unity than any other patriot on the isthmus, was hated by conservatives and died before a firing squad. El Salvador's General Gerardo Barrios, a progressive president who pioneered in encouraging the cultivation of coffee, so beneficial to the economy, was exiled in 1864, took refuge in Costa Rica, returned to his native land a year later, and was captured and shot under a ceiba tree.

Early in the twentieth century the stage became somewhat less cluttered and the spotlight was on the occupation of Nicaragua by the United States Marines, who landed repeatedly at Bluefields from 1912 to 1932 to "keep order." The liberals and conservatives were still bitterly fighting for their principles, but these military Americans, especially in a land where military coups were traditional, cast a long shadow over all of Central America.

Conservative Adolfo Díaz, who was *simpático* with the United States, was president of Nicaragua in 1916 when he signed the treaty giving the United States exclusive rights to the proposed transisthmian canal. Next, the United States supported the election of Diego Manuel Chamorro. Following the withdrawal of Marines in August 1925, the liberals revolted against Chamorro and established a separate government on the Miskito Coast. The Marines returned and reinstated Díaz, whose friendly attitude toward United States policies could be relied upon. Guerrilla patriot General César Agosto Sandino took to the jungles and the mountains and harassed the Marines.

In November 1928, liberal José María Moncada became president of Nicaragua, with United States blessing. The conservatives had made peace with him. Hopefully he represented a coalition. Meantime, the Marines were training the Guardia Nacional (National Guard) of Nicaragua, whose leader was Anastasio ("Tacho") Somoza. Somoza seized power in 1937, assumed the presidency, and the Marines withdrew. Having no more Marines to fight, Sandino came down out of the hills and was promptly assassinated during a visit to Managua.

During the administration of Franklin Delano Roosevelt there was a significant change in the attitude of the United States toward Latin America, with the enunciation of the Good Neighbor Policy. In 1933 at Montevideo, Uruguay, Secretary of State Cordell Hull presented an agreement, which was signed by all conference members, that no American republic had the right to interfere in another republic's affairs. Thereafter the influence of the United States in Central America, while still potent, was brought to bear in an entirely different style.

Today the United States is very much involved as backer-catalyst-teacher on all levels of the Central American economy and culture, but in a manner not so much of imposition as of response to specifically requested help and advice.

In 1960, at Punta del Este, Uruguay, the United States joined its hemispheric fellow-nations in an Alliance for Progress— *Alianza para Progreso*—described as "a great cooperative effort to accelerate economic and social development." Its proclaimed object was "to achieve maximum levels of well-being." Through the Alliance the United States has been making more than nineteen million dollars a year available to the five Central American nations for roads, schools, housing, and medical facilities. Though budgets and policies may shift with administrations and changing times, continuing involvement with and concern for the developing isthmian nations are inevitable.

Dozens of American government and private agencies are pitching in vigorously and effectively. The Peace Corps has many projects, from teaching Central American teachers to developing a Central American Fisheries program—bringing marine biologists, gear technicians, and other indispensable specialists to the Atlantic and Pacific ports of the isthmus. The International Executive Service Corps is sending top men in American business and industry to advise nationals on the development, management, and operation of industrial plants. The A.I.D. (Aid for International Development) has a broad scope; one of its recent projects is the introduction of Guatemalan handicrafts to international markets. The U.S.I.S. (United States Information Service) provides classrooms and education programs, and fosters cultural activities. Private agencies, such as CARE, are fulfilling urgent needs, establishing free-lunch programs and the purification of water systems. The hospital ship *Hope* has brought modern medicine to the isthmus. And this is only a partial indication of American activity there.

Many American individuals are working in training and community development programs on their own. They came, they saw, and were conquered. In Chimaltenango, Guatemala, an American doctor, Carroll Berhorst, has founded a clinic and hospital. He treats the proud highland Indians, descendants of the Mayas, for twenty-five cents a visit (because he knows they would not accept care for nothing). At night, when the long days in the clinic and hospital are over, he trains highly recommended young Indian men to practice medicine in their far-flung communities. His colleague, a Peace Corps volunteer, is showing these same young men how to grow green vegetables to augment their people's inadequate diet of corn and beans. The doctor and the agronomist are not having to beat the bushes to convert the Indians to these particular ideas; the Indians come to them in overwhelming numbers. Thus an entirely new type of community leader is emerging: young men who can practice both modern medicine and modern agronomy.

In Tegucigalpa, Honduras, through the efforts of Mrs. Maxwell Becker, the wife of an A.I.D. official, day nurseries have been set up; not only have these been a great success locally, but they serve as pilot programs for all of Central America's cities.

In poverty-stricken Esquipulas, Guatemala, a middle-aged American woman, deeply moved by the plight of the people, is teaching upward of fifty women to weave and embroider wall hangings for the booming international craft market. Such help is working beautifully. It has really changed the scene.

But the most heartening development on the isthmus has been the cooperation of the five republics in the Mercado Común Centro Americano (Central American Common Market). Tariffs on trade with one another have virtually been abolished, and a common tariff on imports from other nations of the world established; the common tariff now exists for about 98 per cent of all imported items. CACM achievements include the launching of new industries under the aegis of the Central American Bank for Economic Integration, an influx of private investments, a diversification of crops, and a gradual departure from agriculture as the hub of the economy; it is helping numerous citizens to move from *finca* to factory. The five nations provide an impressive market for themselves—thirteen million people with a gross national product of more than four billion dollars.

This upbeat atmosphere has stimulated individual enterprise. A new cement plant in Costa Rica was financed by the sale of stock at $15 a share to upward of three thousand low-income families. It was possible to purchase a share by paying $4.50 down, the balance in payments over a two-year period. The plant obviates the necessity for importing cement, which once cost the country over a million dollars a year. And of course, prior to local investment the profits from this essential construction material were realized outside the local economy.

The individual Central American family has always been wondrously devoted and united, but it has had an autonomous attitude; family strength seemed to end at each front door, and in every state and among the states there was a fatal dissidence. Now Central Americans are becoming community-minded, learning to organize and use community resources. Despite recent altercations between El Salvador and Honduras, the five republics are learning to be "good neighbors" in a sense never before experienced in their history. That Central Americans will increasingly bring their unique qualities and resources to the world family is inevitable.

7 / Digging for_
Pre-Columbian Artifacts

Jewelry, stone sculpture, glazed ceramics, thousands of years old, still lie under the ground from one end of Central America to the other. Nowhere else in the world is there such an abundance of museum pieces that can be dug up like potatoes, each one beautiful without regard to antiquity.

Long before the birth of Christ the isthmus was populated by Mayas and other cultivated Indians who were skilled craftsmen. The narrow bridge of land also served as a trade route between North and South America, so that the artifacts, which have often been shuffled from one earth strata to another through earthquakes or volcanic action, have a fascinating diversity. On a hill near Acajutla (El Salvador) two figures were unearthed that have no relationship to other pre-Columbian sculpture. (They may now be viewed in the National Museum in the capital, San Salvador.) Both Mayan and Aztec artifacts have been found in Nicaragua; some artifacts must have come from as far away as Peru in trade, and some must have been made by indigenous tribes whose culture is as yet little understood.

There is not a patch of soil from Guatemala to Costa Rica that does not promise buried treasure, except those places that have already been painstakingly excavated, and these are few. What can be unearthed are ceramic vessels in an infinite variety of shapes and sizes and functional purposes; sculptured effigies of animal or human figures, footed or ring-based or flanged or in dozens of other forms; tiny jugs and dishes tenderly fashioned for the graves of children. There are ceramic flutes or ocarinas, in the shapes of animals or birds, which still have a haunting sound when blown; ceramic drums whose tops of peccary or iguana hide have long since joined the dust; blue and green conch necklaces; bells like sleigh bells (oddly, to us Santa Claus people, they were funeral emblems); ceramic weights for fish nets.

Among the loveliest objects are jade plaques, which were worn on a necklace of tubular jade beads; these were sculptured in low relief by artisans using cane drills with sand as an abrasive. Ceramic medallions were made in the familiar and beautiful shapes of nature—owls, outspread bird-wings, fish; one was the effigy of a bird with a long bill (like our stork) who was thought to create human life.

The gold jewelry is exquisite, and usually very small, because gold was rather rare, as the conquistadores later found. There are little frogs, parrots, crocodiles, butterflies, lobsters, all less than an inch long. Even the old stone molds for these ornaments can be unearthed; one stone may be incised with the impressions for a number of pendant ornaments. And oddments such as printers' rollers may be found; incised on stone or clay may be totemic designs. They once decorated a warrior's chest, or, when rolled across fabric, they imprinted a design. You can find tiny vessels that once held the venom of serpents used for poisoned arrows; wonderfully, after all these hundreds of years, they retain traces of venom which, when analyzed, is still virulent.

Many Central American families have a hobby of digging for artifacts. You cannot visit a home of any consequence without finding a few representative pieces, and we have seen several exciting and extensive collections. Hundreds of village families make a living out of digging and selling their finds on the street or to hotel-lobby gift shops.

Since world-wide interest in pre-Columbian art is on the increase and anybody can dig anywhere, spadework has been stepped up in recent years. Even if you are a tourist, finders are keepers. The reason a tourist can take away pre-Columbian treasure is simple; his luggage is given the once-over by customs when he enters a Central American country, but it is never looked at when he leaves. Up to now, what a tourist takes out has not been as important to the authorities as what he brings in. This *laissez faire* attitude is not likely to continue indefinitely, however.

Years ago, there was a prophetic occurrence at Puerto Barrios in Guatemala. Some workmen digging a canal found an incised jade pendant dated A.D. 320 in Mayan numerals. It is one of the earliest Mayan pieces of any size anywhere, and it is now known as the Leyden plate, the pride of a museum in Holland. Through the colonial era and since, hundreds of such precious pieces have been taken away. The fact of this plundered heritage is deplorable.

There are many known sites with an established potential where diggers are still taking home ceramics and jewelry from every excursion. Among them are the Nicoya peninsula in Costa Rica, near Puntarenas; Zapatera Island in Lake Nicaragua; and the Lenca mounds near San Miguel in El Salvador. But it is the ubiquitousness of these relics that is remarkable. One woman was digging under a tree behind her house in Nandaime, Nicaragua, when she found two sculptured stone idols, perhaps thrust up close to the surface through the action of an earthquake. Skin-divers have brought up treasures from the bottoms of lakes and inland rivers. Artifacts have even been found washed up on shore, particularly after a storm, and have been picked up by beachcombers. Many farmers have unearthed beautiful vases or ceramic vessels while plowing, and anyone excavating for a house is likely to find pottery if the bulldozer doesn't smash it. Important archaeological pieces were found when Mejicanos, a *colonia* (or development) on the outskirts of San Salvador, was being built. Others were unearthed during the development of Zapote Hill. Near Masaya, in Nicaragua, is Nindirí, an Indian village. A small museum there is filled with pre-Columbian art that was found when the earth was plowed for planting.

There is a whole category of pre-Columbian art known as *"Línea Vieja"* (old line) because hundreds of interesting, intact pieces were found in Costa Rica during the construction of the railroad from San José to Puerto Limón. One of the earliest shapes in the Línea Vieja ware is that of twin jugs, joined together at the handles and at the base.

Each region has indigenous art. Many grinding stones, three-legged and exquisitely sculptured, have been found on the western slope of Irazú volcano in Costa Rica. Even within one small country, findings vary from site to site. In El Salvador the area near Suchitoto yields glazed plumbate ware. Usulután is noted for a unique pottery that bears the archaeological name "Usulután ware." Polychrome and black pottery are unearthed at Chalchuapa, near the ruins of Tazumal.

The ring-based vessel is typical of the Atlantic watershed. In the Ulúa River region of Honduras (banana country), field hands find shell jewelry carved and inlaid with jade. Obsidian tools are actually strewn over the surface of the earth at El Chayal, southeast of Guatemala City; this was apparently the site of a Mayan obsidian workshop, for there are half-finished spear tips, scraping implements, and knives. Burnished, dark brown vessels, known as *cerámica de chocolate,* are typical of the Nicoya peninsula, as are painted vessels in beautiful colors that still endure. Modeled heads are found in the highlands of Honduras. Along the Reventazón River in Costa Rica, which flows toward the Atlantic, vessels with elongated legs and clay appliqué designs turn up. Clay appears to have been snaked out of a funnel, like designs on a birthday cake. The Chixoy Valley of Alta Vera Paz, Guatemala, yields vessels and jars with historically important paintings of Mayan activities. (A noble is borne on a palanquin by slaves; his dog, wearing a fancy saddle, trots along by his side.) And there are remarkable effigy vessels, well-modeled portraits of humans, animals, and birds.

One of the troubles with the relatively unchecked activities of diggers has been the quantities of ceramics smashed and shattered through amateurish techniques. Some dig when the earth is too dry, with disastrous results. Some lift a vessel out intact but do not allow it to become acclimated before handling it, and it breaks in their hands. Or they attempt to wash the earth from the surface of the vessel to uncover the painting and scrub off all the paint. Often an amateur will empty the earth from a vessel without screening it and lose valuable small objects, such as beads or toys. Two people we know, who are now first-rate amateur archaeologists, confess that they smashed more than they took home before they learned how to handle it.

Native archaeologists particularly deplore amateur diggers because often, in searching for underground treasure, they destroy important archaeological material, such as the remains of old campfires or stone work that might be a clue to a ceremonial center. They are especially heartsick over those that use dynamite to blast their way under the surface to open a mound, thus disturbing or destroying valuable historical clues. Most amateurs do not understand the relative importance of what they have found; they do not know the archaeological sequences of pottery manufacture (Old Empire, Chicanel, Tyakol, Tepeu, etc.), nor do they know how to place a piece in time through characteristics of design, shape, material.

Central American archaeologists have a word for these ruthless diggers; they call them *juaqueros,* or grave robbers. This obviously includes the gringo tourist. A tightening up of the opportunity to plunder seems to be taking place gradually, but legislation is not the answer. "The legislation is usually adequate," a professor of archaeology at the University of Costa Rica told us, "but it is difficult to enforce."

There is the problem of policing all the miles of wilderness, and the problem of the private property owner, who has the say-so about what happens on his own land. If he wants to invite diggers for the weekend, who is to stop him?

El Salvador has legislated against the exportation of plundered artifacts but still does not inspect outgoing luggage. And what customs official, in any event, would be able to identify the true pre-Columbian artifact from the fake or copy? A great many fakes are now being manufactured and peddled. Craftsmen cleverly copy an ancient ceramic design, bury it, and dig it up after weathering has given it an authentic look. These plant-now-and-dig-later hoaxers peddle their wares at village markets, on the streets, and in front of tourist hotels and motels. There is even a factory now for such fakes in Masaya, Nicaragua.

But something has recently happened that may be a good omen and shows that conscience is the best legislator. At Cartago, in Costa Rica, a new pre-Columbian site of great historical importance has been excavated on the hacienda of the Gómez family. It is a ceremonial center, including fifteen mounds, ascended by stone stairs from connecting causeways. The covered aqueducts of this ancient city still hold water. The ceramics, jewelry, and tools that have been uncovered are different from any hitherto discovered in pre-Columbian tribal ceremonial centers.

This was an exciting find, but even more exciting, in a way, was the disposition of it. The Gómez family cooperated with the government and regarded it as a public trust, even though it was on their property. Eventually, that center will be preserved as a national park, and the artifacts found there will be exhibited in a museum on the premises. The site will be excavated, meantime, by experts, and a government-posted police guard will fend off all unauthorized persons.

We have been told that there are growing numbers of citizens who now come voluntarily to the Archaeology Department of the National University in Costa Rica to report the existence of mounds or old sculptures on their property. They invite excavation by the experts instead of keeping what they have under their hats to sell, as they would cattle or rice, to avid collectors.

This may spoil the fun for a few but will increase it immeasurably for all who love beauty and are stirred by antiquity.

8 / Saints and Their Fiestas and Other Celebrations

E ach pueblo and city in Central America has its own patron saint, which is present in effigy in the main church or cathedral, and each saint annually celebrates his day with a fiesta.

Patron saints love to celebrate. They enjoy fireworks contests, dancing, good food, flowers, beauty queens, clowns, and marimba bands. Some saints even like horse races and bullfights. To join in the spirit of a fiesta, you must begin to conceive of the central figure, the saint, the effigy of stone or wood or metal or plaster, as an actively participating being, a powerful force in the community.

Once I walked past the stone lions on the steps of the old cathedral at León, Nicaragua. Quite close to one of the entrances, on a pedestal in a shaft of sunlight, there was a small figure, worn-looking, like a doll that has belonged to several generations of children. Standing nearby were two young women, and one reached out and lightly touched the figure. They stood there in a sociable, lingering way and smiled as I approached. I asked about the statue.

"That is San Gerónimo," one said and beamed at him proudly.

As we all stood there together, she told me he was their saint, and I distinctly felt as if I had been introduced to a relative.

We discovered that the effigies had invariably arrived in their communities in charming and ingenious ways.

San Cristóbal materialized at the foot of a tree, several miles from Jutiapa, El Salvador. The tree then burst miraculously into dazzling white blossoms.

The ground rules on the settling in of a saint seem to be that he comes of his own volition, but someone must discover his effigy and recognize him. Then it is better to build a shrine around him, right where he is, than to try to take him somewhere else. You must understand that a saint appears in the place where he wants his church to be. The people built a shrine for San Cristóbal next to the tree, and then the whole village moved close to the shrine.

The image of Santa Úrsula, now patron saint of the village of Jocalapa, El Salvador, was discovered in a cave near the shore. Her people built her a shrine there, overlooking the ocean, since that was obviously where she wanted to be.

It is well known in Nicaragua that San Sebastián of Diriamba and Santiago of Jinotepe are close friends. Years ago they came floating in together on the sea in wooden boxes and fetched up on the Pacific shore near Masachapa. The people on the shore opened up the boxes and the saints managed to let them know that San Sebastián had come to be Diriamba's saint and that Santiago had come to found a city. An altercation arose because Santiago's box had a golden bell in it and San Sebastián's box did not. The people from Diriamba wanted Santiago because of his beautiful golden bell. Arguments led to pushing and shoving, and during the skirmishing the golden bell fell into the sea. But they say that on Viernes de Dolores (Good Friday) you can stand close to the shore and hear the golden bell ring beneath the water—on one condition: that you are without sin.

The story of the arrival of San Sebastián and Santiago closely parallels historical fact. In those days of uncharted harbors and the "Spanish Main," ships did go aground and break up. Then there would be great excitement in villages near the coast, and people would flock to the shore to salvage the flotsam and jetsam.

Many ships would have carried effigies of saints for newly built missions, and no doubt such effigies would have been packed in wooden boxes that sometimes floated ashore.

Santiago and San Sebastián could not celebrate a single fiesta today without the presence of their neighbor and friend San Marcos. His coming to the town of San Marcos was exactly in the tradition of the arrival of all saints. The people needed him desperately. According to Lex: "Water was scarce in the mountains. Even today water carts deliver it to homes and it is measured out like milk. Once, people fought over the water. Sometimes they killed each other with machetes. God punished them by completely drying up the spring. Soon afterward a farmer was plowing when he struck something hard. It was a statue. He brought it to the priest, who traveled from town to town in those days. The priest told the farmer that he believed that this was a saint, San Marcos, and he prayed and asked the saint to give the people water, since they were dying of thirst. The people began to walk in processions, praying, carrying San Marcos at the head of the procession. When they came to the spring, it filled up with water, and the saint is still at the spring in his shelter on a bridge."

Today none of these saints has a fiesta without inviting the others. The festival in Diriamba does not begin until San Sebastián greets Santiago and San Marcos. Each saint has his own procession, and there is nothing in the twilight during the first evening of the fiesta but the eventful silence, broken only by the sound of feet, of horses' hoofs. The processions of the three saints converge at a little place outside Diriamba, called Dolores. Here they bow to each other and the fiesta begins.

"They shoot off fireworks. They shoot off everything they have, including shotguns," Lex explained.

A characteristic of a saint that chooses to watch over a community is often willfulness; this quality, above all others, serves to alert people that here is no ordinary statue.

The effigy of the patron saint of all Honduras, the Virgin of Suyapa, came to a man called Alejandro, as he was taking some rest in a cornfield on his way to the city to buy medicine for his sick child. He felt something sticking into him and pushed it away, thinking it was a stone or a root. But the thing came right back and stuck into him again. He sleepily thrust it into his lunch basket and inadvertently (or so he thought) brought it to the city. There he met a priest who discovered it was an image of the Virgin, and prayed to it to cure the ailing child. Back at home, Alejandro found the boy laughing and talking, his health miraculously restored. (If you want to know whether a statue is actually a saint, ask for a miracle. That's really the only way to be sure.) The ancient little effigy is now housed in a handsome new basilica at Suyapa, Honduras, near the cornfield where she first appeared.

There are at least two other exceedingly willful saints in Central America. In 1635 Mercedes Pereira of Costa Rica found a small stone likeness of the Virgin on a rock. She took it home with her. Back went the Virgin to the rock. Three times the effigy and Mercedes had a battle of wills and the Virgin won. Word of the Virgin's determination spread. The people of the area built a shrine around her, and that shrine became the present church of Nuestra Señora de los Angeles, in Cartago. Her colorful fiesta is held yearly.

The Virgen de la Candelaria (Virgin of the Candles) of Santa María Ostuma in El Salvador was once moved to another location at Santiago Nonualco. She was back in her church at Santa María Ostuma the very next day. Her feet were wet because she had had to wade through the river that runs through a ravine between the two villages.

While effigies of saints are notoriously pigheaded about where they wish to live, they do love to go visiting. They like a change; they enjoy the excitement of a trip. A saint gets all fired up about leading a procession, with music playing, flowers strewn in the road, bells ringing, dogs barking, roosters crowing, and a deafening salvo of firecrackers every few seconds.

In San Vicente, El Salvador, the throng in the procession performs a dance called "Flores del Mayo" in the street, and children throw corn, candy, and flowers in the path of their saint.

Once we were driving through Sonsonate, El Salvador, at

night, and saw, borne close together in the same procession, the effigy of the Virgen de la Candelaria on her pedestal and a dazzling flesh-and-blood beauty queen braced on a float. Occasionally, of course, a fiesta procession will have a penitential character. During the fiesta of the Virgen de los Angeles, the patron saint of Costa Rica (on August 2 at Cartago), persons who have converged from all over the country to walk in the procession carry rocks on their heads; others march with rings of bread around their forearms, following an ancient tradition. When pilgrims visit the miracle-working image of the "Black Christ" at Esquipulas, Guatemala, they often travel the last mile on their knees.

Nora Guitierrez, who works for Lex, grew up in Nicaragua, and saints' days were high spots of her youth. Telling us about fiestas, Nora would stand by the dining-room table in the candlelight, her hands clasped, her eyes popping. Lex would translate. His words would be matter-of-fact, as if the saint were a flesh-and-blood neighbor. I would keep losing the reality that we were actually talking about a statue.

"The Virgen de la Concepción lives on her hacienda near El Viejo. She owns that hacienda and a lot of land around there. Every year, on December 6, people come from all over Nicaragua to what they call *lavada de la plata*. They wash all the saint's clothes and clean her jewels in the river. She has a lot of clothes and jewels that people have given her because of some favor she did for them. While her clothes are being washed in the river, anybody who is sick gets in the water too, hoping for a cure. She has performed a lot of miracles.

"Then the people take her in a big procession from her farm to the church in El Viejo. A band goes with them—trumpets, cymbals, drums, tuba, violin. They play what they call *música del viento*—that means 'music from the wind,' or 'music from the air.' Everybody walks along with the saint, carrying lighted candles. They take her to the church in El Viejo, where she spends the night.

"She goes back to her hacienda, El Hato, on December 12. A big procession takes her home to her chapel there. Music plays, and all along the road the people in the procession are invited by farmers to have refreshments, something good to eat and drink. They keep stopping and having a time."

Some saints have processions on the water, in decorated boats. The patron saint of Puntarenas, a port on the Gulf of Nicoya, Costa Rica, is the Virgen del Carmen. Her fiesta begins on July 16 with a procession on the sea. The effigy's beautifully decorated boat leads a motley procession of craft, also elaborately decorated, and including everything from shrimp boats to dugout canoes.

On the shores of Lake Amatitlán, near Guatemala City, there is a small village with a church that was built in 1635. It houses a miracle-working effigy known as El Niño de Atocha. El Niño's fiesta, on May 2, is signaled by a trip across the lake to the north shore. The effigy travels on a flower-bedecked barge, and smaller boats follow in a procession, with flickering lights and music. El Niño is placed on a flat rock on the north shore called "La Silla del Niño" (the baby's chair). All night long by candlelight the people watch over El Niño, and the next evening he is brought back in a water procession to his own church.

Sometimes, during a fiesta procession, the figure of the effigy is draped until a moment of dramatic revelation.

The patron saint of El Salvador is El Salvador del Mundo (the Savior of the World). During his fiesta at San Salvador in August, he is carried forth concealed in a shell on a large platform, which is borne through the streets on the shoulders of twenty-five men who have committed themselves by a vow to carry the saint. His platform is heavy; they carry him carefully, for there is a superstition that, if El Salvador del Mundo should be dropped, disaster would come to the city. At the corner of the Parque Dueñas, the platform is put down and the procession of gorgeously decorated floats and festive people falls into a hush. Then, as the sacred figure is revealed, everyone kneels at once, as if on a rehearsed cue, but it is spontaneous.

During the procession of the patron saint of San Antonio Abad, El Salvador, the image is also veiled. Little girls in the procession must wear blue dresses and silver ribbons, and carry flowers. A certain dramatic suspense leading to the unveiling is created when men carrying the effigy set it down. The children wail loudly in grief-stricken disappointment until the image is lifted up and carried on to its traditional place of unveiling. When the unveiling occurs, all fall simultaneously on their knees.

Central Americans have a wonderful way of combining such solemnity with fun. Even the Central American custom of decorating graves on All Souls' Day has an air of festivity; graves are completely covered with huge bright homemade paper flowers. During the Fiesta de la Cruz on May 3, rustic crosses are placed in gardens, bedecked with flowers, fruits, candies, and ceramic figures. For the rest of the month—May is "the month of flowers and fruits"—altars are erected in homes and decorated with fruits and flowers. (Superstition decrees that if this is not done, the devil may slip in the door and hang around for a year.)

There is a song sung each July at the fiesta of Santa Ana, at Nandaime, Nicaragua. Nora remembers it from her childhood. This little quatrain has been handed down from the earliest colonial days when some Spanish missionary, less rigid than most, assured the Indians that it was possible to be happy though Christian, and that it was proper to "make a joyful noise unto the Lord." The singers are dressed like *pieles rojas* (red skins), and they sing:

> We are the red-skinned Indians
> And we must forget sadness
> Causing happiness with grace
> On this day, in Spanish.

The explosive, somewhat reckless quality of a fiesta is a startling contrast to the habitual quietness of most pueblos and of even the largest Central American cities after a certain hour at night. The fiesta is a release from the solitude of family life in countries where private lives are very private; where the houses turn blank faces and grilled windows to the street on other days of the year; and where there is a lack of those distractions and diversions that take North Americans "out of themselves" rather too often.

People come out of their homes and throng the streets throughout the night, mingling with strangers, dropping into the homes of persons they may never have seen before, and probably never will again. They become something more cosmic than their individual family selves.

Sudden freedom from family exclusiveness can be seen in the *posadas* of the Christmas season. Central American children are still very carefully controlled, kept within the home. The extent of their social life is decreed by their parents, and teen-agers do not set their own standards or demolish old rules or proprieties. But during the time of the *posadas* boys and girls roam the streets together in a freedom that is all the more exhilarating because of its rarity.

The *posada* (which means "inn"), or going from home to home, symbolizes the Holy Family's search for shelter and welcome as the time for the birth of the Christ child approaches. The children carry a saint with them and knock on the doors of strangers. The doors are opened by the smiling hosts (a fiesta always represents an opening up of worlds), and the visitors are offered refreshments, a fruit or chocolate drink, corn doughnuts soaked in honey, tortillas spread with mashed and seasoned avocado, or fried *plátano* with cream.

On Christmas Eve, Central American families decorate Christmas trees, eat tamales at midnight. Then they place the image of the Christ child in the crèche. El Salvadorans use the famous miniatures of Ilobasco for elaborate nativity scenes. Sometimes such scenes occupy the entire floor of a room, and include farms and villages and roads leading to the crèche.

The Purísima, the annual fiesta celebrating the Immaculate Conception of the Virgin Mary, occurs early in December. Ceremonies blending Christian solemnity and pagan joy are held throughout Central America.

The Purísima begins on December 8, and the night before, each family burns the devil. Bonfires built in front of every house leap and crackle alarmingly, lighting up the cities and pueblos. People stand outside their homes or apartments in excited groups, and the children dance like goblins in the flickering firelight. Once the devil is burned, there is general exhilaration: church bells ding-dong, dogs howl, and roosters crow.

In Nicaragua, the Purísima is vigorously celebrated, especially in the ancient cities of León and Granada. The ritual is known as "La Gritería" (the shout). People all come out of their houses and walk down the middle of the street in crowds, singing songs that every Nicaraguan knows by heart.

Meantime, each household that has a statue of the Virgin decorates the indoor shrine with lights and flowers; the home is then opened to the throng in the street. Anybody passing may enter with the password question, "Who is causing all this happiness?" Visitors pay homage to the Virgin and are offered refreshments.

This goes on from seven in the evening to daylight, building momentum as the hours go by. Crowds traipse down the streets; some people dress in robes and girdles in imitation of the Virgin; firecrackers are thrown into the melee like confetti, exploding in the air, near your ear, at your feet. There is a haze of dust from the scraping of feet, for this is the dry season, and black puffs of smoke from fireworks increase the murkiness.

In León, the Giantess and the Dwarf circulate through the city. The Giantess is a man on stilts wearing the mask and skirts of a woman. He is accompanied by a capering Dwarf who recites witty verses to the crowd. The Giantess and the Dwarf have been figures during the Purísima in Nicaragua since the year 1610.

Since during a fiesta the movement is out of the home and into the streets, many temporary shelters, palm-thatched and festooned with lights, known as *chinamos,* are erected. These house refreshment stands, puppet shows, game tables, bands and dance floors. As you enter one of these open pavilions, you may read a sign, "Please don't put any cigarettes on the floor on account of the ladies." This is because many of the ladies are Indian ladies and they are barefooted.

Although each person in the community has this rare chance to get "outside himself" and his family during a fiesta and join the lovely general dazzle, tradition sets, to some extent, the limits of the action. The broad outlines of what will occur have been well known for years; it's as it was in the beginning, is now, and ever shall be, amen. Fiesta frolicking is not an unknown trip.

The fiesta of the Virgen de la Concepción, the patron saint of Granada, Nicaragua, is heralded by the *atabal,* a very noisy group of drummers who beat their percussion instruments fortissimo. Later, street musicians, going the rounds with guitars, cane flutes, portable marimbas, invent humorous verses in a contemporary vein (much like the verses sung by Calypso groups in the nearby Caribbean Islands). And farmers who come to town perform a dance called "La Yeguita," in which they fence with machetes as they dance. If this were not a traditional rite, it would be easy to suppose that the farmers were about to kill one another.

At the fiesta of Santa Ana in Nandaime, all the musicians who come to town to play gather at the cathedral at five o'clock in the morning. They rehearse together for a while, then wake up the town with a reveille serenade as they drive around in cars. Later, costumed "devils" dance in the streets to traditional refrains of marimba and guitar. They do not conform to the North American image of the devil—no red velvet suits, horns, or forked tails. Nandaime devils wear bloomers, long socks, colored handkerchiefs tied to their belts, and plumed hats. As they dance they wave a big handkerchief in the air and sing:

> We are the devils
> And we come from Hell.
> We are carrying away the mothers-in-law
> Who are not nice to their sons-in-law.

The masks that are worn during many of the dances and moments of pageantry are priceless antiques, passed down from the earliest colonial days. They were originally worn because men played the parts of women. Also, in those days Spaniards did not wish to be recognized when mingling with Indians, so they masked themselves. The oldest wooden masks are of blond, blue-eyed faces. This was the image that the conquistadores assigned themselves.

Traditional fiesta dancing takes you back into history, often farther back than you can travel by reading a book. Sometimes the steps and the music are as old as the sound of surf or of raindrops. And Central Americans, in their most historically meaningful dances, perform to words and music that have been handed down through generations. Since the words have come from the beginning of time, they are often in the Azteca or Nahuatl language. The music, too, has been preserved intact and is performed to this day in the original Indian terms—the instruments are usually the cane flute and drum, or simple portable marimbas with gourds for percussion.

Concursos (contests) are as much a part of the fiesta as processions and dances. Here is a fiesta recipe for a hilarious *concurso*. In the middle of a rather deep pool, secure a pole about twenty meters long. Before raising it, nail a wad of money on the very top and grease the pole from top to bottom. Then let every Juan, Ricardo, and Enrico try to get the money. We were told that the wise contestant waits until the eager ones have worn off most of the grease on the pole by sliding with a splash into the water. Latecomers, if they are shrewd shinniers, get the prize at the top.

There is an appalling but still popular contest that involves burying a rooster up to its neck in the earth. The sport begins when you blindfold a contestant, hand him a machete, and see how fast he can cut off the rooster's head.

At the village of Izalco in El Salvador, during the fiesta of San Juan, horsemen carrying machetes charge at four cocks hung from a pole, the object being to behead the cocks. Afterward, to the ritualistic music of fife and drum, the horsemen try to unseat one another in a grand finale.

The only totally solemn rituals in Central America take place during Holy Week (Semana Santa). Then all normal activities come to a standstill. The stores are shuttered; few cars move along the streets. Instead there are processions, re-enacting the Crucifixion. These processions move very slowly, and the people have the expressionless faces of the grief-stricken; they appear to be groping, blind. There is silence as they pass, some dressed as Roman soldiers or the Tres Marías (the three Marys). Usually the streets are carpeted with intricate mosaics of flowers or colored sawdust. In Antigua, Guatemala, the families who live in each block stay up the night before each solemn procession, working on their knees by candlelight to lay the carpets. As the procession passes, the carpets are instantly scuffed up, leaving a ruin of crushed flowers or muddled sawdust.

There are many celebrations without a religious basis, such as the Fiesta de las Brujas (witches), which is generally observed at the end of October and corresponds to our Halloween. At that time it is customary to go dancing in masks and peaked hats, and little handmade witches on brooms are peddled on the streets and in markets.

The Fiestas Cívicas, beginning three days prior to the New Year in San José, Costa Rica, are a tradition. The festivities begin on December 29, at noon, with the blowing up of *bombetas*. At three o'clock there is a parade, including handsomely caparisoned horses, floats, and bulls. On the 30th there are bullfights, Costa Rican style, *sans* bloodshed but not without bruises and a few torn shirts and pants.

The bullring has a shallow pond with a pole in it—mercifully not greased. A fresh bull is let into the ring, and any citizen who wishes to be matador for the day can take him on. Usually the ring fills with would-be matadors, so that the chance of the bull concentrating on any one of them is greatly diminished. But if the bull should go after one amateur who begins to find the dodging impossible, that Tico (short for Costa Rican) can go gallumphing into the water to escape, and if the bull follows him, which sometimes happens, he can shinny up the pole. This *concurso* can get a little rough; when the bull finally is wearied by his tormentors or shows signs of boredom he is let out of the ring, and a new one is loosed upon the reckless participants.

After the crowning of the Queen of the Fiestas, dancing to bands in *chinamos*, gambling, viewing puppet shows, and so on, the whole city gathers in parks shortly before midnight on December 31. Then bands play the national anthem, balloons are blown, and bells ring in the New Year.

And there is the carnival of San Miguel, El Salvador, with festooned lights and dancing in the streets, while visiting marimba bands compete for audible ascendancy on every corner. The result is a musical melee of contrapuntal confusion; you might not know which band you were dancing to, and if you had had *bastante* (enough) to drink, which is not unusual at this fiesta, you might not even care.

Lex attended the carnival one year with a friend, now a Mormon preacher. "There were marimba bands from all over," he recalls, "a fantastic number of bands, including some from the States. There was a parade of beauty queens from all over Central America. Early in the evening the people who lived there sat around in their houses and all their friends came in to say hello. We took our own food and joined a party in somebody's house. Crowds were streaming down all the streets outside. They began to do the rhumba in chains, loaded. People stayed up all night and went out to El Coco Beach in the morning to recuperate in the sun and sand and salt water."

The San Miguel Carnival, like so much merriment in Central America, has ancient origins. The marimba was a Mayan instrument. The early ones were portable, the sounding boxes gourds with a range of about an octave with no half-tones. Gradually the instrument became more sophisticated, and later keys were made of hormigo wood, which Indians still call "the tree that sings." Today separate marimbas are often grouped so that the musicians can range over ten or more octaves, using quincewood mallets tipped with rubber.

There's nothing like traipsing up a dark cobblestone street with a fiesta crowd, moving in swarms, like fish with mysterious impulses, while rockets burst overhead and firecrackers land at your feet in a shower of colors. You lose yourself in the dazzle and the strange abandon.

Fiestas are as endless as the pueblos and cities of Central America. It should be easy to find one going on somewhere for every day of your trip. But you would probably have to go home on a stretcher.

9 / Handicrafts of the Isthmus

Except for the exquisite tapestry-like weaving of the highland Indians of Guatemala, the handicrafts of Central America are little known, with the happy result that there is little phoniness, and there are few meretriciously baited tourist traps. You can find beautiful, authentic, individual works at remarkably reasonable prices. The most interesting crafts do not wind up in gift shops, so you must know where to look for them.

Artisans of the isthmus are seldom primarily craftsmen; like their distinguished Indian forebears, they are farmers who turn to handiwork when they are not too busy in the fields. Though they may create the most breathtakingly beautiful objects, they do not think of themselves as artists, for these objects fill the needs of farm or pueblo families and are not intended for tourist consumption. What they make is traded or sold on market days: hammocks, for these still serve as beds for much of the populace; woven mats, hats, and baskets; saddles and saddlebags; ceramic bowls, pitchers, and bean pots; masks to be worn at fiestas; paper flowers to decorate graves or lay on the shrine of a saint; and ceremonial jewelry, such as the lovely silver wedding chains of Guatemala. The farmer-craftsman has not been sold on mass production; repeating designs bores him, hence everything he makes is different. The sideline artist is no panderer to commerce, as most gringos think of it; he has integrity that he does not even cultivate; it's just the way he is.

Gift shops in all the hotel lobbies of the five capital cities of Central America offer certain hand-crafted items that are designed for the tourist and are produced by reliable families with whom the shops keep in touch. And so there are silver quetzal pins, hand-woven neckties, cocktail napkins, ashtrays, straw tote-bags, alligator purses, wallets, and belts, seed beads, and the like. But to find truly unusual and not-to-be-duplicated handicrafts you must visit the villages and their markets.

For gorgeous, hand-woven, comfortable hammocks with crocheted edges and fringes you must go to Masaya in Nicaragua. Lacy rugs in the natural color of reeds are to be found only near Tegucigalpa in Honduras. The huge, gaudy pottery roosters with jug-shaped bodies are sold only along the highway near the southern border of El Salvador in Honduras.

Usually there are no signs on home workshops, and you will never see window displays. You have to drive slowly through a pueblo or, better, walk, looking in doorways. If you move through streets fast you will never guess, from the scarred and faded pastel adobe face a village turns to the world, that any notable crafts are created by its families. You should also attend market days in remote villages and be alert along the roads.

For less than a mile along the steep highway that climbs from Esparta to San José, Costa Rica, there are the workshops of Sarchi. Here, in open sheds, are manufactured the gaily painted ox-carts that are still used to transport coffee beans from the *finca* (plantation) to the *beneficio* (processing plant). Lex once stopped and bought a scaled-down replica of an ox-cart, which he now uses as a serving cart. Brightly colored designs cover every inch of it, including the wheels. For this interesting, decorative, and magnificently crafted piece of furniture he paid twenty-four dollars.

Once, returning to Guatemala City from Lake Atitlán, we saw an elderly Indian woman standing under a tree, holding a piece of bright fabric. She offered it as we passed. I gasped, Lex backed up the car, and she handed it to me through the window. It was an exquisitely woven piece, perhaps two and a half yards long, six inches wide, fringed on either end. The color was a rich Renaissance red with bands of green, purple, and orange, and vertical panels of feather-like shapes in the same colors. I had never seen anything like it before and I have not since. I use it as a scarf with suits or as a belt on plain dresses, and it is one of my favorite things. The price was fifty cents, although I probably could have got it for twenty-five. It is perfectly proper to bargain, but since most of the handicrafts are reasonably priced and the people are very poor you should not, in good conscience, bargain ruthlessly.

Guatemala offers the greatest variety of handmade goods. Hand-woven fabrics remain the most exciting products, but recently there has been an unfortunate incorporation of metallic silver and gold threads in much of the weaving. Among the goods that can be bought in local markets are sweet-toned ocarinas charmingly modeled in the shapes of birds and animals; hand-woven blankets, soft and thick, in beautiful colors and designs; wool jackets and sweaters; wedding necklaces of hand-wrought silver; long, hand-woven aprons that Indian women wear; gaily embroidered blouses of fine cotton; tablecloths; light and lovely papier-mâché boxes and ornaments; ceremonial masks; paper flowers; unusual hand-dipped beeswax candles and stuffed dolls dressed in handmade native costumes.

As an indication of prices, I bought, at the central market in Guatemala City, a thick Indian blanket for six dollars, a hand-loomed eight-foot tablecloth with twelve napkins for three dollars, a man's jacket for two dollars, a little wooden home-spun guitar for six dollars. (It was fun to strum, once it had been tuned enough for the strings to hold.) On the outskirts of Guatemala City you could order, from home potters, table settings for twelve—dinner plates, butter plates, soup bowls, serving platters, salad and dessert plates, coffee cups, and water mugs—for thirty dollars.

The village of San Antonio Aguas Calientes near Antigua, Guatemala, is famous for its weavers, who are people of Mayan descent. On the outskirts of the village we saw a woman kneeling on a mat under a tree, working on her loom, which was hung on the tree trunk and slanted into her lap. We decided to stop and look at her fabrics. She was glowingly beautiful. Long black braids hung down her back and were tied with rosettes of blue ribbon. She wore a long, gathered skirt and an embroidered blouse whose colors just *sang*. As she rose to greet us, we saw her weaver's palette, a basket full of balls of yarn. She hung lengths of woven material over a clothesline for us to see. It was amazing to us how one weaver, with only the daylight hours to count on, could produce such a quantity of intricately designed fabric, every row of every inch of which had been exacting and time-consuming work. In one tapestry belt I counted twenty-eight different motifs on backgrounds of black or white; there were stylized white turkeys, an eagle, women with baskets on their heads ranged in a row like paper dolls, owls perched on branches, a pot with a cover and two handles, a row of hands, and all sorts of arrangements of diamonds and circles and zigzags of gorgeous colors. Many of the designs used by Guatemalan weavers are legendary, date from pre-Columbian times; some are doubtless derived from Mayan hieroglyphics.

The miracle of these colors and designs is that they are assertive and yet somehow they do not swear at one another. I bought material for a long skirt, a blouse, and a belt. The skirt is striped red, green, pink, and purple. The blouse is blood-red and covered with motifs in all colors of the rainbow. Nothing matches but, through Mayan magic, there is beautiful harmony.

On a quiet, pale street in Antigua, one late afternoon, I passed a little grocery shop and glimpsed hanging clusters of glowing, softly colored candles. The proprietress, Natalia G. de Cueves, made these translucent, hand-dipped candles out of beeswax. She took me into a storeroom in the rear and showed me fluted five-foot candles for colonial sconces; these are used in restored homes and cathedrals. They were eighty cents apiece. She also made candelabra-like clusters, decorated with flowers, for parties or weddings, for fifty cents. And the señora was very excited about her next dream: she was about to create candles with Mayan motifs. She said: *"Proximamente se harán velas que expresan cultura maya"* (soon we will have candles which express the Mayan culture). She added: *"La primera vela será con el jaguar"* (the first candle will use the jaguar). The jaguar, of course, is a famous Mayan symbol. I left her home and shop with beautiful twelve-inch candles for two cents apiece.

El Salvador, the next country southward on the isthmus, is noted for its wicker and reed weaving and its ceramics, especially the miniatures made in Ilobasco. San Salvador has a craft showroom, in which most of the products exhibited are designed for the modern home: wicker furniture, rugs of reeds or palm fibers, ceramic lamp bases, candlesticks, and vases. But these are not traditional pueblo products. The latter must be bought from the craftsmen, either in their homes or on market days in trading centers.

Ilobasco, a pueblo about twenty-five miles from San Salvador, can be reached by driving east from San Salvador on the Inter-American Highway and turning north just past Cojutepeque. It is a very old village; none of its houses appear to have been patched or painted for years. The pastels are mellower and lovelier, closer to gentle earth tones, than the birthday-cake greens and pinks and blues and yellows of newly painted homes, which can be quite garish.

One day we drove to Ilobasco; on the streets we saw little girls with tangled hair, toddlers who wore skirts but no pants (obviating the need to wash diapers), and women whose costume was the much-washed, baggy dress of poverty. Men were clad in pajama-like suits and straw hats.

We looked into many doorways as we slowly drove through town; in dark rooms that gave on the sunny cobbled streets we glimpsed counters where bright little figures were displayed.

Arbitrarily choosing one doorway, we parked in front and Lex went in to look around. While I waited in the car a small group gathered. Gringos and their cars are still quite a sight down there; we who came to see the quaintness often turn out to be Exhibit A ourselves. I blew the horn to the delight of a pantless boy in his grandmother's arms. She was a billowy person with dark circles under her eyes and a responsiveness to life that you could glimpse in her smile.

Lex appeared in the doorway and beckoned me in. A woman behind the counter showed me a tiny white setting hen that was charmingly modeled; you lifted up the hen and there was a little scene of women grinding corn for tortillas. Among other fanciful miniatures were yoked oxen pulling carts filled with cane or coffee, Lilliputian mariachi bands, marimba players, dancers, baskets of fruit, chickens. I bought the hen for twenty-five cents, and three laden ox-carts for fifty cents, and the woman snuggled them in colored tissue paper.

Through the doorway beyond the counter I could see a small patio of terra-cotta earth. Roses bloomed against the tiles of the steeply slanted roof, and there was an explosion of tropical greenery in the corner. Two tiny black pigs were playing in a patch of sun, and a little girl had baby green parrots perched on her shoulder, her arm, and her head.

The matriarch of the family offered to show me the workshop. I followed her across the jumbled patio and paused to pet a little white goat, silky and warm, tied under the overhanging roof near the kiln. The grandmother puzzled me by saying affectionately to the goat, "She doesn't know anything."

The waist-high clay kiln swelled out from the wall of the rear building. Sculptures were fired simply by putting them into the hot embers. In the shed beyond there was a large pile of powdery white clay. She showed me how it was mixed with water and kneaded to a cool, springy consistency. It was very pleasant to the touch.

Driving home, I idly remarked to Lex, "The grandmother told me that the goat 'doesn't know anything.' I wonder what she meant by that?"

"The goat will soon be eaten and doesn't know it," Lex replied with a touch of grimness or of irony. "And I don't think those pigs have such a bright future either."

"I thought it was a darling family though," I ventured after a moment. "All working together, even the children."

"Yes," Lex agreed, "although it's a little—well, funny, considering some of the things they work on."

I stared at him.

"When I first went in there alone," Lex said, "the woman showed me the same sort of setting hen that she showed you, but when she lifted up *my* hen, the figures were those of a man and woman making love. Imagine all the little kids working on those *sorpresas!*"

Honduras is the next country along the route south. It is particularly rich in valuable trees, such as mahogany and rosewood, and woodcarving is the outstanding craft. You can buy entire doors carved in bas relief. Carved coffee tables, chests, and unique folding footstools that are perfect near fireplaces can be found on the outskirts of Tegucigalpa, halfway up the road to Mount Picacho. Decorative carved wall plaques can also be bought, but we thought they were a little lugubrious. These carvers also turn out some of the world's most beautiful salad bowls and salad servers. Some of the younger sculptors are beginning to be interested in working with "found" sculpture, driftwood from the beaches, swamp wood from the rain forests, and many of these are quite exciting.

Tin ware—tin roosters with feathers of bright enamel, and masks with Mayan faces and agate eyes—can be found in the craft shops of Tegucigalpa. Turn a mask around and you will see that tin ware is pounded out of ordinary cans, as imprints such as Campbell's Soup or Finast attest. Straw purses and hats in beautiful blues, greens, yellows, and reds, and woven reed and fiber rugs are outstanding. The hats are supple and easily packed.

On the spur of the Inter-American Highway that leads from Jícaro Galán up into the mountains to the capital, we passed thatched shelters from which poles of seed beads were dangling. Ordinary as seed beads can be, I bought a string of purple and gold ones that are absolutely unique—for twenty-five cents.

Along this same stretch we saw a few hand-modeled, charmingly uneven, earth-colored pitchers and bean pots, standing in the grass. While the potters, adults and children, came out of the shack to enjoy our decision-making, we chose two to use as planters and flower holders. These primitive vessels are warmly decorative, but we later discovered that water seeps through an unglazed container. This can be remedied by putting a glass inside for flowers, or a can for plants.

In Nicaragua you will find gold filigree jewelry made in the area of Granada and León, and alligator-skin purses, wallets, and belts. These can be bought for half the price that would be paid in the States. The chief craft center is Masaya, where such items as beautifully incised gourd plaque belts and decorative gourd *máscaras* (masks) are made, as well as fanciful straw hats, purses, and woven rugs. But we felt that the handmade hammocks surpassed any on the isthmus. They are not only beautiful to look at, but they are comfortable as only a hammock can be when crafted by those who for centuries have actually used them to sleep in.

We found a home factory for *hamacas* by driving up one street and down another in Masaya. We knew we had struck gold when, through an open door, we saw a calm-faced, barefoot man moving a shuttle with a hummingbird-swift hand on a loom that stretched between polished wooden poles, like a badminton net. We were hesitating at the door when Ramiro Suazo, a short, emphatic man who manages the operation, offered to show us around. Señor Suazo had grown up throwing shuttles and feeding hemp to a giant spinning wheel; then he had discovered the executive gap; nobody wanted to run anything but somebody had to. Now he manages the shop. The output, at the time of our visit, was twelve hammocks a week, priced from fifteen to thirty dollars apiece, depending on the quality of the material, the width, the trimming.

The loom was an astonishingly simple device. The poles were set in the earth about eight feet apart. Between them was strung a cat's cradle of *hamaca* warp. The weaver threw his shuttle over and under, over and under, linking the top strand to the one beneath with perfect tensity; he was creating a flexible, yet sufficiently firm, resting place for the human frame.

Immediately beyond the loom were dim rooms; the darkness in which Central American craftsmen worked was always astonishing. Here women, crocheting tassels, scallops, and fringes, were moving about on bare feet, briefly quitting their crocheting to attend to household chores. In a corner of one room there was the usual raised platform with smoking wood and pots of slowly cooking beans or stew placed on the embers. The smoke drifted through the loosely tiled roof.

Señor Suazo led us past the raised hearth that served as a stove and out into a huge yard, tramped bare by the feet of *hamaca* craftsmen. Shacks in which the factory families lived were situated around the farthest edges of the yard. Women squatted near doorways, combing the *mecate* fiber to be spun; children, chickens, and pigs scurried around.

Close to the main house was a huge, rickety spinning wheel under a canopy thatched with palm leaves. There stood an old woman turning the wheel, while she held a large baby straddled on her hip. Backing away from the wheel, holding newly twisted fiber strands and feeding more fiber as they moved, were several men. Each evolving strand was supported by a tree branch with a crotch in it. The spinners stepped back and back over the bare earth and through the trees until you couldn't see them any more. With the newly spun strands leading off into the woods, zigzagging through the trees in all directions, we were reminded of the thread that Theseus used to find his way out of the labyrinth of the Minotaur.

While some workers walked away from the big spinning wheel, others walked toward it, combining freshly spun strands into two- or three-ply twine, twisted firmly by the motion of the wheel. Many of the women carried babies on their backs or under their arms while they were feeding *mecate* threads to the spinning wheel. Family life and work always go along together in home crafts.

Señor Suazo showed us the hammocks that had been produced thus far that week. They were stored in a large wooden
bin, carefully wrapped in plastic. Some were dogwood white,
with elegantly crocheted fringes and borders. They made you
think of a gracious, dreamy afternoon in sun-dappled shade on a
close-clipped mossy green lawn. You had a Gainsborough revery.
I bought a beauty that was basically off-white with dark green,
orange, and red stripes, and crocheted scallops in the same
colors. It is now hanging from a beam in my living-room and is
the most popular place to be in the house. If ever I feel excited
or anxious, I make a beeline for that hammock; the slight
swaying, the suspended position, the impossibility of maintaining
a stiff spine, are magically soothing. In a hammock, you can't be
frantic.

Costa Rica sounds the Johnny-one-note of isthmian crafts. Its
forte is bright enameled over-all designs, lovely whorls on wood,
that originated in ox-cart painting. Nowadays craftsmen are
transferring these exuberant designs to garden furniture, wall
plaques, even to earrings. In Sarchi you can buy an oxen yoke
to put up over your door; you will find that it is a happier choice
than a horseshoe.

Today, sophisticated designers who travel to Central America
predict that isthmian artisans will soon be contributing to the
hungry international market, but with new ideas, pitched to
today and tomorrow rather than harking back to the Mayan
yesterday. We can see this beginning to happen. In Esquipulas,
Guatemala, fifty women are producing hand-woven and embroidered wall hangings and shipping them out to world-wide
gift shops through the Alianza para Progreso. Giving them
guidance and encouragement and making contact for them with
buyers in the United States and Europe is an American whom
we'll call Bertha. Until she came to live and teach in Esquipulas,
the Indian women and their families were starving. Bertha has
brought them into the international economy.

All over the world, genuine handicrafts are becoming scarce.

Sophie, who runs the gift shop in the lobby of the Gran Hotel in Managua, Nicaragua, shrugs. "Girls used to stay home and embroider. Now they are all bilingual secretaries for Pan Am."

However, Central America still remains one of the most exciting and relatively undiscovered areas for crafts. Before all the *hamaca* weavers and ceramic *sorpresa* makers become mass-production-minded, there is likely to be an international burst of enthusiasm for the beguilingly beautiful products of their old-fashioned, innocent, casual creativity.

10 / What's on the Menu in Central America?

Papusas, Turtle Eggs, Palmito Salad, Fried Parrot

A tourist can order virtually any international dish he has ever heard of in Central American cities. The hung-up diner, who wants the same old scrambled eggs or medium-rare steak, will have no problem either. If sampling new and different dishes is part of the adventure the tourist seeks in his travels, we guarantee fantastic fun with isthmian food. Most menus have both English and Spanish listings. (Slightly off-putting was a translation for *bistec corriente*—steak; the English side read "Run of the Mill.")

The gourmet will discover that certain foods, such as the invariable side dishes of rice and beans, are served throughout the isthmus, while others are regional. On Monday nights in El Salvador, fighting cock is served in a gravy seasoned with *chicha* (Indian corn liquor). Cockfights are traditionally held on Sunday, so on Monday you eat the losers. And only at Tipitapa, Nicaragua, can you find fried fresh-water fish called *guapotes*, a tasty type of trout.

Everywhere on the isthmus, the *boca* is served before meals and with drinks. *Boca* literally means "mouthful." Each restaurant has its special *bocas;* they are brought as surprises from the chef.

They may be tiny, succulent ears of corn, pastry wedges with meat or cheese filling, slivers of charcoal steak, or soft-boiled turtle eggs the size of ping-pong balls.

The eggs of the sea turtle are one of the most popular foods in Central America. Along the Atlantic and Pacific Coasts, entire families make a living out of robbing nests of their eggs and bringing them to market. The huge green *tortuga* rides to shore on the surging of a wave to lay her eggs in the warm sand above the tide line. She plods patiently along the beach looking for the perfect nest site. If undisturbed, she will dig a deep nest with her back flippers, lay several hundred eggs, tenderly cover them with sand with her front flippers, and go back to sea. However, chances are that a turtle-egg merchant will find her tracks and follow her. With a stick or a shell he will leave his particular mark in the sand near her first tracks as a sign to other hunters that this *tortuga* is spoken for. One of the reasons the turtle is so helpless is that she is a compulsive egg-layer; once she lays a single egg she can't stop until she has laid them all. A hunter can pick them up as fast as she lays them and pop them into a big basket; you'll see women walking through the streets with baskets on their heads, each containing enormous heaps of eggs, the output of a single turtle.

We were told that a turtle always weeps during egg-laying. We have never seen a lachrymose turtle, but, considering how few, if any, of her eggs will ever get to be big turtles, we understand her discouragement. Lex's sympathy is no deterrent to egg-gobbling, however. Let some *other* turtle's yummy eggs grow up to be big turtles is his attitude.

Other isthmian delights are the *refrescos* (cold drinks) and *helados* (sherbets) flavored with an exciting variety of tropical fruits, offering a new realm of adventure for the palate. I once counted over thirty different flavors, such as passion fruit and mango, on a big blackboard in a *refresco* pavilion. You double the fun by drinking your refreshment in one of the beautiful places where they are served. I remember one warm night when we took a long walk along the big crescent beach at Puntarenas, Costa Rica. The shape of the harbor, the brightly lit ships offshore at anchor, and the sidewalk on the edge of the beach made me think of the Bay of Naples. We rested at a table in an open pavilion. Lex had a *refresco* of *piña* (fresh pineapple) while I had *mandarina* (fresh tangerine). We could see the breakers frothing in the night. We were aware of the tempo of the waves, each pulse with its crescendo. Accompanying the waves in a sort of bossa-nova rhythm were the palm trees, rattling and shooshing in the breeze. It would have been very difficult to be grumpy. One Sunday afternoon we joined the Sunday celebrators on a stone terrace overlooking lovely Lake Jiloá outside of Managua, Nicaragua. Inside the pavilion a band was playing, and it was festive. And I remember what fun it was driving to the top of Mount Picacho, up from Tegucigalpa, Honduras, and pausing at a drive-in to drink in the mountain atmosphere along with the *refresco*.

The ice-cream and cold-drink "parlor" is far more usual than the liquor bar in Central America. Generally, bars are found only in hotels, motels, and night clubs, and restaurants of course serve alcoholic beverages, but bars are not the popular meeting places that they are in the States.

Once you cross the border from Mexico to Guatemala you will have seen the last of the red-hot seasoning that is characteristic of Mexican cooking. Such hotness obscures the flavor and makes you feel like a circus side-show fire-eater. The isthmian chef does not overseason; he has a respect for the subtleties of flavor. He is wonderfully creative with soup; I have never had a bowl of dull or wishy-washy soup down there. No matter what the crucial ingredient is—say, chicken or tomato—his sensational version will not taste like any other chicken or tomato soup in the world. There is a great variety of fresh fish and seafood, and these are handled superbly. Rice and beans are served with each meal everywhere on the isthmus, but great pains are taken to provide the perfect texture and flavor.

A dessert-loving tourist will find the last course the least interesting part of the meal. The sweet tooth is not a characteristic of isthmian eaters. Custard or guava paste or ice cream is about all you can find unless you patronize a hotel that features "American-style" cooking, and then there will be pie.

You will seldom be out of the sight or smell of snacks. Vendors are stationed on every stretch of sidewalk, at bus stops, crossroads, border crossings. There are so many of them at every place that anybody could possibly want to eat, that I would not be surprised to meet a huckster with fruit, candies, or hot *papusas* at the top of a mountain or on a jungle trail. On the streets there are always little wooden carts carrying hunks of ice and bottles of fruit juice. The vendor shaves off some ice, heaps it in a paper cone, and pours over this whatever fruit juice you choose. They are like the snow cones I made as a child, with orange or apple juice to flavor the blizzard-provided snow. Under a tree on a lonely stretch of highway, in an empty lot on a village street, there will always be women behind homemade charcoal grills, stirring blue or white enamel pots of hot food—beans, sausages, stew, or fish steamed in corn husks. This food is delicious but, in general, untrustworthy. It has probably been prepared under unsanitary conditions in a tumbledown shack, with grunting pigs cozily stretched on the earth floor and hens and roosters wandering in and out.

A tourist walks a tightrope when he is traveling outside the big cities of Central America and the places well known to be "safe." To be over-finicky is a kill-joy attitude; yet there are certainly small towns where one should not drink the water or order an iced drink or eat a salad. The best advice is, when in doubt, order beer (always cold and delicious) or a soft drink instead of water, and refrain from salad. You may be counseled by old-timers to immunize yourself gradually, to build up a resistance to tropical stomach disorders. If you followed their program, you would take a tiny bite of salad one day and very gradually increase the amount until you are chomping great heaps of lettuce, blithe as a rabbit. However, doctors of tropical medicine say that this is nonsense; exposure to the amoeba, for instance, does not diminish its virulence. Don't listen to anybody who tries to con you into the vaccination-through-eating plan. Even if you are in the wilds, there is always something available that is quite safe to eat.

Fruit, protected by its skin from contamination, is a good bet. Once, under the magnificently outspreading branches of a giant ceiba tree in Palín, Guatemala, we bought from some Indian women the oddest collection of miniature fruit—tiny bananas and tangerines ornamentally arranged in little hand-woven baskets. These were delicious morsels. And I remember finding what was called "marzipan" in Antigua, Guatemala, quite unlike the almond paste at home. At the end of a long day on my feet, I was hungry and tired, yet still far away from my hotel. I stopped by a little grocery and bought, for seven cents, a round wooden box that held a gruel of ground nutmeats. You broke the cover of the box into pieces and used them to spoon up the marzipan.

For what's known as "square meals," it is never difficult, in a city, to locate reliable first-class restaurants. As elsewhere in the world, they may be found in the luxury hotels or fashionable resorts, or look for Diners' Club, A.A.A., or other internationally accepted insignia. Also, there are always many fine "foreign" restaurants. We have enjoyed wonderful cheese fondue, wine, and strawberries with cream at the Swiss Chalet in San José, Costa Rica; the best pizza that we have eaten anywhere, including Italy, at the Roma in Tegucigalpa, Honduras; egg rolls and sweet and sour pork at the Mandarin, in Managua, Nicaragua; paella at La Fonda in San Salvador, El Salvador.

But it is possible to dine beautifully—and safely—in the most unexpected places. Once, traveling from San Miguel to San Salvador, Lex took the "back road" over the mountain and stopped in Tres Ríos. The restaurant was a thatched open platform with a few tables and many hammocks hanging from the rafters. This was a favorite gathering place of the cotton farmers. They could loll in the hammocks, sipping a beer or a Coke, or spooning up a bowl of food. The specialty here was warm black beans mixed with chopped onions and sour cream.

We had a memorable meal at an old run-down hotel in Poneloya, Nicaragua. We were the only ones on the rickety porch that day, looking out over the sea and the brown rocks. The meal began with a fresh shrimp cocktail in a delicious sauce. A fish called *pargo* was the main dish, served with cabbage and carrot salad, boiled yucca, rice and beans. The waiter-proprietor-cook brought us candied wild beach plums for dessert.

In Nicaragua it is a tradition to eat iguana seven days before Good Friday. Hunters usually set forth on Wednesday because the process of cooking an iguana is long and ceremonious. The best hour for iguana hunting is midmorning, around ten o'clock, when the hapless creatures can be spotted sunning themselves on the branches of the trees where they live. The first step in cooking an iguana is to smoke it over wood coals for two days. It is then simmered, seasoned, and served with a topping of iguana eggs, garnished with fried *plátanos.*

Once, on the Inter-American Highway at the turnoff to the Pacific seaport of Acajutla, El Salvador, we stopped at a brightly lit, clean, plain little box of a restaurant. Anywhere else, its looks would have been a guarantee of no imagination in the cooking, but you can never be sure of that in Central America. We had shrimp soup, bouillabaisse style, and it was delicious.

Every locality has its traditional dishes, although these will not always be found on the menu in hotel or international restaurants most likely to be patronized by tourists.

Conch, sea snail, and turtle soups are served in Honduran seaports such as Tela and La Ceiba. In Guatemala you will find *chuchitos* (pork meat wrapped in corn paste), fried iguana, boiled iguana eggs, and fried or baked parrot, often served with *chimol* (a piquant tomato sauce containing *chitepe,* a little green pepper). Typical of Nicaragua is *mondongo* (tripe soup), yucca with *chicharrones* (cracklings), *ajiaco* (pork ribs cooked with green *jocote* (a fruit) and fresh pineapple in the leaf of the *quelite* tree), and *tajado* (fried pork topped with fried *plátano* and a salad mixture of chopped cabbage, tomatoes, and onion seasoned with an oil-and-vinegar dressing).

One of the most delicious and unusual foods in Central America is the fresh *palmito* (hearts of palms) salad of Costa Rica. *Empanadas* (meat-pie wedges) are popular in the capital, San José. *Pejivalle* (palm nut) soup is a treat; you will sometimes find manatee (sea cow), armadillo, or *tepeizcuinte*, a small game animal, on the menu.

El Salvador's outstanding specialty is hot *papusas* (corn paste filled with cream cheese); you can buy them in the afternoon in shops on the outskirts of San Salvador. I had my first *papusa* when we came down from climbing to the top of the volcano Boquerón, and it was really not a fair test as I was hungry to the point of wanting to chase chickens like a fox. But I discovered that they were delicious even when the hunger pangs were not so frantic.

It was in San Miguel that brown lizard soup was highly recommended to me. A friend of Lex's, a doctor-druggist, said, "It is wonderful if you are tired. It picks you right up." The reason for this, he explained, is that the brown lizard is known for its astonishing stamina; it is almost impossible to kill one. Its stubborn longevity makes a cat's proverbial nine lives seem relatively unimpressive. Salvadorans believe that whoever takes the soup imbibes the brown lizard's too-tough-to-put-down vigor.

If you are the faint-hearted type who is afraid to sample *conchas negras* (black clams), iguana, armadillo, or sea cow with its fabled seven flavors, how about a nice big bowl of brown lizard soup? After that, you'll try anything.

11 / Green Grows the Economy

To Get Closer to Central American Life,
It Helps to Know the Crops

Agriculture has always been at the very heart of life in Central America. The cultivation of maize three or four thousand years before Christ was the indispensable prologue to the great civilization of the ancient Mayas. Botanists believe that the original progenitor of corn was a perfect-flowered grass. Once the Indians had a source of food at hand they, who had been nomadic hunters, could settle down and evolve a community life; for the first time they could think beyond the desperate pursuit of game. Basic to the development of the extraordinary Mayan calendar was the cycle of planting, the seasons of growth and harvest; because of this recurrent need to know the approaching hour the Indians began to measure time.

The Mayas believed that God, having destroyed previous races of unsatisfactory men by floods, finally created a more pleasing man out of the dough of maize. And Central Americans are corn men indeed. To this day, their life revolves around the agricultural economy. The United States alone imports upward to 350 million dollars' worth of products, mainly coffee, cotton, and bananas.

Corn still provides 85 per cent of the food of the descendants of the Mayans. The Indians of the Guatemalan highlands cultivate that basic food crop exactly as it was done in the beginning. It is known as *milpa* agriculture, *milpa* being the Mayan word for cornfield. The *milpero*, or farmer, plants his corn in a cleared, burned-over plot, using a dibble stick to make the hollows for his corn kernels. Between the rows he may plant squash or peppers. After several seasons, the land being exhausted, he moves to a new plot.

Mayas of the Old Empire prayed to rain gods before and after planting corn. They beseeched North Chac, South Chac, East Chac, and West Chac to bring the rains so that their seed would sprout and grow.

Today, at the first full moon in May, just before corn is planted, the Maya-Quiché, now nominally Christian but combining and modifying their Christianity with ancestral rituals, pray to the idol of the rain god as of old. From high on a mountain slope above the idol's station comes the haunting sound of reed fifes and drums. Maya priests swing incense burners containing the traditional *pom*. They are followed by farmers carrying handfuls of seeds to be blessed. The native priests approach the idol, make the sign of the cross, kneel, and pray, "We beg you to protect our plants so that they may bear good and abundant fruit. . . . Here are your seven sticks of turpentine, your seven pieces of incense, and we have said our seven prayers of love and faith. . . ."

Seven is a number of religious significance to the Indians. Although the original Mayas had no connection that anthropologists and archaeologists can establish with the ancient tribes of the Middle East who wrote the Bible, they, too, believed that God destroyed the earth by flood. The rainbow, with its seven colors, signaled the end of the deluge and a hopeful new beginning.

As the rainy season approaches—what would coincide with early spring in New York State—the Indians of Izalco in San Salvador revert to Mayan rites. Twelve men wearing helmets of feathers do a dance and shout, "Let the rains come!" Then four poles of corncobs, painted in the colors of the four persons of

Chac, the rain god, one for each of the corners of the earth, are flourished to the north, east, south, and west.

But the annual anxiety over the coming of the rains is not limited to Indian villages; toward the end of the dry season, when the dust blows and the foraging cattle are scrawny, when many fields are charred by the sun and the *cuchara* crickets sing (their rasping at full crescendo is reminiscent of a power saw), you can feel the tension, even in city-dwelling people, all over the isthmus. The *cucharas* are said to be praying for rain, and only quit their unnerving chorales after the first cloudburst.

The mood is uneasy, edgy. Because agriculture accounts for 70 per cent of the exports and is absolutely basic to the economy, this anxiety is understandable. Still, the rains have always come, and they will come again. But the waiting becomes painful, weary. The dust blows. The heat is unrelieved and very trying.

One day in April, Lex wrote me, "Life gets pretty unbearable here before the rains come." Then, early in May, "Today everybody has felt rain. And sure enough here it is. It is coming just as it did last year, with the wind, and hard. Really smells good. Now the trees will cover out. What a great dust settler."

Once it rains, a new mood can be felt all over the land; there is a lot of work to be done, planting the crops. There is elation and hope and a new importance to life.

Wherever you travel, you will be aware of the money crops: bananas, cacao, African palm, rubber, in the low-lying areas; coffee in the cool highlands; cotton, rice, and sugar cane on sunny slopes and plains. Coffee, cane, and cotton, the Big C's, are the most lucrative, though vegetables are coming up fast as an important export. There are many minor crops of commercial importance, such as lemon grass, which smells so pungent in the sun; tobacco; and medicinal herbs in variety and profusion. So many drug companies now have headquarters in Guatemala City that their conglomerate location is known as "Pill Hill." There is a great deal of breath-holding in Central America about a plant called *calajuala;* exhaustive laboratory work is going on now in Tegucigalpa to establish whether it is a cure for cancer. Flowers and seeds are grown for markets, and their shipment to other parts of the world is on the increase.

There is undoubtedly pure magic in the soil due to the minerals deposited through volcanic action. Even a field of porous lava will support plant life if it is watered. Topsoil gradually covers old lava fields and is mixed with ash, providing what Lex simply calls, "The best soil in the world."

Lex knows a farmer in Honduras who was embarrassingly successful with watermelons. One year they grew to such a monstrous size, weighing about a hundred pounds, that they were almost frightening. He drove around a truckful, trying to give them away, but he was more successful in amazing than in nourishing his neighbors. The things were just too discouragingly huge to be eaten.

Of course, after the first elation at the onset of the growing season, farmers are beset by their ancient enemies, weeds and insects. "Some small farmers plant a strip of corn around their cotton to attract the insects," Lex says.

The large *fincas* now use planes to spray insecticides and fungicides; the big farm generally has its own landing strip. As you ride along the highways of Central America, you will see hundreds of agricultural-spray planes, flying spectacularly low over fields of cotton, cane, and rice. They seem to be as common as bees.

Once we visited Xolotlán, a small airfield outside Managua, Nicaragua, a base for pilots who fly these planes. The pilots told us what their jobs were like, and how they trained to fly under such arduous conditions, between volcanoes, through rainy-season squalls, close to the ground in the wind, dodging trees, fences, and other hazards. A farmer told us that once when he was having his cotton sprayed "the pilot flew so low that one of the help jumped off a mule's back."

Before he learns to fly an agricultural-spray plane, each pilot must have logged two hundred hours of solo flying. Then he is required to have a minimum of a hundred hours of training for agricultural spraying, making tight turns, flying low and through obstacles, his maneuverability hampered by a heavy load of insecticide or fungicide. It is tricky, but one pilot said, "I'd rather fly insecticides than drive in Managua." These pilots have a big investment in training, at twenty-five dollars an hour. But during the growing season they make about fifteen thousand dollars in four months for four or five hours a day. They are paid six cents for every gallon sprayed.

Their planes are small; behind each wing is a long spray pipe with nozzles. The tank for agricultural chemicals (this payload weighs from 700 to 1200 pounds) has an average capacity of from 90 to 150 gallons. Inside the cockpit there is a lever to release the spray as the pilot buzzes low over the crops, and another emergency lever, painted red and white, to dump the load if he should get in a tight spot and need to climb fast. The planes are kept in good shape, for the industrial spray companies that own them and hire the pilots insist that they return to a qualified base every night; there is a thorough check by mechanics every fifty hours, and a complete overhaul at fifteen hundred miles. Besides Xolotlán, there are three other qualified bases in Nicaragua, at Chinandega, León, and Granada.

A pilot usually services several *fincas*, spraying as many as two thousand acres, with frequent landings to take on more chemicals or fuel. They prefer to work in the early morning when there is less wind. Often they take off at 5:30 A.M. and are through for the day at 9:30 A.M. From the time crop-spraying starts (July in Nicaragua) until it ends in late December, upward of a hundred and fifty pilots fly out of Xolotlán. About a third are nationals; the rest are Americans, Peruvians, Canadians, Argentinians. In 1962 there were only six pilots flying spray planes, which gives some indication of how rapidly this modern farming method has developed.

Throughout Central America (although to a lesser extent in Costa Rica than elsewhere) the land is privately owned and managed by a very small percentage of the population. These wealthy farmers often live in style in the capital cities and commute to their *fincas* in their own planes.

Every large *finca* is a world of its own with executive offices, a chapel, a commissary, a soccer field, clusters of huts for the

permanent help, dormitories slung with hammocks for the migratory workers. The housing standards for the permanent help are
not high; the shacks are often flimsy, with one or two rooms, dirt
floors, and a little land around them for chickens and pigs and
small truck gardens. There is seldom a school for the children
or a clinic to minister to the families' health. And the *finca* worker
averages about eighty cents a day.

In a sense, the lot of the field hands has not greatly changed
since early colonial times, when the *encomienda* system was the
rule. A Spaniard would be given a "protectorate" over a certain
number of Indians; it was considered his duty to watch over
their physical and spiritual needs in return for their labor. The
attitude of the individual *encomendero* determined the quality
of the paternalism.

Although *finca* owners at the present are more and more concerned with modern agricultural methods, they have not been
as quick to apply concepts of modern social welfare. The individual *colono,* or resident field hand, is still helpless and dependent. He has no "upward mobility"; he is stuck for a lifetime
in the status quo.

In judging a "backward country" situation, however, you come
up against a more and more apparent truth: the flaws of a backward country differ only in degree from those of our own. Which
great nation in the world today puts human welfare, as it can
be specifically promoted by health, education, housing, recreation, a chance to work creatively, ahead of technological con-
siderations, such as space exploration, prowess in science, military
equipment, and the development of modern conveniences?

When you drive along the dirt or gravel roads of a huge *finca*
you are not so aware of the struggles of the poor as you may be
in a city slum either in Central America or in the States. Those
close to the land are more resilient, less inclined to melancholy.

One Sunday—which always has the quality of a fiesta in all of
Central America—we drove through a huge *finca.* Lex explained
that this *finca* was diversified in its products; it included a cattle
ranch, a coconut-processing plant, and thousands of acres of
cotton and rice. It was bossed by a superintendent, with a sub-

superintendent for each of the four operations. At its hub was a red-brick administration building, a simple (and astonishingly lovely) wooden church, painted blue, and the home of the owner, a really rather unimposing stucco structure with a tiled roof and a swimming pool. We passed a big field where soccer was being played. The grandstand was a huge, fallen tree; men and boys were sitting along the trunk and the great branches with their legs dangling, and along the road in front of the shacks the barefooted women, stationed behind charcoal tables, were selling hot foods from the usual huge blue enamel pots and white basins. Children and roosters and pigs and dogs were underfoot, and everybody seemed happy.

The climate and the greenery and flowers and sunlight combine to produce the most potent drug that has ever been invented, which peps up and tranquilizes, puts people into a happy dream-state. Those in favor of social reform should first change the weather down there.

Since money crops are so much a part of the Central American scene, it is interesting to visit plants that process any of the three Big C's, cotton, cane, or coffee. We particularly recommend visiting a coffee *beneficio;* the end product is so universally popular. *Beneficios* can be found on the outskirts of the cities in all five republics; you can be directed to one by hotel desk personnel, or join a guided tour.

We visited a *beneficio* in Costa Rica and were shown around by a man in a clean khaki suit and straw hat and very white false teeth. He had worked there for thirty years, he told us, adding with a smile, "*Poquitico*" (just a little while).

Coffee berries when red and ripe look like cranberries. They are brought in by truck, then dumped into a large vat of cool water. The water keeps them from fermenting until they are processed.

The first husk of the coffee berry is taken off by machine; at that time the two halves of the coffee bean are separated. The beans are then conveyed by a gravity-powered stream of water to a succession of vats of water. Water-grading deposits some beans in a near vat, some at the end of the line of vats. The graded beans are then spread in the sun on clean cement to dry; they are constantly raked by a special wooden tool and turned for even drying. Then they are taken to hot blowers inside the plant where the drying and parching process is completed and the second husk removed. The beans, which look as white as pea beans, are then divided into three grades, packed in burlap bags, and shipped off. The roasting is not done in Central America but at the coffee plant that imports them.

The agricultural product most associated with Central America is certainly the banana. Because of the enterprising and vast operations of the United Fruit Company and, later, the Standard Fruit Company, the countries of the isthmus have been known as "banana republics"; this inadvertently did more to create a tourist-intimidating image of steaming jungles throughout the isthmus than any other single happenstance.

Bananas do indeed grow in hot and humid coastal areas, in cleared jungles, and 95 per cent of banana shipments to the world are out of Central American ports.

The banana plant is slash-leaved and relatively short for its heavy burden of fruit. According to Lex: "An interesting plant. Related to the lily." Most independent farmers turn over a spadeful of earth, plant "bits" of rhizomes with buds. When the plant sprouts, they clear out the jungle around it. All but the most vigorous sprouts are pruned. Seven to nine months after planting, the tree blossoms and the stem begins to form. One of the most common disasters is known to the banana community as a "blowdown" or "tipover." Here the whole tree is lost by being uprooted through gales. Ill supported by the spongy jungle earth, down it goes with its precious load of immature bananas.

It is interesting to visit a banana "division," not only to see how bananas are grown, harvested, and shipped, but to feel much better about the enterprising Yankee presence in Central America. The United Fruit Company has been much criticized for its monopolistic character. United Fruit is the biggest private landowner in Guatemala; its yearly budget, until recently, was larger than that of Costa Rica's national government. However, this first North American company to take hold in Central America has contributed much to education and to social welfare as well as to the economies of its host countries. The advantages to Central Americans of working for United Fruit or Standard Fruit have been great; few of the native *finca* owners have ever operated with such a high degree of concern for human happiness and comfort.

Workers on banana divisions have the best jobs in agriculture today. They make about three dollars and fifty cents a day, as opposed to eighty cents elsewhere. They are supplied with good housing, laundry and cooking facilities, non-profit commissary services, clubs, schools and hospitals, playgrounds, swimming pools, and movies. Schools take the children through the sixth grade, which is still generally the ultimate in Central American education. Where parents desire to cooperate for secondary education, the United Fruit Company will furnish the facilities, the building, the equipment, and assist in finding the faculty. If it is paternalistic in structure, it has brought some better standards of living to field hands.

The fruit companies pay taxes to each of their host countries. Each nation profits from the cleared jungle, the developed land. Roads, airstrips, railroads, and wireless and telephone communications have been brought into the wilderness, and remain when the fruit companies withdraw. When Panama disease strikes banana divisions, for instance, the land, then impossible for bananas, is good for any other crop.

One of United Fruit Company's great contributions has been its experimental stations, such as the one at Lancetillo, Honduras, in the Tela Division, which has concerned itself with the nurturing and use of all tropical plants. United Fruit Company founded and is maintaining a unique training school for tropical agronomists at El Zamorano, near Tegucigalpa.

There is today an interesting repetition of the original linking of agriculture with civilization in Central America. Once the growing of crops triggered one of the most advanced early civilizations. Now again, agriculture is the key; a "backward" country begins to industrialize in ways that complement its greatest natural strength. Under the aegis of the Common

Market, there are new plants that are producing agricultural chemicals; there are sugar refineries, tanneries, cotton gins. A new textile industry is based on the cotton crop. Oil from citronella grass and lemon grass is being refined close to the fields where the grasses are grown. Predictably there will be the manufacture of products that use oils as a base, such as soaps and perfumes.

Leading into tomorrow, the path for Central Americans is now, as it always was, green with growing plants.

II / Where to Stay, Eat; What to Do, See

12 / Guatemala

The Tiger with the Tender Smile

Guatemala's Mayan heritage is what gives this colorful country its particular character. Fifty per cent of the inhabitants are pure-blooded Indians who wear hand-woven costumes that have been traditional for centuries. Of the rest, more than 80 per cent are of mostly Indian blood.

The Adam of the Maya-Quiché Indians was a *cacique,* or chief, called Bakam-Kitze, the tiger with a tender smile. His oldest son became the people's Moses, who led them to the present Quiché region, near Lake Atitlán. Prior to the exodus, the tiger with the tender smile went to heaven.

Two of Guatemala's national emblems are straight out of Mayan tradition: the quetzal, the bird of freedom, with the long, iridescent green tail-feathers that once sprouted from the war helmets of Mayan nobles; and the ceiba, the Mayas' sacred tree. The national hero is the Maya-Quiché Prince Tecúm Umán, who was slain by the conquistador Alvarado.

Fireplaces are a necessity in the mountains. When you are staying in the highlands, at Chichicastenango, Antigua, or Quezaltenango, it is fun to watch an Indian make a fire. He uses no kindling, only split pitch pine. He makes a teepee-like structure of the wood and places under it a single burning splinter of pitch pine. The wood soon is burning briskly.

Guatemalan scenery is magnificent; many of Central America's active volcanoes are within its borders. The climate, except in tropical coastal regions, is cool.

This country has been more popular with tourists than any other in Central America, and it is better known than the other four republics. Its attractions range from the colorful Indian villages of the highlands with their exciting crafts and markets to the important Mayan ruins of the Petén region (see p. 160). Its wilderness areas lend themselves to hunting, fishing, and bird-watching safaris.

Accommodations outside of the capital, Guatemala City, are more plentiful and comfortable than in any other part of Central America, so that side trips, of which there are many tempting choices, can be made in style.

Guatemala has an extremely active and creative tourist bureau, which is making a great fuss over arrivals these days. Large tours are greeted by a marimba band, and the ladies are handed corsages. The bureau is opening more branch offices all over the country; their personnel can be very helpful in working out an individual project or trip. They are happy to mark maps and make suggestions.

DRIVING THROUGH

Border stations: La Mesilla or Tapachula.

You leave the light blue sky and khaki earth of Mexico behind at the border for the dark green and deep blue of Guatemala. Guatemala has a quickly perceptible character of its own, with a burning brightness at noon, and a chilly gloom at dusk, and sensational sunsets.

The Guatemalan *quetzal* is on a par with the United States dollar. You will be charged 2.40 quetzales ($2.40) for temporary Guatemalan license plates, which will be wired over your permanent United States plates.

There are two main routes from the Mexican border to Guatemala City. The Inter-American Highway, CA-1 (from La Mesilla), leads over the El Tapón Pass. El Tapón can be tricky in the rainy season, prone to landslides and washouts. For the Ruta Pacífico, the coastal route (CA-2), cross the border at Tapachula, Mexico; generally, we have found it more comfortable.

From Border to Border on Inter-American Highway (CA-1)

Huehuetenango. After descending from El Tapón, 6 miles beyond the bridge at Puente Tepepul, turn left on Route 9N for Huehuetenango. Magnificent scenery; surrounding mountains are 11,500 feet high. It is four hours from here to Guatemala City.

Nearby, the ruins of Zaculeu have been partially restored. The *Hotel Zaculeu* is a good place to stay; European plan $6-$7; American plan, $9.50.

Quezaltenango. (See p. 148 for more details.) This ancient Indian-colonial city is historical, a true highlands community. Turn right shortly after San Cristóbal Totonicapán; as you climb up to Guatemala's second largest city, watch for the active volcano Santa María (12,434 feet) on your left, which has a new and dangerous volcano, Santiaguito, growing out of its flank. Plumes of smoke or steam will be ascending. You will notice that the Indian villages off the road are of quiet, earth-colored adobe with dim tile roofs. You will pass the adobe bricks drying in the sun. Along the road, here and there, you will see boys driving flocks of jogging sheep and goats, the primary source of hand-woven goods (blankets, sweaters, shawls, jackets).

Pensión Bonifaz has fireplaces, tastefully furnished rooms, a colorful patio with singing birds, a roof garden with a beautiful view; a dining-room in the colonial manner, with high, beamed ceilings; hand-woven Guatemalan linen and fresh flowers are on the tables, and Indian waitresses are in native dress; excellent food, relaxing and friendly atmosphere; American plan, single

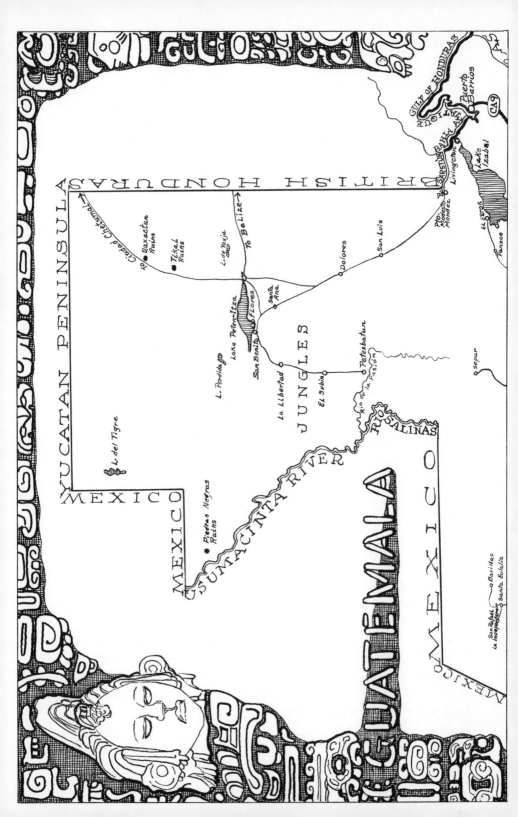

$6-$10; double $16-$18. The *Hotel Modelo* is pleasant; single $6, double $10.

Zunil. South from Quezaltenango toward Retalhuleu on Route 9S. Ancient Indian village where Mayan rites may still be observed. Visible are the volcanoes Santiaguito (active), Zunil, San Pedro, and Santo Tomás (11,567 feet). Zunil volcano is the source of a flowing mineral spring with healing powers.

Totonicapán (8225 feet). Left on spur of CA-1. Cool highlands Indian country; wonderful ceramics and textiles are sold in market. Look for blankets from Momostenango. Magnificent scenery.

Nahualá. Indians wear interesting costumes. Between Nahualá and Sololá, CA-1 climbs to almost 11,000 feet. If you are a bird-watcher, look for bush tits, mountain trogons (including, of course, the famous quetzal), painted redstarts, and a variety of sparrows.

San Francisco el Alto (8650 feet). 3 miles north of Totonicapán. This is a typical highlands village; buy hand-woven wool goods at Friday market.

Sololá. Turn right off CA-1 on RN-1. On sapphire Lake Atitlán, natives speak Cakchiquel, wear traditional costumes. Market has interesting textiles, ceramics. Visible are volcanoes San Pedro, Santiago, and Tolimán.

Patzicia. On RN-1 between Sololá and Antigua. Mountainous region where bird-watchers may see bluebirds, rufous-colored robins, acorn woodpeckers, and unicolored jays.

Santo Tomás Chichicastenango. Left near Sololá. This famous village is usually called just Chichicastenango, and affectionately "Chichi." (See special report, p. 150.)

Santa Cruz del Quiché. 10 miles north of Chichicastenango; can also be reached from Huehuetenango. Isolated Indian village, once capital of the Maya-Quiché nation. Near it are the ruins of Utatlán, rich in legend, dating from earliest Mayan times.

Panajachel. Right on RN-1, past Sololá. Resort on the shores of Lake Atitlán. Adding to weekend fun of boating and swimming is Sunday market day.

Hotels are all American plan. Rates are $3-$12 single, $6-$18 double. The following hotels are listed from lowest to highest priced: *Rancho Grande, Monterey, Regis, Tzanjuyu, Casa Contenta;* all have gardens. *Hotel Tzanjuyu* is on the lake, with a gorgeous view; it has comfortable accommodations with fireplaces in bedrooms, a dock with launch services, terraces in the sun, a dining-room with a marimba band. Hotel will arrange inexpensive launch trips to lakeside Indian villages. (There are twelve, named after the Apostles.)

Bird-watchers: take launch to Santiago Atitlán, with its reed beds; this is the world's only home of the rare giant pied-billed grebes; interesting water fowl abound; Lake Atitlán is a national water-fowl refuge. Around the lakeside town itself, watch for nightingales, wrens, and redstarts.

Ranged near the lake are the volcanoes Atitlán (11,565 feet), San Pedro (9921 feet), Tolimán (10,270 feet).

Tecpán. Nearing Chimaltenango, to the right of CA-1, you will find the village of Tecpán, with the ruins of Iximché, an ancient Mayan center of the Cakchiquel Indians, a short distance away. Restaurant.

Chimaltenango. A small colonial city, trading center for tiny mountain villages. A visit to Dr. Carroll Berhorst's clinic, on the street downhill to the right of the main plaza, is inspiring.

Chimaltenango is the take-off point for Mixco Viejo, a Mayan site with temples, plazas, palaces, ball courts.

Antigua (5030 feet). Right off CA-1 on Route 14. The most important colonial city in Central America, long the headquarters for the government of all Spanish colonies on the isthmus. It has beautiful hotels, exciting restaurants, wonderful shopping and sightseeing possibilities. Impressive historic volcano, Fuego, is still active. (For details, see p. 48.)

Guatemala City. (See p. 143 ff.)

Cuilapa. The bridge over the Los Esclavos River is of historic interest; construction was begun in November 1591. Restaurants in area serve excellent seafood.

Jutiapa (2939 feet). An industrial little city. Good restaurants, hotels. Beyond, left of highway, is Suchitán volcano (6698 feet). *Asunción Mita.* Close to El Salvador border. Uncelebrated but wonderful Mayan ruins.

San Cristóbal. Border station.

From Border to Border via the Ruta Pacífico (CA-2)

This is a far less curvy and climbing route to drive; it avoids El Tapón but it does not take you as close to the villages of the highlands as does CA-1. Still, it is possible to cut north to CA-1 on Route 9S (see below) and visit Quezaltenango, Totonicapán, Sololá, Chichicastenango, Panajachel, Chimaltenango, and all the picturesque pueblos.

Bird-watching is especially rewarding on this route. Watch all the way.

San Sebastián. South of the village, Route 9S intersects the coastal route. Turn left (north) on 9S to join CA-1, right to visit Retalhuleu and Champerico.

Retalhuleu. Agricultural, cattle-raising center. Cathedral, gracious central park. This is a good overnight stop. *Motel Royal* (at turn-off to Retalhuleu), has excellent accommodations, good food; American plan, single $4, double $8.

Champerico. A Pacific Ocean port, 25 miles south of Retalhuleu on route 9S. It offers beaches, boating, fishing.

Mazatenango (1247 feet). Volcanoes in view are Santo Tomás, Santa María, Zunil. Good and reasonable hotel accommodations.

Escuintla. A crossroads: left on Route 14 takes you to Antigua (see p. 151); left on CA-9 to Palín and Guatemala City (see p. 143); right on CA-9 to port city of San José. Aside from being a hub of travel, between mountain and coastal routes, Escuintla is known as the "City of the Palm Trees." Agricultural; the scent of citronella is exuded here.

Bird-watchers: Ask for El Salto Estate near Escuintla. Running water here attracts many species.

Satisfactory overnight accommodations; recommended is *Hotel Tahormina,* American plan, $4-$5 single, $8-$10 double.

Palín. Left at Escuintla on CA-9. Old Indian village in fruit country. Close to the highway, a giant ceiba tree, two hundred years old, spreads 180 feet. It shelters the picturesque market place.

San José. Right at Escuintla on CA-9. An important Pacific Coast port, with beaches, boating, good deep-sea fishing. Restaurants, hotels. *Hotel Viñas del Mar* has salt-water pool; American plan, single $7-$8, double $12-$13.

Bird-watchers: Near San José are fresh-water marshes where black-bellied tree ducks, jacana, tiger bitterns, swallows, kiskadees, wood ibis, roseate spoonbills, and herons can be found.

Taxisco. Continuing on CA-2 from Escuintla, the volcano Tecuamburro (6383 feet) is to left of highway.

Chiquimulilla. Picturesque canal; rent a launch for an enjoyable trip or rewarding bird-watching: sun grebes, caracas, laughing falcons, four species of kingfishers, mangrove swallows, northern water thrush, euphonias, blackfish crane hawks, wood creepers, and others. Beautiful beaches—look into La Avellana and Las Lisas.

El Pijije. Border station.

Guatemala City

At 4900 feet, with an average temperature of 68 degrees, Guatemala City has a cool climate. This mystifies many Americans in foreign service who are paid extra for living in "the tropics" in a "hardship post" and often go around with their teeth chattering.

The handsome capital, white as San Francisco, is surrounded by volcanoes. When last seen, Pacaya was huffing and chuffing and shooting out fountains of fire and furious columns of smoke. Fuego, also nearby, never stops glowing; among capricious volcanoes, it has a history of steady activity.

Mayas, who once lived here, called the city Kaminaljuyú. Ruins of Kaminaljuyú can be seen within the present city.

Widespread Guatemala City is very modern, with many high-rise buildings. A landmark is a copy of the Eiffel Tower down-town; at night it is brightly outlined by lights. Many of the new administration buildings have giant stucco sculpture on their walls. Residential sections have prosperous modern mansions, walled gardens, beautiful trees and vines, and are invariably watched over by vicious dogs, predominantly German Shepherds or Boxers. There are a number of new low-cost housing develop-ments covering acres on the outskirts. You are not as aware of slums in Guatemala City as in other capitals.

Because the city is divided into zones, it is important to know the zone of any address you wish to locate. Avenue numbers are repeated within each zone, and trying to find an address without knowing the zone number can be a real wild-goose chase.

If you want to expedite mail to the States, use the small post office at La Aurora Airport, near the terminal building. There is no delay and far less confusion than in the rabbit warren of a huge post-office building downtown.

Familiar sounds at night in Guatemala City are the whistles of the night watchmen on patrol, calling to each other like birds. Some strangers have been known to mistake them for owls.

Transportation: Buses are cheap and there is good service. You can ride anywhere in the city for 5 centavos. Taxis charge up to $2 for trips within the city limits. It is also possible to rent a car by the day or week from Avis or Hertz for about $69 to $79 dollars per week. Aviateca, the national airline, is one of the most active of the local airlines in Central America; a flight of a half hour or less will get you to Mayan ruins, shore, or mountain resorts.

WHERE TO STAY, EAT

In the case of the capital cities, we have made representative rather than exhaustive suggestions of hotels and restaurants, which should not prevent your doing some inquiring and explor-ing on your own.

Hotels

Camino Real: $15 single, $25 double; pool; good accommodations.

Guatemala Biltmore: $11-$14 single, $16-$20 double; pool; good service.

Continental Ritz: $13 single, $20 double; beautiful dining-room overlooking the city; nice rooms.

Maya Excelsior: $8.50 single, $15 double; pool, Turkish baths.

Continental: $7 single, $10 double; restaurant serves Spanish food.

Motel

Plaza: $9 single, $15 double; pool; good restaurant; nice rooms.

Pensions

La Reforma: $7 with food and no bath, single; $8 with food and bath; $11.50 double; colonial decor; comfortable.

Casa Shaw: $7 single, no private baths; $11 double; good American food; downtown.

Asturias: $6 single, $10 double, no private baths; with meals.

Restaurants

La Puerta: $3-$6; broiled steak; rustic atmosphere.

Nuria: $3-$6; broiled steak; popular, nice surroundings.

Vittorio: $3.50-$4.50; good broiled steak.

Hostería Don Pepe: $3-$4.50; colonial atmosphere in the center of town; guitar some evenings.

Lys: $3-$4.50; serves seafood.

Hidalgo: $4-$5.50; elegant atmosphere; violins on Friday.

Bodegón: $3.50-$4; rustic; good food.

La Tablita: $2.50-$4; rustic and small, eat by candlelight; serves wine.

Canton: $2.50-$4; good Chinese food; downtown.

Petit Suisse: very expensive and elegant; continental cuisine.

Ritz Hotel: $3.50-$6; continental cuisine; beautiful view of the city.
El Camino Real: $3.50-$6; continental cuisine; nice atmosphere; orchestra nightly.
Chez Lisette: $4-$7; good continental cuisine.
El Parador: $2.50-$5; specializes in Central American dishes (try the stuffed peppers); typical decor.
La Mesa Larga: $3-$5; Central American dishes served buffet style.
Simon: pastry and coffee; downtown.
Corinne: pastry; downtown.
Café de Paris: good snacks.
Hawaii: sandwiches, good food; downtown.

WHAT TO DO

Night Clubs

These come and go, so it is better to telephone in advance. Travel agencies can also arrange night-club tours for you.
El Gallito: típico; marimba, loud and touristy, dancing.
Señorial: no cover, drinks $1; orchestra, dancing, food.
Old Tiquila: discothèque; popular at present.
Brasilia: on top of Ritz Hotel; romantic; orchestra.
Hotel Camino Real: combo; dancing, food.

Sports Facilities and Events

Visitors' cards can be arranged through a travel agent for the Tennis Club, Guatemala Club, Mayan Golf Club, Guatemalan Country Club.

Soccer and basketball every Sunday (and occasionally weekdays) at the Olympic Stadium and Gymnasium; baseball at the Olympic field in Minerva Park.

Lake Amatitlán, seventeen miles south of the city, offers swimming, sailing, good water sports. Take the road around the shore for a beautiful view. Behind the lake rises the active volcano

Pacaya. Skin-divers have found pre-Columbian artifacts on the lake bottom. Dine at Club Guatemala. Marked trails for hiking around the lake.

Cultural Activities

Guatemala City has its own symphony orchestra and ballet company. Chamber music and recitals are regularly scheduled at the Capitol and Palace Theaters. Excellent little theater companies present plays at the National and Gadem Theaters. There are exhibits of contemporary paintings and sculpture.

WHAT TO SEE IN GUATEMALA CITY

National Palace. Unusual pale green stone building on central square. Historical state rooms, chandeliers, carved wood panels. Murals of the Spanish conquest of Guatemala. Beautiful view of the city from the balcony.

Minerva Park. Relief map of Guatemala covering approximately 11,000 square feet. Makes the volcano system vivid.

Aurora Park. Large zoo, flower gardens.

Campo de Feria. Once the site of a world's fair. The buildings now house the Archaeological Museum with a fine exhibit of Mayan sculpture, jade jewelry, and ceramics; the Museum of History and Fine Arts, which features paintings and sculptures of contemporary Guatemalan artists; and the Natural History Museum with displays of flora and fauna.

Kaminaljuyú. Mayan ruins within the city.

Mercado Central. Block-square building behind Metropolitan Cathedral: hand-woven fabrics, blankets, jackets, baskets, pottery, and all the handicrafts of the highlands Indians for sale along with fruits and vegetables. Interesting to walk through.

Church of Nuestra Señora de las Angustias. Completely atypical in style, this quaint brick church on the edge of town began as a chapel for the family who still live in the mansion next door. The head of the family, on the eve of an eye operation, made one of those *promesas* typical of Central American Catholicism: if God would restore his sight, he would build him a church. Inside this unusual edifice, at shoulder height, in a panel on each wall, are carved stone eyes.

Cerrito del Carmen. Church dates from 1550; Santa Teresa willed the gold-embossed altar to the church. Located on a height over the city, the church looks as if it had once doubled as a fort, with its thick walls and lookouts.

AROUND THE COUNTRY

To reach the colorful villages of the highlands, sea shores, lakes, and jungles, there is excellent air-taxi service from La Aurora airport; or you can travel by bus or car. Upward of eighteen travel agencies offer package tours to Mayan ruins and resorts.

Quezaltenango and Environs

We recommend spending the night in Quezaltenango (see p. 137), proceeding next day to Huehuetenango and ruins of Zaculeu, or to nearby Indian villages.

We stopped at Quetzaltenango for lunch en route to Guatemala City from the Mexican border at Tapachula. We saw the highland country at a bright time of day, the sea of mountains drawn in big black-green strokes against the sky.

From our log: "As we climb to Quezaltenango, we pass Indian boys and men, in colorful wool costumes and jackets, driving flocks of sheep and goats along the footpath that skirts the highway. There is the fleeting sound of their tinkling bells in the big silence. The shepherds seem self-contained, do not glance our way, as if neither we nor the highway were real. Lex says, 'To me, the Indians have sad faces.' They are certainly withdrawn. The mountains are chilly. Babies are carried papoose style, are tenderly bundled up, wear bright knitted stocking caps. Horses and burros carry big arching loads of turpentine sticks for fuel.

"Beyond the deep purple blossoms of a shrub along the highway, we see the volcano Santa María, with its new cone, Santia-guito, smoking furiously.

"The Indian villages that we pass as we climb are usually in a valley to one side of the road. Indian adobes are the color of parched earth with dim red-tile roofs. They fade into the earth, but the inevitable church is dazzling white with its bell tower rising over everything.

"We pass a small market in a field. White muslin canopies, which make one think of Arab tents, shelter the people and their produce.

"Quezaltenango has the look of a long-established colonial city. Wherever you walk, it seems you're on a steep slope. *Pensión Bonifaz,* where we eat, is charming, beautifully decorated, hospitable, quiet. Lex shows me the flowering roof garden high over Quezaltenango's tile roofs and chimney pots. Beyond roof-tops are the fantastic shapes and shadows of giant mountains. The air is keen, golden, exhilarating.

"We walk through the rooms downstairs. There is a new bar-night-club, with a bandstand. In a central patio, near the dining-room, a series of colored flower pots are set all along the tiles on the first floor and the first-floor balcony, and canaries are singing in competitive trills.

"The dining-room waitresses are attractive, mature, gracious highland Indians, their ribbon-trimmed hair in braids; they wear hand-woven skirts and beautifully embroidered blouses. Each table has a hand-woven cloth with designs of red and pink, and vases of fresh pink daisies. Wonderful food. The rice is fluffy with flecks of green and red pepper in it."

It is about two hours by car or bus from Quezaltenango to Huehuetenango and the important and extensive Mayan ruins of Zaculeu, including temples and a ball court, which have been restored by the United Fruit Company.

Not far from Quezaltenango are some Indian villages, famous for their crafts, which can be reached in an hour or less by private car or taxi.

San Cristóbal (15 minutes). Hand-woven textiles. Outstanding colonial Franciscan church.

Totonicapán (30 minutes). Pottery, wooden ceremonial masks, textiles.

San Francisco el Alto (20 minutes). Hand-woven woolen blankets in striking designs.

Momostenango (40 minutes). Famous for its woolen blankets.

San Pedro Sacatepéquez (1 hour). Market days: Tuesdays, Thursdays, Sundays. This is a large market with outstanding hand-woven Indian textiles.

Olintepeque (10 minutes). Hand-woven textiles. Site of bloody battle between Mayan Prince Tecúm Umán and Alvarado.

Chichicastenango and Environs

Chichicastenango (6447 feet) is probably the most famous village in Central America, due to its colorful Indian customs and costumes, its mixture of Mayan and Christian rituals, its scenery, and its exciting market, with a large selection of handicrafts from neighboring villages.

From our log: "The road to Chichi is well gravelled but can be dusty or muddy. Very steep with short, hard turns. Nonetheless, the road is fun, because of the breathtaking views and the traffic on the footpaths alongside. Here Indians walk along in the fascinating costumes of their various villages, carrying produce to market in Chichicastenango, sometimes leading several tiny black pigs with leashes of colored ribbons. The cobblestone streets of Chichi are narrow and steep with the one-story adobe houses shoulder to shoulder, with blossoming vines climbing up to the sun and tumbling over tile roofs."

The *Mayan Inn*, which is not to be missed for an overnight stay, is right off the main square, site of the famous market. It is of colonial architecture with hand-carved doors; high walls screen its bright and beautiful patio gardens. You can have your choice of mountain view or patio room ($14.50-$26). Accommodations are comfortable and beautiful; each room has its share of priceless colonial antiques. The beds are heaped with hand-woven Guatemalan blankets. When you arrive, your fireplace is lighted and a rum drink is served. Bar and dining-room are attractive, relaxing; the food is memorable, served by Indian women in their graceful village costume. A marimba band plays on Saturday nights.

We suggest arriving on Saturday evening, before dinner, enjoying the festivity, and visiting the market next morning. We warn that you will be tempted by the wool blankets, jackets, knitted sweaters and scarves, bedcovers, table linen, masks, carvings, pottery, and the silver jewelry from the nearby Indian pueblo of Sacapulas, famous for its silversmiths. Pre-Columbian pottery (some real, some of it fake) is also for sale.

For sightseeing on foot, hire one of the Indian youngsters who will crowd around, begging to be your guide. They speak English. Pay your young guide a dollar for showing you around.

Ask to see the shop where ceremonial masks are made; visit the nearby stone idol to which live chickens are still sacrificed; look over Father Rossback's Museum of Mayan relics, including the original manuscript of the Popol Vuh, a combined bible and history of the Maya-Quiché.

When you visit the church of Santo Tomás, remember that it is not wise to take pictures without permission. Religious customs of the Maya are still being observed along with the more recently acquired Christian rituals. Indians pause on the stone steps to burn *pom* to the old gods, swinging it in clay censers before entering the church. Inside, they kneel in the aisle to set candles ablaze on the floor; they lay a trail of rose petals or pine needles to the effigy of Santo Tomás. If he does not heed requests for favors or help, the Indians may later place his effigy out in the rain for punishment.

Antigua

La Preciosa bus line leaves 15 Calle 3-37, Zone 1, Guatemala City, every hour from 7:30 A.M. until 7:15 P.M.; a round trip costs 80 centavos. It takes about an hour and a quarter.

Antigua, the most historical of all Central American cities, is now a carefully preserved national monument. It is small enough to be seen during a leisurely walking tour. The Tourist Bureau, on the first floor of the old Palace of the Captains-General, will be glad to mark a free map for you. If you want a guide, there are responsible teen-aged boys around the shady central plaza who speak English. Your guide will stay with you for as long as you can stay on your feet in the bright cobbled streets, and a quetzal or two will make him very happy.

It is a dazzling little city, so high as to suggest Shangri-la. For contrast, the great volcano Agua looms over it with a faintly disturbing, incongruously gloomy air. When we were there, purple-blue jacaranda trees were in bloom, the wide-open blossoms of clematis climbed walls, and bougainvillaea cascaded from red-tile roofs. The houses were low; their pale mellow colors were red, yellow, blue, green, pink, and they had heavy carved doors and windows with grilles. Sometimes, walking, you heard only the sound of your own feet; the hush of history seemed to have fallen over Antigua.

The most interesting time to visit Antigua is during Holy Week. The Easter processions are magnificent and moving. The families on each block fashion by hand an intricately designed mosaic carpet of colored sawdust or flowers; usually this takes all night and is done by candlelight. Slowly shuffling over these carpets the next day 'are men and women carrying enormously heavy wooden platforms with images of Jesus, Mary, and the saints. A deeper than usual silence settles over the city then; there is nothing to be heard but the sound of feet. Men dressed as Roman soldiers, with helmets and capes and spears, march in the procession. Those who love Antigua have told me that it is *triste;* it is never more *triste* than on Holy Thursday or Good Friday, with great, brooding Agua blocking most of the sky, and the people watching in Indian silence with the sudden acrid sweetness of incense in the air.

There is a street off the north side of the central square and running east that is full of small shops. I found that what was offered was repetitious, tended to be expensive, and that it was wiser to visit the market for shopping. The market is active daily with more of an influx on Monday, Thursday, and Saturday.

There are some fine pensions and hotels, ranging from very

reasonable to average-expensive. The *Hotel Antigua* is a favorite, tastefully and comfortably furnished, with a fireplace in each room. Each room has a view of the great green patio with its clipped lawn, flower borders, and trees, where gaudy parrots and long-tailed red macaws sit on their perches and Indian women weave for the guests. The waitresses serve in Indian costumes: they wear ribbons in their hair, blue or rose-red; two huge rosettes blossom in satin at the nape of the neck, with braids hanging down the back.

For a luncheon break during a walking tour, there are pleasant places, all reasonably priced, close to the Central Square: *Hotel Aurora* ($1.50, $2 on Sundays); *Hotel Antigua* ($2.25, $2.75 Sundays); *Pensión Rojas* ($1.75, $2 Sundays).

WHAT TO SEE IN ANTIGUA

El Carmen Church. In ruins. Fine façade.

Las Capuchinas. Convent with circular Tower of Retreat; two cells have been rebuilt to show nuns at prayer.

La Merced Church. Only church not destroyed by 1773 earthquakes. Large fountain in convent ruin at left. Note arch where nuns passed overhead to church without being observed.

La Recolección. Now more of a monument to the earthquake than anything else; the tumbled roof that fell about two centuries ago helps you realize the force of an earthquake.

House of the Lions. Façade of colonial mansion with carved stone lions.

Museo Colonial. In the old University Building. Library, colonial art, portrait of Don Pedro Alvarado.

Santa Clara Church. To visit the choir loft and the roof, you must ask the guard to open the gate. Wonderful view of Antigua from roof.

San Francisco Church. To the left is the chapel where Brother Pedro Betancourt, a candidate for sainthood, is buried. It is a local custom to knock on his crypt with coin offerings. Every

Independence Day, San Francisco's huge bell tolls one stroke for each year of Guatemala's independence.

Popenoe House. Arrive between 4 and 5 P.M. Housekeeper will show you around restored colonial home, furnished authentically.

Belem. One of the most enlightened spirits of his or any other age was Brother Pedro Betancourt. In 1563 he founded the Hospital of the Bethlehemites, the monastery had only twelve brothers, in memory of the Apostles. The old monastery was converted into the present Posada Belem, an inn, by Guatemalan architect Rafael Pérez de León. The gardens of Posada Belem are a delight, filled with many birds—hummingbirds, tanagers, orioles, goldfinches, swifts, parakeets, manakins, and wood-peckers.

Compañía de Jesús. Completed in 1626. The ruins of the Jesuit Order are now used as a public market. On Fridays, a marimba band plays in the Central Park.

SIDE TRIPS OF INTEREST

A taxi can be hired reasonably for trips to adjacent villages. Walk to the Central Square, where the taxis park, or ask the hotel to arrange the trip and the fare for you.

Ciudad Vieja. The "old city" is only three miles away from the Central Square, closer to the foot of the ever-present Agua. Here, in the playground of a boys' school, you will see the ruins of the chapel where Doña Beatriz, Alvarado's wife, perished in a deluge from Agua's crater lake which slopped over during an earthquake.

The day we visited, school had just let out and swarms of eight- and ten-year-old boys in uniform, dark short pants and jackets, hovered near us, wondering at our interest in their fa-miliar surroundings. They played all their games round the old stones of the ruined chapel. It was a wonderful picture of the present and the past, with a promise of the future.

San Antonio Aguas Calientes. An old village famous for its weavers. Though you can buy its produce in the Antigua market, it is worth a trip just to see this picturesque village. As seen from the road that winds down to it, it lies, white and beautiful, in a little valley surrounded by towering mountains, with its church reaching up over the adobe houses. Along the road you see women weaving, kneeling with their looms slanting down to their laps. Many homes have fiber ropes strung up between trees, or under thatched shelters; bright tapestries are hung out on them to attract passers-by.

El Progreso—Quiriguá—Lake Izabal—Puerto Barrios— Livingston

It is 184 miles by car or bus from Guatemala City to Puerto Barrios on the Atlantic Coast, on an excellent highway, CA-9. The fare by Litegua Line bus, 8a Avenida 15-42, Zone 1, is $6 round trip.

El Progreso. Fruit-growing district. Bird-watchers: in dry stream beds, look for wrens, lesser roadrunners, kites, falcons, and sparrows.

Salamá. Turn left off CA-9 on Route 17 past El Progreso. Grows particularly delicious oranges; has famous Zacualpa Waterfall and a lake in which there are blind fish.

Zacapa and Chiquimula. Turn right off CA-9 on CA-10. Natives are often blond and blue-eyed, have the reputation for wit and hospitality. In recent years the hills of Zacapa have served as retreats for guerrillas.

Quiriguá. Turn off CA-9 on Route 4 past El Progreso. One of the most interesting of Mayan ruins (for details, see p. 159). It is possible to hire a launch at nearby small towns, Izabal or Mariscos, to cross over Lake Izabal to San Felipe.

Bananera. Left off CA-9 on the approach to Matías de Gálvez is an important United Fruit Company division.

Puerto Barrios. At the very end of CA-9 on the Atlantic Coast, this old settlement and picturesque port is a good center for side trips by boat. The *Hotel del Norte,* on the shore, operates on the American plan ($6-$8 single, $12-$16 double).

From Puerto Barrios you can travel by launch to Livingston,

a historic colony, one-time British stronghold. At Livingston you can take a boat trip up the Río Dulce to Lake Izabal, through spectacular canyons and jungles, stopping at Fort San Felipe. Built by the Spaniards to guard Lake Izabal from such British pirates as Sir Henry Morgan, Fort San Felipe is located at the point where the lake flows into the Río Dulce.

For an overnight stay, the *Hotel San Felipe* offers singles for $5.25, doubles for $10.

JUNKETS BY PLANE: ARCHAEOLOGICAL SITES

There are some important and beautiful trips into the Guatemalan hinterlands that can only be made by plane, including the most important Mayan ruins. Skilled pilots, flying staunch prop planes, are available at reasonable prices.

Cobán. A half-hour flight to Cobán; by taxi to the Caves of Lanquín. With a miner's lamp, a guide will take you down into the caves. They are labyrinthine; one could wander for days without reaching an exit. You will see stalagmites and stalactites, gleaming and translucent as icicles. Indians used to punish recalcitrant persons by tying them in a cave overnight with nothing but bats for company.

Cobán's *La Posada Hotel* offers accommodations and food; European plan, $3, American plan, $6.

Esquipulas. Close to the Honduran border. Famous for its great basilica, which houses the miracle-working Black Christ, the five-foot carved image of balsam wood, blackened from candle smoke. Pilgrims come here from all of Central America each January 15. Grateful supplicants have left miniature gold likenesses of healed members—heads, legs, arms, hands. Walking to Esquipulas over old trails, pilgrims traditionally wear large straw hats decorated with mosses and fruits.

Flores. On an island in Lake Petén Itzá, in the heart of the land of the ancient Mayas, Flores is important archaeologically and serves as a take-off point for expeditions to Mayan ruins in the jungle. It is the foremost chewing-gum center of the world.

You can hire dugout canoes rigged with an outboard motor for a trip around Flores. Wonderful for bird-watching, fishing.

Tikal

Fly Aviateca; one hour from Guatemala City; fare, $33. For overnight, the *Jungle Inn* is good; American plan, single $12-$16, double, $18-$24.

If you plan to visit Tikal from December through February, bring a warm jacket. June through October is the best time as far as climate is concerned. Rainwear is usually unnecessary from February through May.

You fly into the oldest and largest of ancient Mayan centers over high-reaching white limestone temples and palaces and come down on a jungle landing strip. Enthusiasts recommend a three-day stay. In the six square miles of Central Tikal, the University of Pennsylvania, whose special project this has been, has mapped over three thousand separate constructions—temples, palaces, shrines, ceremonial platforms, etc. There are more than two hundred stone monuments, sculptured or plain stelae, and altars. But it is conceded that many of the most important sites can be covered in a day or a day and a half.

For briefing, visit the Tikal Museum, where the best of the million-odd potsherds, a hundred thousand tools, ceremonial objects, personal ornaments, incense burners, and other objects that have been unearthed are on exhibit. Also available is literature on Mayan history, art and architecture, and culture.

One of the most interesting exhibits is Stela 29, believed to have been carved and erected about A.D. 292; it is the earliest stela discovered so far with carved hieroglyphic texts. It is believed that Tikal was first inhabited about 600 B.C. Evidence of life at that time has been found on bedrock beneath the North Acropolis, one of the great plazas of the Mayan Empire. By 100 B.C., Tikal was an important center and architecturally wondrous.

It is about a mile's walk from the landing strip to the plaza at the heart of Tikal. Here you will find Stela 11, carved and erected in A.D. 879, when time was running out for Mayan civilization.

Tikal has the tallest temples of any in the Mayan area. The tallest, Temple IV, measures 229 feet. The flight of steps that were probably climbed by the *halech uinic,* the priest-governor, is steep. Don't try if you are subject to dizzy spells. Notice particularly the carved sapodilla lintels over the doorways in Temple IV. Archaeologists agree that wood carving reached its highest development here.

The most important mathematical monument in Tikal is Stela 10, on which 5,042,277 years are recorded.

If, leaving Tikal, you feel that you have scarcely scratched the surface, this is also the reaction of archaeologists who have been working there for a decade. Future discoveries within these historical miles are absolutely predictable.

The 222 square miles of Tikal National Park are a wild-life preserve. The park is crisscrossed by cleared trails, a delight to naturalists. Birds of brilliant plumage fly through the jungle. Upward of three hundred species have been identified, including trogons, warblers, woodpeckers, forest falcons, barred antshrikes, swallow-tailed kites, king vultures, parrots, puff-birds, vireos, honeycreepers, and Montezuma's oropendulas. Spider monkeys move from tree to tree in the late afternoon. Howler monkeys are rare but can sometimes be heard hooting.

Uaxactún

This site is 12 miles from Tikal. Stay at Tikal's *Jungle Inn.*

Uaxactún was one of the longest occupied of Mayan cities; One of the earliest dates on commemorative stelae anywhere in Mayan ruins can be found on Stela 9 (A.D. 328). Structure B XIII has the finest and oldest Old Empire wall painting, in tones of yellow, gray, and black on white, dating from the sixth century of the Christian era. In the temple, one of the murals shows singers shaking maracas or beating drums. The earliest pottery finds here, in the strata of black earth, are crude and date from the second century B.C. And the earliest astronomical observatory has been found here.

Quiriguá

This Old Empire city, where you can see some of the earliest Mayan carving and architecture, can be reached by plane and car. Currently, one guided tour costs from $30 to $80, according to the number of persons; it leaves at 8 A.M. and returns between 4 and 5 P.M. (box lunches included).

The most beautiful chipped flint art has been found here. The stone carving is thought to be among the best; the hardness of the stone held the sculptures to simple and forceful designs. Spectacular is Stela F, with beautiful and inexhaustibly imaginative hieroglyphs carved on stone. Zoomorph B (dedicated A.D. 761) may be the most ornate anywhere. There are seventeen *Hotun* markers, to celebrate the endings of each *Hotun* (five-year period). Stela E is the largest shaft of stone ever quarried by ancient Maya; it weighs 65 tons, measures 35 feet in height.

Piedras Negras

In the opinion of many archaeologists, Mayan sculpture reached its highest development here. Wall panel 3, Structure 3-08, is thought to be the most beautiful stone sculpture among all the Mayan ruins. It combines high and low relief, showing a *halech uinic* on a throne decorated with fourteen sculpted figures. The elegant costumes worn during the Old Empire are clearly shown.

At Piedras Negras there is the best front view of a human figure sitting cross-legged that can be found in any Mayan sculpture. There is an interesting repetition of that cross-legged figure in some of the niches. The earliest has a rather wooden look. Eighty years after this first effort, a sculptor tried to do better (Stela 11). Forty-three years later, another attempt was made to excel the earlier techniques and resulted in a deeper, more fully expressed job. And thirty years after that, on Stela 14 (761 A.D.), the figure was repeated for the third time. Thus, over a period of 153 years, a series of sculptors strove for perfection, and finally one of them said, "That's it."

There are sweat baths at Piedras Negras with benches and drains, and a large sculptured throne.

Petén Region

There are more Mayan ruins worth visiting in the Petén region: Calakmul (in Mexico), Naranjo, and Nakum. *Calakmul* is the most interesting; it has 103 stelae, more than any other Mayan city. Here ancients sculptured giant figures in a great outcrop of limestone, 9-foot-high captives with bound hands. *Naranjo* has extensive architectural remains, including 47 stelae. *Nakum* is believed to have been settled very late; its few stelae are dated A.D. 771 to 849, but its ruins show that latter-day Mayas were adhering, even if half-heartedly, to old customs.

Sayaxché. Southwest of Tikal, this is the take-off point for many less visited archaeological sites. Fly Aviateca on these very interesting safaris. Excellent accommodations are to be found at the *Río de la Pasión Lodge*, single $16, double $24.

"Baul," a privately owned sugar plantation, is worth seeing.

Seibal, two hours upriver by canoe in the Río de la Pasión Valley. The Peabody Museum of Harvard is doing some restoration; ceremonial center, well-preserved stelae.

Aguateca has Maya bridges, stelae.

Dos Pilas—a long hike in high humidity; plan on camping.

Yaxchilán, northwest of Sayaxché on the Mexican border, along the banks of the Usumacinta River, is famous for its 59 carved lintels. The most beautiful is Lintel 26, Structure 23. (The British Museum has Lintels 24 and 25.) The finest stelae are 1, 4, 3, 7.

MARKET DAYS

Antigua	Saturday, Monday, Thursday
Chichicastenago	Sunday, Thursday
Chimaltenango	Monday, Thursday, Friday
Cobán	Saturday
Guatemala City	Monday through Saturday
Huehuetenango	Daily

Momostenango	Sunday
Nebaj	Thursday
Olintepeque	Tuesday
Palín	Wednesday, Friday
Panajachel	Sunday
Quezaltenango	Monday through Saturday
Quiché	Saturday, Sunday
San Cristóbal	Sunday
San Francisco el Alto	Friday
San Lucas Tolimán	Tuesday, Friday
San Martín Jilotepeque	Sunday
San Pedro Jocopilas	Tuesday
San Pedro Sacapulas	Monday, Thursday, Friday
San Pedro Sacatepéquez	Tuesday, Thursday, Sunday
San Raimundo	Thursday, Sunday
Santiago Atitlán	Daily
Sololá	Tuesday, Friday
Totonicapán	Tuesday, Saturday
Tecpán	Thursday
Zaculeu	Daily

FIESTA CALENDAR

DATE	PLACE	CELEBRATION
Jan.		
2	Santa María de Jesús (Sac.)	Dulce Nombre de Jesús
6	Salcajá	Día de los Reyes
6	Comalapa	Indian Dances
12–15	Esquipulas	Christ of Esquipulas
15	San Pedro Sacatepéquez	Christ of Esquipulas
15	San Jorge La Laguna	Christ of Esquipulas
15	Totonicapán	Christ of Esquipulas
15–18	Chicalajá	Local Fair
20	San Antonio Aguas Calientes	Local Fair
20	San Sebastián Lemoa	San Sebastián
22–26	San Raimundo	Local Fair
23–25	San Pedro Jocopilas	Local Fair
25–29	Rabinal	Local Fair
Feb.		
1–2	Chinautla	Virgen de Candelaria
	San Juan Ostuncalco	Virgen de Candelaria

DATE	PLACE	CELEBRATION
Feb.		
1–2	*Santiago Sacatepéquez*	Virgen de Candelaria
	Mixco	Feria de Morenos
March		
19	*San José Pinula*	San José
	Chichicastenango	San José
28–31	*San Pedro Sacatepéquez*	Feria de Dolores
	Sololá	Feria de Dolores
3rd Sunday	*Panajachel*	Xocomil Fiesta
Holy Week	*Entire country*	Semana Santa
April		
22–30	*San Marcos*	Local Fair
May		
1–5	*Lake Amatitlán*	Feria de la Cruz
2	*Chichicastenango*	Feria de la Cruz
13–20	*Patzún*	María Auxiliadora
24	*San Martín Jilotepeque*	María Auxiliadora
	Chichicastenango	Pentecostés
	Guatemala City, Antigua	Pentecostés
Corpus Christi	*Guatemala City*	Corpus Christi
	Patzún	Corpus Christi
June		
10–13	*San Antonio Aguas Calientes*	San Antonio de Padua
12–13	*San Antonio Palopó*	San Antonio de Padua
23–24	*San Juan Sacatepéquez*	Local Fair of San Juan
24	*Olintepeque*	San Juan Bautista
	Comalapa	Local Fair
27–29	*San Pedro Sacatepéquez*	Local Fair of San Pedro
29	*San Pedro La Laguna*	San Pedro
	Chichicastenango	San Pedro
	Rabinal	Local Fair
July		
12–18	*Huehuetenango*	Fiestas Julias, Local Fair
23–25	*Santiago Sacatepéquez*	Local Fair
23–26	*Patzicia*	Local Fair

DATE	PLACE	CELEBRATION
July		
24–25	San Cristóbal	Local Fair
26–	Momostenango	San Cristóbal
Aug. 2		
26	Chimaltenango	Local Fair
29–30	Palín	San Cristóbal
Aug.		
1–4	Sacapulas	Local Fair
1–6	Cobán	Local Fair
12–18	Guatemala City	Feria de la Asunción
	Santa Cruz del Quiché	Feria de la Asunción
13–14	Sololá	Local Fair
25	Salcajá	Local Fair
26–29	Sumpango	Local Fair
Sept.		
11–15	Quezaltenango	Departmental Fair
15	Entire country	Independence Day
16–21	Salamá	Local Fair
25–30	Totonicapán	Departmental Fair
Oct.		
1–4	Panajachel	San Francisco
	San Francisco el Alto	San Francisco
1–8	Tecpán	Local Fair
10–11	Momostenango	Octava de San Francisco
11–13	Zaragoza	Local Fair
15	Palín	Santa Teresa
15–18	San Lucas Tolimán	San Lucas
17–19	San Lucas Sacatepéquez	Local Fair
Nov.		
1	Entire country	All Saints' Day
2	Entire country	All Saints' Day
11	San Martín Jilotepeque	Local Fair
21–22	Santa Cruz del Quiché	Santa Cecilia
24–25	Santa Catalina Palopó	Santa Catalina
25	Nahualá	Local Fair
	Zunil	Local Fair
Dec.		
6–8	Huehuetenango	Concepción

DATE	PLACE	CELEBRATION
Dec.		
6–8	*Ciudad Vieja*	Concepción
6–12	*Escuintla*	Concepción
6–13	*Retalhuleu*	Concepción
8	*Guatemala City*	Concepción
	Chichicastenango	Concepción
	Chiquirichapa	Concepción
12	*Guatemala City*	Virgin of Guadalupe
12–14	*Santa Lucía Utatlán*	Fair of Guadalupe
15–21	*Chichicastenango*	Local Fair, Santo Tomás
23–27	*Cuilapa*	Santo Tomás
24	*Entire country*	Christmas Eve
25	*Entire country*	Christmas Day
31	*Entire country*	New Year's Eve

13 / El Salvador

Nine Angels Standing on the Head of a Pin

The Mayan word for El Salvador was Cuscutlán—land of precious things. Being tiny—it is 190 miles long and 70 miles wide at its widest point—it does have a jewel-box quality, with its amazingly varied terrain, flora, and fauna. Jaguars, pumas, and ocelots are still hunted in wilderness areas; game fish abound off its coast; islands in the Bay of Fonseca are a world-famous area for observing migratory water fowl. Good game birds abound— partridge, snipe, quail, pheasant.

This little nation has volcanoes, thermal springs, caves with pre-Columbian graffiti on the walls, lakes, rivers, ocean beaches, estuaries, islands, Mayan ruins, picturesque Indian villages rich in handicrafts, such as Izalco or Ilobasco. Exciting artifacts have been unearthed, and are still being dug up, all over the land: especially at Tehuacán, Atehuan, Quelepa, Juayúa, Chalchuapa, Usulután, Mejicanos, San Miguel. The buried remains of ancient civilizations have scarcely been touched.

The remark that is always being made about Central America is that it is a "land of contrasts." This is especially true of El Salvador. The smallest nation in all the Americas, it is the most populated on the isthmus; the average is 392 persons per square mile and increasing. At the same time, El Salvador is the most sophisticated industrially.

As you drive through the country, your first impressions will not confirm these facts. You will not see great crowds of people apparently short of space, jammed like the proverbial angels on the head of a pin. Nor will you encounter much of the stigmata of an industrial economy—treeless acres, smokestacks, factory buildings.

What strikes a first-time visitor most forcibly is the astonishing difference between one Central American country and another. The big difference begins with the people. Salvadorans tend to be short, stocky; their noses are less aquiline and severe, their mouths are more mobile, their expressions are less withdrawn than those of pure-bred, grave Indian Guatemalans. Salvadorans are products of a uniquely Central American melting pot of Toltec, Mayan, and European stock.

Except in a handful of Indian villages whose people still adhere to old customs (Izalco, Nahuizalco, Panchimalco), you do not see tribal costumes as you do in Guatemala. Women's clothing is fairly nondescript, running to blouses and skirts that show the beating they've taken on riverside rocks on washday; but part of every woman's ensemble is the traylike basket without handles that she balances on her head. Its contents are often as decorative as trimmings on an Easter bonnet—pink carnations and white lilies, green and red peppers, brightly feathered chickens. She moves along in bare feet swift and silent as a wraith. The men tend to wear pajama-like slacks (sometimes colored sky blue), frayed shirts, straw hats; part of their uniform is the machete and the water gourd slung over their shoulders as they walk to and from the fields along the shoulders of the highway. You will sometimes see a woman riding a horse and carrying a red or blue parasol; it is a pretty sight, especially if there is a small child behind her, with its arms around her waist.

Typically Salvadoran are the river bathers. Women wash clothing alongside the banks of rivers everywhere in Central America, but only in this country is bathing on washday customary. When the family wash has been draped over the bushes and sunny grass to dry, the women wade out into the river, happily naked; they can often be glimpsed from the highway as it crosses bridges, especially near Sonsonate.

As you drive into El Salvador you will notice a type of water jug being carried that you will not see in any other Central American country. It is bulb-bottomed, giraffe-necked, and has the dim patina of pewter. The design is perfectly lovely and centuries old.

You first notice the population explosion in the number and urgency of people at a crossroads where you slow to a stop, or at a garage where you pause for gas. Then you will be anxiously surrounded by vendors who offer you homemade sausages in bristling clusters, candles wrapped in bright paper, minced meat or white cheese rolled in tortillas. These roadside stands are typical of El Salvador. For most families, the homemade foods or home-grown fruits and vegetables sold by the women provide the only source of income. In the cities, the men sell lottery tickets or shine shoes in a land where, ironically, there are very few shoes to be shined.

Another indication of desperation in the countryside is the cultivation of land right up to the very craters of volcanoes. Family gardens are sometimes planted on such steep slopes that, as a young sociologist put it, "People are always falling out of their cornfields."

I once marveled over how much wilderness there appeared to be despite the fact that I had heard that the land was exhausted. Lex pointed out that coffee, the money crop (cotton is second), is in a sense a hidden crop, for every coffee tree is sheltered by its own shade tree, botanical *nanas;* when you look at miles planted to coffee, even from a short distance these appear to be woods.

As you drive around the cities you may glimpse shockingly squalid slums, flimsy little shacks in ravines or arroyos. Some of these dwellings are actually made of cardboard, pieced together like a child's house of cards.

The younger Salvadoran leaders are motivated by a greater social conscience than that of the previous generation. Until recently, the fact that wealth and power were in the hands of a very few families (they are still called the *Catorce,* the fourteen) was accepted as inevitable. The growing ranks of the poor and ignorant were out of sight, out of mind. Now progressive leaders are backing low-cost housing projects, day nurseries, adult education, to bring the helpless and illiterate into the urban economy. Despite this, of course, the numbers of the desperately poverty-stricken are such that these programs cannot possibly reach out in time to help every family here and now.

The jumbled cardboard shacks and naked children are not necessarily the face of yesterday; unless the world grows wiser, this may be the face of tomorrow for many nations. In our own prosperous land, one out of every six persons now lives in extreme poverty. El Salvador's Malthusian predicament, too little land to support the people, is simply more evident because of her smallness. Her limitations are more dramatic, and the way she copes with this emergency, the way she strikes a balance between industrialization and agriculture, will be of keen interest to sociologists and economists in every nation of the world. She is a very important guinea pig.

A visitor may never see a slum section in El Salvador's beautiful colonial or modern cities, or walk through the pathetic squalor of some of the urban markets, where a small bowl of peppers may be a whole family's only hope of income. He can limit his view to the elegant hotels, the beautiful suburban homes, the private clubs, and the fine restaurants.

Even if he does sense some of the misery of those who are too numerous for the land, he can wake up on an effervescent morning, for which El Salvador is famous, and understand completely why even the most desperate can still have life and feel hope here.

DRIVING THROUGH

From Guatemala City, there is a choice of three routes to San Salvador: the Inter-American Highway (CA-1), which crosses the border at San Cristóbal, is routed via Santa Ana. CA-8, which crosses at Paso el Jobo, also goes through Sana Ana. The Carretera del Litoral (coastal highway), CA-2, crosses the border at La Hachadura. On the coastal route, turn north near Acajutla on Route 12, then east on CA-8; or north at La Libertad on Route 4.

Equate 1 Salvadoran *colón* to 40 cents, 2.50 colones to the dollar.

El Jobo to Santa Ana (CA-8)

Ahuachapán. Nearby, one acre of fumarolic activity; bubbling mud, steam, and sulphuric mists rise from fissures. Los Ausoles has thermal springs that benefit sufferers from rheumatism and arthritis.

Chalchuapa. The ruins of an ancient center, Tazumal, can be found southeast of Chalchuapa's central plaza; the large pyramids have been reconstructed, and artifacts and black pottery found during excavations are on display in the museum.

Santa Ana. El Salvador's second largest city was once known as Sihuatehuacán (City of the Priests). The largest coffee mill in the world is on its outskirts.

Metapán. 25 miles north of Santa Ana, on Route 12, back in Indian village country. On the way you will pass Laguna de Güija, a lake of crystal-clear water, where flooded-over Mayan ruins can be seen. This is also great fishing and hunting territory. The village of Metapán has some of the finest Spanish colonial churches in the Americas. La Parroquia has a famous altar with silver and gold decorations, and the wood carvings of its interior are beautiful. Beyond Metapán there are Mayan ruins worth visiting.

Santa Ana to San Salvador (CA-1)

Lake Coatepeque. South on CA-1; turn right just beyond El Congo. This favorite lake, situated in a valley and ringed by hills, is green with islands. Hotels, restaurants. *Hotel del Lago* serves superior meals; gourmets order lake crabs. Excellent fishing, water sports. Local pros make rafts out of two-by-fours, sit on a chain strung between them, and fish from that position. There are hot-water springs at hand.

Cerro Verde National Park. Turn right, past Lake Coatepeque, for Cerro Verde National Park, 17 miles from highway. From Cerro Verde's 6200-foot summit you can look into the 600-foot crater of Izalco volcano. The best viewing spot is from the balcony of the ill-fated Hotel Montana (see p. 46).

We recommend that the village of Izalco, one of El Salvador's most interesting Indian villages, be approached via Sonsonate on Route 12 (see p. 171).

Ruins of San Andrés. Between kilometer markers 32 and 33 on CA-1, turn left to ruins of Mayan pyramids, two of which have been restored. The ruins are located on a *finca,* near the San Andrés Agricultural School. Tourists still find artifacts here.

Santa Tecla (3028 feet). In a coffee-growing area near San Salvador, this city, also known as Nueva San Salvador, is considered part of the capital. In fact it was the capital from 1855 to 1859, when the old city was destroyed by earthquake. Now it is the capital of the department of La Libertad.

Nearby are some good swimming spots; on the road to La Libertad (Route 4 south), the Ayagualo River has good bath houses.

Los Chorros, an extraordinarily beautiful sylvan park with three crystal-clear natural pools fed by waterfalls, is three miles from Santa Tecla; picnic sites, restaurants.

In the immediate vicinity of Los Chorros is Antiguo Cuscatlán, an Indian village that was the center of Pipil Indian life before the Spanish conquest.

From the height of Santa Tecla you descend into the Valley of the Hammocks, where San Salvador is located at 2200 feet.

San Salvador. See p. 179.

From La Hachadura to San Salvador via Acajutla and Sonsonate (CA-2, Route 12, CA-8)

Acajutla. Where CA-2 meets Route 12, turn right (south) on Route 12 to reach this Pacific seaport. Acajutla offers the contrasts for which Central America is famous. It has one of the most modern dock installations in the world, with a mile-long pier and an observation tower. It is the Common Market's principal Pacific port. There are hotels and restaurants, a good beach, and a lingering quaintness despite the modern dock.

At the Acajutla turn-off, there is an excellent restaurant, very unpretentious in appearance. A good milk bar, Botella de Leche, is between kilometers 3 and 4. At kilometer 5 there is a fine restaurant aptly named "Kilo Cinco."

West of Acajutla on CA-2, is Barra de Santiago, one of the most beautiful beaches in Central America. It is an ocean channel. No overnight facilities.

Sonsonate. Turn left (north) on Route 12 at the junction with CA-2. A colonial city, with a unique old cathedral that has seventeen cupolas and a shrine to San Antonio del Monte to which miraculous powers have been attributed. Restaurants, hotels, swimming at nearby Nahulingo Springs. Market is important because the crafts of Izalco are sold here.

Village of Izalco. North from Sonsonate on a secondary road going toward the Izalco volcano. While driving, keep an eye out for glimpses of the Pacific Ocean at strategically panoramic places. At the foot of Izalco volcano (6138 feet), you will find the ancient Indian pueblo, with cobbled streets and faded adobe houses and a profound stillness that is shattered only when the church bell rings.

There are legends and superstitions about this Lady Bell in the tower of the church at the foot of the mountain. It was cast in 1580 in Seville, Spain, and was given a personality by its inscription: "My name is María Asunción. I weigh 1000 pounds and if you don't believe me, pick me up." The bell is considered to have sovereignty over village inhabitants.

Here live the Nahuatl Indians, who are of mixed Mayan and Toltec blood. They still speak Nahuatl and adhere to old customs. The village has a chief and an Indian Court of Justice. Some of the finest handicrafts in El Salvador are made here. The Indians are renowned hemp-weavers, makers of mats, hampers, and baskets. Rushes from which these are woven are planted

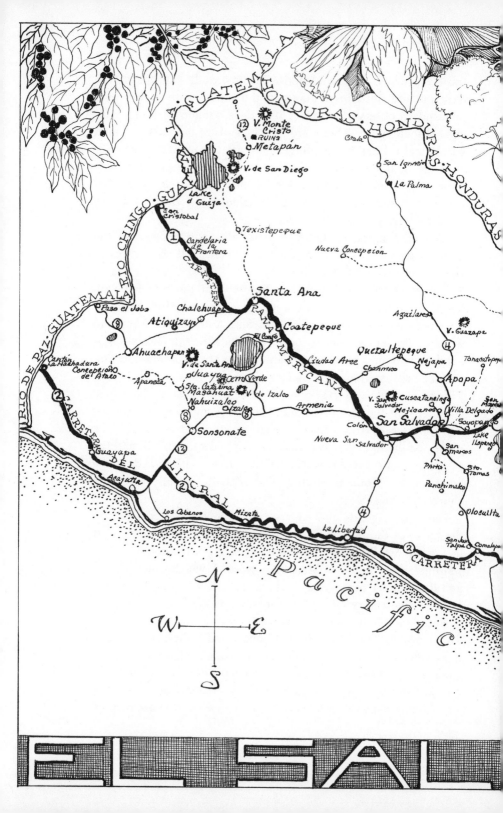

when the moon is new. When about seven feet tall the rushes are cut, dried, slit with knives, colored or left in their natural state, then exposed to the dew to make them pliable for weaving.

Nahuizalco and Santa Catarina Masahuat. From Izalco return to Route 8 and turn right to Sonsonate. Proceed through the city and bear right onto an unpaved section of Route 8. Next village beyond Sonzacate is Nahuizalco, which is joined by a rough country road to Santa Catarina Masahuat.

Nahuizalco means "four Izalcos" and is said to have been established by four families of Izalco Indians at the time of the conquistadores. Its specialty is hand-woven mats and baskets.

"Masahuat" is Nahuatl for "river belonging to the deer owners." The local craft is basket and mat-weaving.

Parque Atecozol. Eastward on CA-8 is a sylvan park with giants of wonderful shade trees. Swimming pools, restaurant.

Armenia, Ateos, Colón. You pass through these three small villages as you near San Salvador on CA-8. Armenia is in an agricultural and cattle-ranch area, near Los Lagartos River. Its ancient Mayan name, Guaymuco, means "frog talk." Ateos and Colón are altogether unnoteworthy except for agricultural output.

San Salvador. See p. 179.

From San Salvador to Honduran Border via San Miguel (CA-1)

Lake Ilopango. Outside San Salvador, watch, eyes right, for sapphire-blue water. A road leads right to the resort town of Apulo on its shores. Hotels, restaurants, swimming, boating, water sports.

Cojutepeque. On the north slope of a mountain, Cerro de las Pavas; restaurant, picnic pavilion on top. Dates from 1571; rich in historical incident. General Gerardo Barrios was declared general-in-chief of the army here in 1863, having fought back the invading Guatemalans. Woven goods made from a morning-glory-like vine in market. Delicious salami, sausages, and tongue can be bought in private homes.

Ilobasco. Turn left on Route 11. An ancient Indian village famous for its ceramic crafts. (See p. 109 for details.)

San Vicente. Off to the right before crossing the Río Lempa. There are outstanding colonial buildings, some reconstructed. Nearby San Vicente volcano (7197 feet) has broad shoulders and conical peak.

Capital of El Salvador from 1834 to 1839, San Vicente was one of the earliest settlements to be granted the title "Ciudad" by Spanish colonists. There are many legends and historical tales about San Vicente. For instance, during an Indian uprising in 1833, led by Anastasio Aquino of Santiago Nonualco, Aquino entered the Church of La Ermita de Nuestra Señora, lifted a gold and emerald crown from the statue of the image, put it on his own head, and was carried through the town on the shoulders of his triumphant army. Aquino also abducted ladies of the town, the most famous of whom was the beautiful Matilde Marin. Aquino intended to marry her, but Matilde managed to escape during a battle. Aquino was eventually captured and hanged. The church can be visited today. Also, look for the venerable *tempisque* tree under which early colonial families met to organize for mutual protection. San Vicente was the center of the cultivation of indigo.

Two miles from San Vicente is Amapulapa Park; its unusually beautiful natural swimming pool, on three levels, is surrounded by gardens and ancient shade trees.

On a slope of San Vicente volcano are the ruins of Tehuacán. Not easy to visit, but a guide can be hired in San Vicente. Nearby are the Indian villages of San Sebastián and Apastepeque, with its beautiful lake, famous for its indigo fair; and the Laguna Vita, which attracts interesting water fowl.

Río Lempa. At kilometer 90, between San Vicente and El Triunfo, you cross El Salvador's most important river, the Lempa, over the longest suspension bridge in Central America, the Puente Cuscatlán. Lex says he has heard that on one side of the Lempa the ox-carts have solid wheels, on the other they have spoked wheels—just another indication of the many regional differences. To the west of the river once lived the Lenca Indians in their kingdom of Chapparestique. Their chief was the hero Lempira. Indian mounds can be found in the plains of the area, well known for its wealth of archaeological material. Many crucial battles between conquistadores and Indians were fought on the banks of the Lempa. At its mouth, at high tide, the river is as wide as the Mississippi. There is good fishing on the Lempa, whose main port is La Barca. The week before Holy Week, fishermen and their families camp on the banks of the river at La Barca, dry their fish over fires.

Quelepa. Approximately 10 miles northwest of San Miguel, slightly to the left of CA-1 on a secondary road, is the site of an important pre-Columbian city, much of which is still unexcavated. Archaeologists believe that the Indians covered their sacred buildings with clay and dirt to prevent their seizure by Spaniards.

San Miguel Volcano (7029 feet). On CA-1 toward San Miguel, 125 kilometers from San Salvador, its huge shape is broadside to the road. From a distance, the volcano is a blue shadow. It has a wide crater, which is usually smoking, and its body hulks up into the sky. Scops owls live near the crater, and so do red-billed pigeons. (See pp. 50–51 for more details.)

San Miguel. Turn left off CA-1 onto Route 7. This is a mostly colonial little city. Some portions of it have been rebuilt because of earthquakes and the eruptions of San Miguel volcano. One of the meanest of all the conquistadores, Martín Estete, made his presence cruelly felt in this area.

Millian's Motel is tops for good food and comfortable lodging. And there are unpretentious but memorable restaurants. The most unlikely gourmet spot, the Shell Station cafeteria, located at the intersection leaving the city for La Unión and Usulután, has black clams, turtle eggs, dreamy shrimp soup.

Routes to Puente Goascorán

From San Miguel there are three routes to the Honduran border at Amatillo. CA-1 wanders southeast, then heads north to the border. CA-2, the coastal route, can be joined south of San Miguel and hugs the Pacific shore to La Unión; there you make a left turn and proceed on CA-1. The Ruta Militar, Route 7 left from San Miguel, is the shortest, rejoining CA-1 approximately 6 miles from the border.

From San Salvador you can head south on Route 4 to La Libertad and pick up CA-2 there to La Unión.

La Unión. Just a jog from CA-1 is this old port on the beautiful and wild Gulf of Fonseca, where coves were once hideouts for pirates. Look down the cobbled streets lined with faded adobe house fronts to deep blue water and bare golden mountains ringing the shores. The docks at Cutuco (a modern installation including formidable storage tanks) handle over half of El Salvador's imports and exports. You can go deep-sea fishing from La Unión; you can also hire a motorboat for bird-watching the islands around La Unión. Aside from one of the greatest collections of native and migratory seabirds in the world (coots, whimbrels, pelicans, whistling ducks, sandpipers, killdeers), you will find unbelievable varieties of wrens, indigo buntings, blue-headed macaws.

There are no suitable hotels. Use the motels at San Miguel or Usulután as a base.

Nearby is lovely El Tamarindo beach. The waters are calm, clear, comfortably shallow for an unusual distance, safe. King-sized oysters are sold locally and should be sampled. They too are safe.

Puente Goascorán. As you approach the border station, the character of the land changes; you begin to see the bare, golden mountains characteristic of Honduras. Along the highway on the Honduran side, there are displays of gaudy and wonderful clay hens and roosters, made locally and sold only in these few miles.

San Salvador to La Unión on CA-2

La Libertad. About 15 miles south of San Salvador, on Route 4 through the suburb Colonia San Benito, to where Route 4 meets CA-2. The beach is of black volcanic sand. Undertow can be treacherous. It is an interesting, active port. Hotels, restaurants.

Lex observes: "From about three to five in the afternoon fishermen come home to the pier at Libertad in their dugout canoes, bringing in their fish. There are about sixty or seventy of these little boats; some are run by motors, some have sails, and some are moved along by oars. Five or six lobster boats come home too."

Near La Libertad you will find the only stand of balsam trees, uniquely Salvadoran, useful in medicines and cosmetics. Once the balsam sap traveled to Spain by way of Peru and was mistakenly called "Peruvian balsam." *Balsameros,* skilled natives who understand the trees, harvest the sap.

If you bird-watch, look for spectacled owls, band-tailed pigeons, Inca doves, warblers, blue-headed macaws.

San Pedro Masahuat. Past Comalapa, turn left off CA-2 onto a secondary road. Here is an opportunity to get off the highway and visit an old Indian village famous for its hand-woven palm-leaf hats.

Santiago Nonualco. On another secondary road left off CA-2. This was the home of the Lenca chief Aquino (see p. 175).

San Juan Nonualco. Known for its ceramics.

Zacatecoluca. Natives make the best saddlebags in the country. They also weave shallow, strong baskets without handles, which the women carry on their heads. This little city was established early in the eighteenth century.

Jiquilisco. Near the blue waters of Jiquilisco Bay, this is a lovely little old village. Much pre-Columbian pottery, called "Usulután ware," has been dug up in this area.

Usulután. Located on the south slope of Usulután volcano. Waterfalls from the El Molino River form swimming pools. There are hot springs too; you can hear their boiling water for two miles. Excellent new motel.

Chirilagua. Close to the Pacific, this quiet village is known for its reed mats, palm-leaf hats, and fiber products.

Playa el Cuco. One of the most beautiful Pacific beaches. At sunset it is unbelievable; a wide, wonderful, lonely stretch of smooth sand against the charcoal and flaming pink and gold of the sky.

La Unión. See p. 177.

Puente Goascorán. Border station. See p. 177.

San Salvador

San Salvador has more modern buildings than any other Central American city. Repeated earthquakes have destroyed it, and, except for a very few sections, it has been rebuilt and has largely lost its colonial look.

It lies in a valley at 2200 feet, with its enormous volcano, green all the way to the crater, as a dramatic backdrop. Close to the city, to be seen from many vantage points, is Lake Ilopango, a luminous blue that changes its shades with the hour and the weather; at dusk it often seems to gleam with a light of its own. The climate of San Salvador is particularly heavenly, bright and clear and clean, warm during the day, cool at night.

Long before colonial days, San Salvador was at the hub of Indian trade routes that crisscrossed the country. Later, it was a favorite stopping place for caravans of Spanish colonists, carrying gold, silver, quinine, balsam, indigo, and other products to be exported to Spain. The city was given its name by Central America's most famous conquistador, Alvarado. Now some 350,000 people of El Salvador's total population of three million live here.

If you fly into San Salvador, you will drive from Ilopango Airport through the new, tastefully landscaped industrial section. Notice the modern factory buildings in tropical pastels, and the absence of the garish signs that make so many industrial sections of the United States hideous. Going into the city, the highway temporarily becomes the divided and landscaped Avenida Franklin Delano Roosevelt. You are instantly struck by the prosperous, modern look of the city, and by the way its planners have kept beautiful shade trees and stretches of lawns and gardens to relieve the severe urban look. Perhaps one advantage to having the city originally under the control of the Catorce, or fourteen wealthy families, is that they were educated and cultivated and their influence was fortunate in planning San Salvador.

You'll observe that one truth about these "backward" countries is that they often make a clean break from old ways and jump into the most modern of worlds without any in-between stages. This is true of all the new buildings. Here there is little of the gradual march of time that is reflected in the architectural styles in the States, which went from the early salt-boxes to Federal to Victorian gingerbread and only gradually got to the Frank Lloyd Wright.

The residential sections, a series of new developments called *colonias,* have modern, beautifully designed homes; only the indispensable patio with pool and garden has been retained from colonial architecture. When you are sitting in one of these patios, it is hard to believe that you are anywhere near a city. In the late afternoon flocks of parrots fly over, gabbing as they go. *Colonias* for middle-income groups are part of the outspreading city, and there is an increasing incidence of low-cost housing.

A good place from which to get a view of San Salvador is the Hotel Intercontinental, located in an exclusive residential section overlooking the city. A good time of day to do this is when, in pale twilight, the lights first come on in the valley. Much later, as the night goes on, the lights become concentrated in the center of town, like a turned-down lamp. If you drive through the city at night, coming home from a club or the movies, you'll see mariachi groups playing on corners all over town. The mariachis are combos, mostly guitars, cane flutes, and gourds, though sometimes a portable marimba or a trumpet is included.

It is not considered wise to walk around the streets of San Salvador alone at night. (Nor is it in New York, or Washington, or any number of cities in the United States.) The reason is the same all over the world; an intense concentration of people includes the poverty-stricken and the desperate.

Transportation: Buses crisscross the city in every direction. One in particular, Bus 29, takes you on a complete trip around the city for a few centavos. Taxis are reasonable, less than a dollar within the city limits. It is possible to make individual deals with drivers for local sightseeing trips.

WHERE TO STAY, EAT

Hotels

El Salvador Intercontinental: $13 single, $20 double.
San Salvador Gran Hotel: $11 single, $17-$19 double.
Nuevo Mundo: $6-$7 single, $9-$10 double.

Motels

El Patio: $7-$8 single, $10-$11 double.

Pensions

Casa Clark: $6.75 single, $10 double. (See special report, p. 183.)
Parker House: $7 single, $11 double.

Restaurants

Siete Mares: $3-$6; seafood; music Friday nights.
Casuela: $3-$5; Spanish cuisine.
La Fonda: $4-$6; international cuisine.
Chez Balta: $3.50-$5.50; seafood.

WHAT TO DO

Night Clubs

Safari: combo, dancing.
El Salvador Intercontinental: $6-$8; dancing, floor show.

Sports Facilities

There are a number of private clubs for which guest cards are available. The Club Campestre Cuscutlán has a 9-hole golf course; the Corinto on Lake Ilopango has an 18-hole golf course. The Círculo Deportivo Internacional offers swimming, tennis, volleyball.

The Club Hipatico is a riding club; visitors flock there on Sundays to watch the horsemanship for which Central America is famous.

At the National Stadium soccer games are played every Sunday. Built for the Olympic Games, it seats 35,000. There is also an Olympic-sized swimming pool.

El Campo de Marte, on the west side of the city, is an extensive public park with tennis courts, a racetrack with a grandstand, volleyball and basketball courts, soccer and baseball fields. Beautiful setting, with green lawns, giant shade trees. In the early spring the concentration of *matilishuat* trees, with their pink and red clusters of blossoms, makes it a favorite Sunday strolling and trysting place.

WHAT TO SEE IN SAN SALVADOR

Santa Tecla, or Nueva San Salvador. On the road to Santa Tecla, pause to visit La Ceiba Park. Among its beautiful shade trees is an ancient ceiba, long venerated by the Indians.
El Boquerón. A landmark of San Salvador, the view from the volcano's 6333-foot summit is spectacular (see p. 44). Drive through Santa Tecla, inquire for the gravel road to the crater.
Parque Modelo. Within this spacious park is the Jardín Zoológico, or zoo.
Parque Infantil. Charming park for children. Adults have fun riding with them on the park touring train and watching them on merry-go-rounds, driving mechanical toy cars, and flying high

in little planes. There is a large roller-skating rink, a refreshment pavilion. Ventriloquists carry dummies around and play to the crowd for tips.

Balboa National Park. Take the road to Los Planes de Renderos. Beautiful, with lookout points for viewing the city. Take a short walk to Puerta del Diablo (Devil's Door), from where you can see the Pacific Ocean and the coast.

Cuartel de El Zapote. Old fort located on a hill on the south side of the city. While visiting the fort, don't miss the Church of La Candelaria in the El Zapote colony, which has an unusual mark on its outside walls. It shows the crest of the flood of the Acelhuate River that once cut off the entire district from the rest of San Salvador for a week.

Apulo. Resort on Lake Ilopango. Lakeside park, restaurants, bath houses, swimming, boating.

Cathedral. The image of San Salvador del Mundo, patron saint of the capital, is kept in this new, modern cathedral. In early colonial days, sculptor Silvestre García carved the effigy of the saint out of the wood of an orange tree that grew in his yard.

El Rosario. Church next to Archbishop's Palace. Padre Matías Delgado is buried here.

Bell Tower of Nuestra Señora de la Merced. From this tower Padre Matías Delgado called for freedom from Spain in 1811. The church and the adjacent convent were ruined later, but the bell tower remains.

National Museum. Interesting collection of Indian relics.

El Ateneo. Home of the historical and literary society. Lectures of international scholars and scientists are regularly held here.

Public Buildings. The Palacio de Comunicaciones, the National Theatre, the National Palace, the Military School, the Post Office, and University Complex.

THE LEGENDARY CASA CLARK OF SAN SALVADOR

Casa Clark, at 7A Calle Oriente No. 144 in San Salvador, is a favorite pension of those who travel through the isthmus. Guests include Peace Corps representatives, doctors down to study tropical medicine, technicians, salesmen from foreign countries, students, professors, priests, and missionaries. This friendly pension is in the city, close to parks, movies, clubs, and bus stops. Trips or excursions to nearby beaches and resorts are easy. The Casa is managed by American citizens, Mr. and Mrs. B. M. Simpson. U.S. money. The price (see p. 181) includes three hearty meals daily and all the second helpings you wish; your laundry washed and beautifully ironed twice a week and mended, if necessary, by the "mending lady"; the use of a nearby club with excellent tennis and squash courts and an Olympic-size swimming pool. It also includes being mothered, kissed hello and good-by, by Eva Marguerite Simpson, affectionately called "Mommy," or "Sonny."

You enter through a huge worn green wooden door; inside, a wide flight of stairs goes to the pension's reception area, an open tile-floored living room with a sunny green patio beyond. All bedrooms open on to one of the three patios in the sprawling, one-story building. Each room has swinging screen doors, half covered by cretonne panels. There are no locks, only a hook and eye to keep them closed.

A newcomer always receives a briefing from Sonny or Jimmy. He is given a key to the front door and warned not to lose it. ("You can imagine how terrible it would be if some stranger walked in here, since we don't have any locks on the doors.") One's name and room number are printed in chalk on a big blackboard so that the maids will know where to find a guest in the event of a telephone call. Refreshments are available on the "honor system," one is told. Help yourself to cold beer, Coca-Cola, or pop, which are stocked in a large refrigerator near the dining-room, sign an IOU (or *vale*), and drop it into a little box nearby. Bathrooms are shared; there are four on each corridor; freshly painted and clean, each with a shower and hot water. After you use a towel, drop it into a hamper; next time take a clean one from a pile on the shelf. Breakfast is served from seven on. . . .

You wake up at Casa Clark to the sound of canaries trilling, bells ringing at San Francisco, the *iglesia* directly across the street. Step out of your room and onto a patio and you're in the middle of a glorious San Salvador morning. What's radiant outside makes you feel sunny inside. In the joyously golden patios diminutive russet doves peck on the grass, and up above the green of the banana palms the sky is absolutely blue.

Around the patio on the way to the dining-room there are easy chairs, sofas, desks, lamps, tables. Pendant baskets holding trailing plants hang from the edge of the roof, and there are cages full of peeping and trilling canaries; large ceramic pots painted different colors line the open side of the living-room. On the wall under the tiled roof there are photographs and paintings, shelves full of knickknacks and doodads and crossed machetes in tooled leather cases.

The dining-room is open on one side, giving on a large mango tree that has a large frilly lavender orchid blooming on its trunk. There is a plastic cover on each table, and a cluster of catsup and hot-sauce bottles and jam pots in the middle. Except for one place, you may sit anywhere you like. This is at the head of the far table; its chair is a carved Jacobean one with arms, and a permanent "reserved" sign is posted under the plastic cloth. This sacrosanct place belongs to coffee taster Joe Brown, who has lived at the Casa for over thirty-five years.

At the buffet, you help yourself to coffee, cold cereal, juice. Then one of the several maids on duty in the adjacent kitchen asks you whether you would like your eggs *fritos* (fried) or *revueltos* (scrambled). You are also served *jamón* (ham) or *tocino* (bacon) with *pan tostado* (toast).

Vociferous greetings are common at every meal. Old-timers who walk in after a long absence are given a really big hello. Sonny, more frequently hailed as "Mommy," always circulates, with a hug here and a kiss there. "Never can tell what you're going to find around! Oh, *there's* my boy with his feet on the ground!" In her "Mommy" role, Sonny is able to exert a certain amount of affectionate control over her boisterous bachelor guests.

Nicknames have been given the habitués: Uncle Red, the

White Whale, etc. Joshing is the most frequent form of communication. Said an engineer to a priest, just down from his mountain mission, "Father, they tell me it's so dry up there that they use sand for holy water."

Boss of the kitchen is Angelina, who has been the cook since the Casa was founded by Sonny's mother, "Ma" Clark, in 1931. She plans all the meals, which are "American style" with the usual international dishes, such as spaghetti or curry, and local foods (fried *plátanos*, sliced papaya, mango pie).

Every morning, at eight o'clock, Angelina walks to the Central Market, a quarter of a mile away. To have produce transported to the Casa, Angelina hires a "basket lady," who carries up to seventy-five pounds on her head, on a crown of twined rags, or *yacqual* cloths. Angelina pays the basket lady one colon (about forty cents). This is more than they usually receive.

If a guest has a favorite dish that he looks forward to during his stay at Casa Clark, Angelina will gladly put it on the menu. Her assistants in the kitchen are cheerful girls. "They eat what the guests do," Sonny says, "not only tortillas and beans." It is not usual in Central America for the help to be allowed the same food as the employers.

For most guests, breakfast is over by seven-thirty, and the men, in shirt sleeves and carrying dispatch cases, go off to begin their tropical work day at eight.

Then, except for Sonny's heels clacking on the tiles, there is a hush. Her dachshund, Toughie, naps in the sun. Doves, with their paper-sounding wings, fly up to the mango tree. Maids wipe up the tile floors, using large rags tied onto the mop handle and a mixture of water and kerosene. ("No soap or wax has ever touched them," says Sonny.) Canaries' cages are cleaned. Out in the patio, the porter shines dozens of pairs of shoes with painstaking buffing. In an area near the kitchen, women wash guests' clothes, by machine and by hand. The wash is hung up on the roof and taken down in the late afternoon because of the danger of marauding snatchers.

There is an influx shortly after noon, when guests return for a hot lunch and a siesta, and another one before dinner. At the companionable sunset hour guests sit in groups around the patio near the dining-room, their feet often sharing the same hassock, swapping stories.

Casa Clark is part of the modern history of San Salvador; it marks an important moment in the city's growth, its shift from one age to another. The Casa's existence is the result of the coming of international airlines to the airport at Ilopango, and the subsequent influx of foreigners, preponderantly gringos, on errands of commerce or of mercy.

The two most important people to the Casa's beginning, the ones most responsible for its character, its homeyness, actually met in San Francisco, California, a city dear to all Salvadorans. These were Leona Clark, Sonny's mother, and Angelina, who still plans and sees to the preparation of the food.

In San Francisco, Leona and Angelina both worked for the coffee-wealthy Alvarez family of San Salvador. Leona was the nursemaid; Angelina, Leona's assistant. Leona had been married and divorced; had left her children, Sonny and her brother, in Pennsylvania for her mother to raise while she set forth to seek her fortune. Angelina was born in a small pueblo in Honduras and came to the Alvarez family through an aunt who worked as a cook on their coffee *finca*. When the Alvarez family returned to San Salvador from San Francisco, Leona and Angelina traveled with them. It was Leona's first look at Central America. Angelina helped open Leona's eyes to the beauty of the old city, with its then all-cobblestone streets.

Leona intended to return to the States when the Alvarez children had outgrown their need for a nursemaid, but a vice-president of Pan American Airlines, which was soon to fly in and out of San Salvador, was in the city looking for a woman to run a boarding house for Pan Am pilots and mechanics. North American women were then even scarcer than they are now. Morrison met Leona and asked her to manage the Pan Am hostel; the job included packing lunches for the passengers and crew of outgoing flights. Leona said "yes" conditionally; if she could persuade Angelina to assist her. Angelina agreed.

A large house was located near the Ilopango Airport. Pan Am

furnished it, and Leona and Angelina moved in and set to work on June 1, 1931. "Cooking was done on a wood stove," Sonny says. "There was no pasteurized milk or sterilized water."

After serving dinner to Pan Am mechanics and crew, Leona and Angelina would make an assortment of sandwiches and cookies, put up tea, lemonade, and hot consommé in Thermos bottles, for up to twenty-eight passengers on the early flight. "We would go to bed at twelve," Angelina recalls, "and get up at three-thirty to make breakfast."

Then, in December, 1932, Pan Am moved its headquarters to Guatemala City, and Leona decided to open a pension of her own. In time, Leona became "Ma" Clark; she was a pillar of the growing American community. Old-timers say, "Every Christmas, Ma entertained the entire American colony at Casa Clark. There would be two great big tables full of presents, one for the men and one for the women."

Sonny was then happily married to Jimmy Simpson and living in Miami, Florida. Jimmy was an officer in the Police Department and Sonny was a waitress. Their children were grown.

Early in 1956 a wire from a stranger at the Casa Clark telling of her mother's death threw Sonny into a flap. She had inherited a going business; she was saddled with a legal responsibility; and she was not overjoyed. Sonny had a chilly reception at the Casa, a contrast to her own warm welcoming today. The guests and the help all mourned Ma, to whom they were devoted, and they resented Sonny.

"When I took over, all I heard was Ma did this and Ma did that," Sonny says. "I cried for six weeks and I was ready to quit. Then Jimmy wound up his job in Florida and came down. Jimmy told everybody off. He said, 'If there are any god-damned people around this place who don't like Sonny, they can get out, and I'll help them pack their bags.' "

After that, there was an abrupt improvement in attitudes, Sonny says, adding, with a hint of grimness even now, "We toughed it out."

Sonny took Spanish lessons, but the teacher made her feel

"tongue-tied," so she picked up what she calls "kitchen Spanish" by "just talking."

Sonny and Jimmy gradually made improvements in Casa Clark, ran the place in their own style. Under their management, the Casa expanded from seventeen rooms and four baths to forty-four rooms and fifteen baths, including the area around the farthest patio that is known as "Hogan's Alley."

"One night, here came a big wheel from the U.S.," Sonny remembers. "I told him we were filled up. He said, 'I'd rather stay here and be a little bit uncomfortable than go to some damned hotel.' So he slept on the chaise longue here in the patio. Those kinds of things make you feel good."

Jimmy nods. "A lot of these people have big expense accounts, could go anywhere they please, but they prefer to come here and have a big time."

The doves fly up to the mango tree with their paper wings; the palms make their swishing dry percussion; there is the familiar clang of bells from San Francisco; and a canary calls, sounding plaintive as a robin in the rain.

"People keep coming and going and coming and going," Angelina says, with a gleaming, dark-eyed smile, "just like a river."

SIDE TRIPS FROM SAN SALVADOR

Because El Salvador is such a small country and almost any area within its borders can be visited in a day, we have covered most of the possible junkets in the "Driving Through" section. Here are some others.

La Chacra. Large swimming pool fed by Acelhuate River; dressing rooms, restaurants, sports.

Panchimalco. Beyond suburban Los Planes de Renderos, 6 miles south of San Salvador, is an Indian village where natives still speak Nahuatl; tile or thatched roofs, stone-paved streets; one of the very few places where you will find traditional costumes, perpetuated customs. Hand-woven textiles and ceramics can be

bought here. Women wear necklaces of blue and white decorated
with old Spanish coins. Note the church and large *amatle* tree
that shelters meetings and markets.

Ruins of Sihuatán. Take Route 4 north approximately 20 miles
to Aguilares. Turn northeast here and you will find ruins, "the
place of the goddess Cihuacoatl."

La Palma. Take Route 4 north approximately 40 miles. This
resort area in the mountains has a wonderful climate the year
around. Hotel, cabins, a good bet for a weekend.

La Toma. On the outskirts of Quezaltepeque (take either CA-1
or Route 4), 12 miles north of San Salvador. Swimming pools are
fed by streams in a gorgeous setting; dressing rooms.

La Herradura. Located on a calm estuary of the Pacific Ocean,
the Estero de Jaltepeque; along the shores are the docks of
rustic summer cottages (some of which can be rented for an
overnight stop). At the end of the road through Herradura,
there is a town dock. Here you can rent an outboard motorboat
for an all-day fishing junket for twelve dollars a day; less expensive is a boat ride to the wild and lovely beach where breakers
froth on the white sands at the mouth of the estuary. The boats-
man will know where a cottage can be rented, but if you plan
on staying overnight, it would be well to take along sleeping
bags (you will find shelter and a bed for two dollars, or five
colones, a day, but no service) and food, for there is none available after leaving the refreshment vendors at the dock.

One Sunday morning Lex and I made this trip to the Estero
de Jaltepeque. We headed south from San Salvador, turned
toward Panchimalco and Comalapa, cutting across to CA-2. After
passing through Comalapa we took the first road right toward
the Pacific, to La Herradura.

From our log: "The main (and probably only) road through
La Herradura is narrow; lined by outjutting, tumbledown, picturesque thatched huts. Sunday refreshment stands and Sunday
festivity—Sunday always has the quality of a fiesta—are in
progress. We could scarcely make our way through the happy
hodgepodge, all sorts of goods in baskets, hanging from make-
shift canopies, children and dogs and little pigs criss-crossing.

"There is absolutely nobody at the dock except for a girl selling cold drinks and black clams in baskets. Lex tells me that she has a 'typical Salvadoran face.' It is round, amiable, black-eyed, pug-nosed; her body is stocky, inclined to overweight, with a fulsomeness both of stomach and behind. Lex inquires about renting a boat, and a couple of young men turn up like magic; Lex agrees to pay fifteen colones (or about six dollars) an hour for a trip to the beach at the mouth of the estuary. The young men skid a large skiff over the mud of low tide, then shove it through shallow water to a float at the foot of the dock.

"We step into the skiff, which needs baling. It also needs painting and caulking; the wood seems bone-dry and fragile; some of the planks over the deck are loose and broken. But the outboard motor is steady and strong, and we start out on the quiet, glossy estuary, trees crowding both banks; we pass dugout canoes full of produce being paddled toward La Herradura. It is fun riding along with the wind in our faces. Every turn in the estuary reveals another stretch of water-mirrored trees and natives slipping along close to the shores in dugout canoes.

"We stop at one dock to the right to look at cottages that can be rented by tourists for two dollars a night. They are very simple frame buildings, under palm trees, but they are adequate shelter, and it would be fun to stay in this quiet place and see the moon on the water, and wake up here. Close to the dock there is a large pavilion, now in need of sweeping and painting. The boatman tells us that every Holy Week (always as madly festive in the resorts of Central America as it is solemn in the cities) a band plays here for dancing; there are dugout canoe races, and the Queen of the Islands is crowned.

"As we proceed, a blue heron flies across the river. Now we can see the haze over the gentle Pacific water, ahead the shimmering white sand, the slow-motion pulsing of breakers. Our boat put-puts close to the shore; Lex and I jump out of the boat into the shallow water. Bare-footed, we go walking on the lovely, hard-packed sand, and ahead of us in the sky we see a flight of ducks, with their unmistakable long necks and wavering V formation. There is nothing here but miles of lonely beach and the sky and the sound of the water. Miraculously, there's no dearth of wild and lovely places even in crowded-up-to-the-hilt El Salvador."

MARKETS

In diminutive El Salvador, craftsmen of outlying pueblos tend to bring their wares on foot or by bus to central markets that are open daily. Handicrafts gravitate to San Salvador's teeming market near the central plaza: incised gourds and woven belts from Izalco, palm-leaf hats from San Antonio Masahuat, hammocks from Chirilagua, hand-molded ceramic figures from Ilobasco, pottery bowls and pitchers from Quezaltepeque, hand-loomed textiles from Panchimalco, baskets from Santa Catarina Masahuat, huge hampers from Zacatecoluca. San Miguel is in the henequen country, and its market offers a large selection of woven hammocks and saddlebags. Sonsonate is outstanding for fine baskets woven from a vine resembling the morning glory, and for hats, mats, and hampers.

An alternative to shopping in the central markets of the cities is to visit the pueblos where the craftsmen work.

To combine shopping for crafts with sightseeing, here are the most famous products and the villages that produce the best of them.

Ceramics: Ilobasco, Quezaltepeque, Izalco, Panchimalco, San Juan Nonualco.

Hammocks, woven bags: Chalatenango, Suchitoto, Chirilagua.

Palm-leaf hats: Chirilagua, Chilanga, Tenancingo, Olocuilta, Izalco, San Antonio Masahuat, Sensuntepeque.

Baskets, mats: Zacatecoluca, San Pedro Perulapán, Nahuizalco, Chirilagua, Olocuilta, Santa Catarina Masahuat.

Hand-woven fabrics: Izalco, Panchimalco, San Sebastián.

FIESTA CALENDAR

DATE	PLACE	CELEBRATION
Jan.		
1	*Alegría*	La del Niño
5–6	*Jocoaitique*	Los Reyes
6	*Corinto*	Los Reyes
8–18	*Juayúa*	El Señor de Juayúa
11–15	*San Pedro Masahuat*	El Señor de Esquipulas
12–15	*Usulután*	Feria de Jesús
12–21	*Coatepeque*	Concepción
	Cojutepeque	Concepción
13–14	*San Alejo*	El Señor de los Milagros
13–15	*Colón*	El Señor de Esquipulas
15	*Texistepeque*	El Señor de Esquipulas
15– Feb.16	*Guayabal*	Jesús del Rescate
16–18	*San Antonio Abad*	San Antonio Abad
17–20	*Villa Delgado*	San Sebastián
19–20	*Pasaquina*	San Sebastián
20– Feb.2	*Jucuarán*	Candelaria
20– Feb.5	*Sonsonate*	Candelaria
21–22	*Ciudad Barrios*	El Señor de Roma
31– Feb.2	*Yayantique*	Candelaria
31– Feb.4	*Candelaria de la Frontera*	Candelaria
31– Feb.5	*Usulután*	Candelaria
Feb.		
1–2	*Ishuatán*	Candelaria
13–16	*Jocoro*	Santo Niño de Atoche
15–22	*San Miguel*	Carnival de San Miguel
24	*Metapán*	El Señor de Ostúa
March		
1–8	*Sesori*	Corazón de Jesús
15–20	*Berlin*	San José

DATE	PLACE	CELEBRATION
March		
16–20	El Paisnal	San José
17–19	El Tránsito	San José
	Ataco	San José
18–19	Cancasque	San José
	Guatajiagua	San José
	Jocoaitique	San José
	Verapaz	San José
18–20	Guayabal	San José
Holy	Everywhere	Semana Santa
Week	Sonsonate	Jubileo de San Antonio del Monte
April		
22–		
May 3	San Juan Nonualco	Romería de la Cruz
24–26	San Marcos	San Marcos
May		
3	Everywhere	Fiesta de la Cruz
14–15	Ereguayquín	San Benito
22	Apastepeque	Santa Rita
24	Jocoro	María Auxiliadora
June		
7–8	Quelepa	Concepción
15–24	San Juan Nonualco	San Juan Bautista
15–30	Cojutepeque	San Juan
18–24	Izalco	San Juan
22–24	Chinameca	San Juan
22–25	Nahuizalco	San Juan
23	Olocuilta	San Juan
24	Chalatenango	San Juan Bautista
24–25	San Alejo	Candelaria
	Yayantique	San Juan
25–29	San Pedro Masahuat	San Pedro
26–29	San Pedro Nonualco	San Pedro
27–30	Coatepeque	San Pedro
28–29	San Pedro Perulapán	San Pedro
28–30	Nueva Esparta	San Pedro
29	Metapán	San Pedro
	Alegría	San Pedro

DATE	PLACE	CELEBRATION
June		
	Corinto	San Pedro, San Pablo
	Usulután	San Pedro
July		
2–25	Santiago Nonualco	Santiago
16	El Carmen (La Unión)	El Carmen
17–21	Chalchuapa	Santiago
17–26	Santa Ana	Santa Ana, Fiestas Julias
19–22	Chilanga	María Magdalena
19–25	Apastepeque	Santiago
20–25	Santiago de María	Santiago Apóstol
23–24	Jucuarán	Santa Ana
23–25	Guatajiagua	Santiago Apóstol
24–25	Santiago Texacuangos	El Señor Santiago
25	Quelepa	Santiago Apóstol
26	El Carmen (Cuscatlán)	El Carmen
	Villa Delgado	Santiago
Aug.		
Whole month	San Salvador	Fiestas Agostinas
1–8	Chinameca	Fiestas Agostinas
1–15	El Tránsito	El Tránsito
4–6	Pasaquina	El Salvador
6	San Salvador	El Salvador del Mundo
14–16	San Marcos	El Tránsito
15	Ahuachapán	El Tránsito
15–16	Mejicanos	Virgen del Tránsito
15–20	Jiquilisco	El Tránsito
Sept.		
Whole month	Everywhere	Independence
7–8	Jocoaitique	Virgen de la Merced
13–14	Chilanga	María Exaltación
13–15	Nueva Esparta	El Señor de las Misericordias
13–16	Panchimalco	Santa Cruz de Roma
20–21	Santiago Texacuangos	San Mateo
26–29	Villa Delgado	San Miguel Arcángel
27	Comazohua	San Mateo
28–29	Guazapa	San Miguel Arcángel
	Ilobasco	San Miguel

DATE	PLACE	CELEBRATION
Sept.		
29	*Huizúcar*	San Miguel Arcángel
29	*Alegría*	San Miguel
29–30	*Nejapa*	San Jerónimo
Oct.		
2–5	*San Francisco Morazán*	San Francisco de Asís
5–12	*Soyapango*	Virgen del Rosario
13–16	*Anamorós*	Santa Teresa
16–18	*Ataco*	San Lucas
21–		
Nov.5	*Chalatenango*	Feria de los Santos
25–30	*Jucuapa*	San Simón
Nov.		
1–5	*Santiago de María*	San Rafael Arcángel
6–12	*San Martín*	San Martín
10–13	*San Francisco Morazán*	El Rosario
12–16	*Ilopango*	San Cristóbal
14–15	*Candelaria*	Dulce Nombre de María
20–21	*Tejutepeque*	El Tránsito, San Rafael Arcángel
20–25	*Santa Catarina Masahuat*	Santa Catalina
20–30	*Ishuatán*	Santa Isabel
21–25	*Usulután*	Santa Catalina
22–25	*Apopa*	Santa Catalina
25–		
Dec.8	*Sensuntepeque*	Santa Bárbara
27–30	*Anapaca*	San Andrés
Dec.		
1–8	*La Libertad*	Concepción
1–10	*Izalco*	Concepción
1–20	*Izalco*	Virgen de los Remedios
2–7	*Tonacatepeque*	San Nicolás
6–8	*Chilanga*	Concepción
6–13	*Suchitoto*	Concepción, Santa Lucía
7–8	*Jucuapa*	Concepción
	Ilobasco	Concepción
7–9	*Cuscatancingo*	Concepción
8	*Teotepeque*	Concepción
8–13	*Chirilagua*	Virgen de Guadalupe
8–14	*Juayúa, Chinameca*	Santa Lucía

DATE	PLACE	CELEBRATION
Dec.		
8–18	*Ataco*	Concepción
10–28	*Zacatecoluca*	Virgen de Guadalupe
12	*San Salvador*	Santa Lucía
	La Unión	Concepción
15–27	*Quezaltepeque*	General Fair
19–25	*Santa Tecla*	La Pascua de Navidad
19–26	*San Vicente*	San Vicente Abad
20–25	*Tejutla*	Santo Tomás
22–25	*California*	Niño Jesús
24–25	*Everywhere*	Christmas

14 / Honduras

Chameleon Mountains, Progressive People

Honduras is the second largest state in Central America (Nicaragua is first); it is the least populated, has been the least developed, but is now showing more action and promise industrially, culturally, and socially, than most of the other republics. You can feel life bubbling up and over in Tegucigalpa, the capital, and in San Pedro Sula, an extraordinary boom city. As a matter of fact, all of Honduras has an infectiously buoyant atmosphere.

The country is scenically breathtaking; it is the most mountainous of all the republics, and that's like saying that so-and-so is the tallest basketball player, because Honduras has plenty of competition in her sister republics. She is the only country without a single active volcano, although her mountains were once heaving and active and cannot be ruled out as extinct. They are sensationally beautiful and have the quality of reflecting light and color; a rosy sunset will turn them to burning rose. A bright sun will wash out the color and leave them vague and pale and mistily Japanese. Her Caribbean coast probably has the most beautiful beaches of any on the Atlantic Ocean, and her hundreds of beautiful miles are largely undiscovered by hunters, naturalists, archaeologists, and all lovers of wide-open spaces. The strongest present tourist attraction is probably Copán, one of the greatest cities of the Mayan Old Empire. The ninety-four-mile stretch of Inter-American Highway that runs through Honduras to the border of Nicaragua, is beautifully maintained.

Though her highway system was late in developing, Honduras was a pioneer in plane travel; the first passenger and freight flights to hitherto inaccessible parts of the country were initiated in the late 1920s. The nation jumped from the ox-cart to the air age overnight.

Incongruously, the airport at Tegucigalpa has the shortest landing strip of any of the Central American capitals. Located on a short mesa between deep abysses, every inch of the strip is used on take-offs or landings. Taking off, you think you'll never be airborne before you plummet over the edge; landing, you think you'll never come to a stop before the end of the runway.

We recently logged a landing at Toncontín Airport, Tegucigalpa: "Our captain had to get his little jet down between towering mountains on very short notice; to lose speed with the necessary dispatch he brought us in sagging and bumping. The plane reacted like a wasp sprayed with insecticide. A Honduran next to us made a face and held his hands up, pressed together, in the traditional attitude of prayer. The moment the wheels touched, the captain braked. One felt the strain of desperately checked speed; there was a wild shuddering. We all pressed our feet on the floor to help. The jet rolled to a stop just short of the edge of the runway; the captain wheeled it smartly around, and we were down safe among the ancient cathedrals and red-roofed pastel adobes. Getting out, still shaken up, we smelled the sweet wind of an agrarian economy."

SAHSA, the Honduran airline, has an impressive safety record. It and the other Central American airlines, accustomed to dodging mountains and landing on short strips, come into Toncontín regularly. Pan Am and foreign airlines, using larger jets, prefer to land at San Pedro Sula, where there is a large international

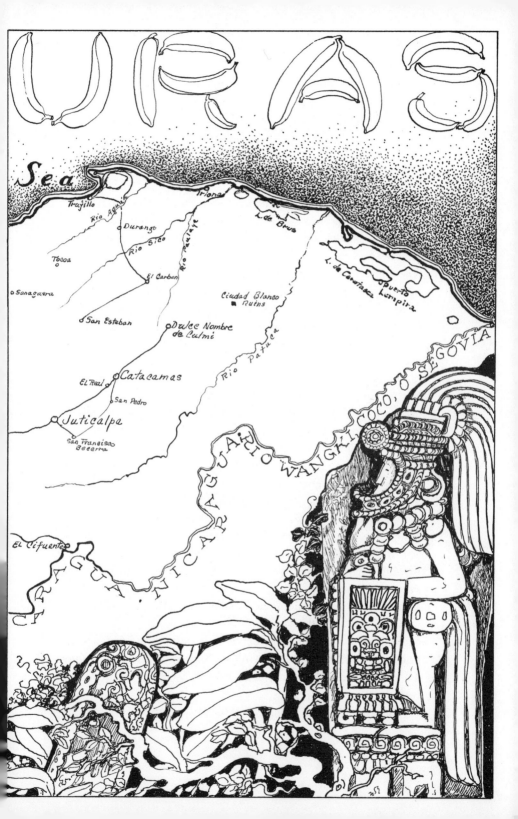

jet airport; passengers for Tegucigalpa are transferred to airborne taxis, manned by pilots whose experience qualifies them for the tricky runway at Toncontín.

DRIVING THROUGH

The Inter-American Highway, CA-1, cuts across the narrowest portion of Honduras between El Salvador and Nicaragua.

Amatillo. Border station. The Honduran *lempira* equals 50 cents American.

Nacaome. First right turn after Amatillo. Gold and silver mines. Manufacturing. Sixteenth-century church. Hotel, restaurant.

Jícaro Galán. At this junction, 25 miles from the border, a scenically spectacular spur of the Inter-American Highway leads (left) to Tegucigalpa (see p. 203). The 63 miles to Tegucigalpa are curvy but the road is excellent and well graded. The vistas are among the most beautiful in Central America. About halfway to the capital you reach an altitude of 5100 feet.

To proceed to Nicaragua by private car or bus after your visit to the capital you must double back to Jícaro Galán junction. It is seventy-one miles from there to the Nicaraguan border. Along this stretch you'll see beehive-like mud ovens in front of the thatched houses along the highway.

San Lorenzo. Right off CA-1, between Jícaro Galán and Choluteca. Old fishing port on an inlet from the Gulf of Fonseca; it is completely undeveloped, sleepy, untidy, full of little black pigs and ragged children. The *Miramar Hotel* juts out on pilings over the inlet, where motor-propelled dugout canoes go put-putting out over the dark green glossy waters in the early morning, and fishing boats chuff off to the Pacific. The Miramar has recently updated accommodations.

Cedeño Beach. Right from CA-1. A 25-mile stretch of relatively undiscovered beach, on the Gulf of Fonseca, close to Choluteca. This is an Eden for those who love to swim in beautiful, protected waters.

Choluteca. 28 miles from Jícaro Galán junction. (If you have forgotten to have your passport visaed for entry into Nicaragua there is a Nicaraguan consulate here.) This is a coffee, cattle, and cotton center, a small, authentic, colonial, unusually lovely, and unspoiled city. There is a brand-new motel with air-conditioning, swimming pool, and good food.

San Marcos de Colón. From Choluteca to San Marcos the high-way climbs to an elevation of 4500 feet. Look to the right; if it's a clear day, you will see the Gulf of Fonseca and volcanoes Consegüina and Conchagua.

Fraternidad. Border station, 7 miles beyond San Marcos. The Nicaraguan border station is El Espino.

Tegucigalpa

Though this is the most picturesque and other-worldly of Central American capitals, there is architectural unity here, even in the bright new housing developments on the outskirts. Much of the city is halfway up Mount Picacho; many of the cobbled streets are as steep as ski jumps; some are actually stairways.

There are many modern, high-rise buildings downtown, but most of the city consists of mellow pastel adobes, a lovely topsy-turvy clutter of intensely rose tile roofs. From Mount Picacho, Tegucigalpa looks like a toy city, an imaginative jumble of bright houses, as if drawn by a cheerful and energetic child.

At 3200 feet above sea level, the climate is delightful; the air is crystal clear. The average temperature is 73 degrees. Even during the rainy season, from May to December, the days are usually sunny; the rains come at night. The rains are welcomed especially here in the dry mountain area. Residents look to May 3, the Day of the Cross, for the first happy downpour.

Tegucigalpa, originally a mining community, was founded on September 29, 1598, when the Spaniards came in, attracted by the silver mines. Actually the capital is a twin city, with a river running through it; three bridges connect Comayagüela and Tegucigalpa. But it doesn't feel a bit different on the other side of the bridge.

Inconsistent with Tegucigalpa's quaintness is an enterprising quality that can quickly be sensed. It's a tomorrow-oriented society. Here it is possible for a family to rise socially, moving from one kind of housing development to another as children become educated and pitch in to contribute to the family income in new kinds of jobs in business and industry. The residents are beginning to have true "upward mobility." Of course, there are still some dreadful slums and poor people whose situation is stubbornly unaffected and who are sometimes too hopeless to seize on an existing opportunity.

But this is one city where you will not see babies and small children spending uncomfortable days in the markets with their mothers. The upper stories of the buildings at the Los Dolores Market in Tegucigalpa and the San Isidro Market in Comayagüela have been turned into cheerful, airy day nurseries for preschool children. Mrs. Maxwell (Margaret) Becker, the wife of an A.I.D. emissary to Honduras, got those day nurseries going as a volunteer. The result is far-reaching. The young are getting the sort of start they've never had, with good food and such innovations as toothbrushes and clean smocks. And the older ones are receiving preschool training. Mrs. Becker has collected a library of over seven hundred children's books. She has enlisted American wives to convert the English captions into Spanish. Mrs. Becker has also instituted a training program for teen-aged girls, who are becoming professionals at child care. After a year of classes and working with the children, they are given certificates. As trained *niñeras* they can command a good salary in the community. (The average *muchacha*, or maid, has no such advantage.) Market mothers, who leave their children in the morning and call for them at night, are bringing new ideas home to their families. Situations like this are behind the strikingly cheerful on-going atmosphere of Tegucigalpa.

And then there is cultural liveliness to an unusual degree. Director of all cultural activities for Honduras is Arturo López

Rodezno, probably Central America's greatest contemporary painter, and one-time Ambassador to Italy. He has offices in the Escuela Nacional de Bellas Artes, where there are presently upward of ninety young artists enrolled. Rodezno told us that the people of Tegucigalpa are appreciative of cultural activities; during a recent exhibit of contemporary Italian art, over thirty-five thousand attended in two weeks.

Community enthusiasm for the arts is reflected in the programs at the elegant National Theater; there is a concert, a play, or a ballet every night. Both the ballet and the National Folklore groups, who specialize in the native "Sique," are composed of dedicated amateurs who rehearse each night after work. Rodezno and his staff arrange for skilled teachers, and the result is professional. Gifted veteran Mercedes Agurcia directs the ballet and theater productions.

The Instituto Hondureño de Cultura Interamericana, a group of Americans and Hondurans provides interesting programs and small halls for lectures, concerts, movies, plays, and art exhibits.

Transportation is cheap and plentiful. There is a steady procession of buses and taxis through all the main streets. Taxis charge thirty centavos per zone, buses ten. Tour vehicles will call for you at your hotel. Rent a car for $7.50 to $10 per day. Small planes can be chartered for three or four persons for special junkets. Inquire at SAHSA office or aero sources.

WHERE TO STAY, EAT

Hotels

Prado: comfortable rooms, midtown, $9-$11.50 single, $15 double; nice dining-room.

Lincoln: same price as above; small rooms; nice roof-top dining-room.

Savoy: $6-$7.50 single, $10-$12 double; apartments available; poor dining-room.

Boston: American plan, $8 single, $12 double; fair rooms, good food.

Motels

Remus: $6 single; outside of town; small clean rooms, no meals.

Pensions

Doña Teresa: Peace Corps stays here; inexpensive; with food.
American Boarding House: with good food.
Casa Pomerania: excellent German food, clean rooms.

Restaurants

Roma: good Italian food, especially pizza.
El Chico Club: $3-$4.50; Spanish food, colonial atmosphere.
La Parrilla: $2.50-$3.50; good steaks.
Barbacoa: steaks; good service, taped music.
Villa Adriana: $2-$4; informal, American food, also typical foods.

WHAT TO DO

Night Clubs

Club de la Llave: orchestra, dancing, $1 drinks.
Petunia: discothèque, dancing.
007: combo, dancing.
Centro Arabia Hondureña: Arab club.
Rilos: drive-in night-club restaurant; 3 guitars, dancing.
La Caverna: no orchestra; artists sometimes perform informally.
La Fontana: dancing, with combo; nice atmosphere.

Sports Facilities

Facilities for golf and tennis through the president of the Country Club of Tegucigalpa. Soccer every Sunday at the National Stadium. Or ask hotel management or tourist bureau about guest privileges. Hunting and fishing safaris can be scheduled through travel bureaus.

Cultural Activities. See pp. 204–205.

WHAT TO SEE IN TEGUCIGALPA

Parque Concordia. A small block-square beautiful walled park. Not another one like it in this world; stone carvings, plants, bridges, temples, arbors, walks, trees, ponds, reproductions of Mayan ruins, statues. If there is a pillar to an arbor, it is carved within an inch of its life, as are legs of benches. If there is a tile floor, each tile is different. Walk through it in the twilight and you'll think you're dreaming.

United Nations Park. On Mount Picacho's summit, lookout stations, with benches and arbored vines overhead, hang 1200 feet above Tegucigalpa. Sensational view. Replica of Mayan temple, formal garden with boxwood hedges, fountains, and roses, playgrounds, walks. Natural rock outcroppings are unusually beautiful. At the top of the road to Picacho, bear right for a drive-in that serves fruit drinks, ice cream, and food. Take a bus or taxi up for $3.

San Miguel Cathedral. The national cathedral of Honduras is on the east side of the Parque Central (main square). Original church on this site was wooden; it burned to the ground December 24, 1742. The priest, Father José Simón de Zelaya, vowed to build the largest and loveliest church in Honduras. Father José worked for nineteen years to raise funds, round up materials and workmen, but died before the edifice was completed. Lime, milk, and eggs (five million yolks, they say) were used to mix the plaster. The church was consecrated at last on September 29, 1782. The bells of San Miguel are said to have been cast in the square—precious gold and silver jewelry of devout Tegucigalpans were put into the melting pot. In 1927 San Miguel was named the national cathedral. There is a hand-worked silver altar and tabernacle. Chapel to the right of the altar is supposed to be lucky for lovers who pray there. Stunning tiled floors.

Los Dolores Church. Dates from 1732. To the right, the chapel of Fatima, imported from Spain, is very beautiful and unusual. Los Dolores Market is close to the church; women crouch on the stones in dark draped clothes, selling huge baskets of lilies, carnations, roses.

Church of the Immaculate Conception of Comayagüela. Original building dates from 1570. Early missionaries taught Indians the New Testament story through pageants, still re-enacted by the parishioners during Semana Santa (Holy Week). On Holy Thursday there is a Silent Procession. Men carry a statue of Jesus and clank a chain as a symbol of captivity. There is no sound but the clanking of the chain and the shuffle of feet. On Good Friday the cross is carried to twelve stations. During Holy Burial, men of the parish, twenty-five at a time, take turns carrying a glass casket weighing over two tons. During the Procession of the Sorrowful Virgin, later, the women of the parish each carry a lighted candle.

The University and its nucleus, La Merced Chapel. In the late 1500s Franciscans built a monastery; La Merced was its chapel. In 1829 President Francisco Morazán, trying to gain control, confiscated the property for the State. In 1845 a group of young students banded into a group that they called "The Society of Learning and Good Taste." In 1847 their academy was granted the status of a university. Today over two thousand students attend classes in the Schools of Medicine, Law, Liberal Arts, Dentistry, and Engineering ($30 per year tuition, $50 for books). Many of the faculty are volunteers. New, exciting modern buildings to house the university are going up on land near the Basilica of the Virgin of Suyapa.

Escuela Nacional de Bellas Artes. Across the bridge in Comayagüela. Open for visitors from 8 A.M. to 11:30 A.M., 2 P.M. to 5 P.M., Monday through Friday. Always an interesting contemporary art exhibit on the main floor; murals by López Rodezno decorate the walls facing center court; ancient Mayan pottery on display. The school is government-sponsored; students pay no fee and receive scholarships for their ability.

Presidential Palace. This Moorish-turreted fantasy was built in

1918, overlooking the Choluteca River and the old Mallol Bridge. There are crystal chandeliers, hand-carved wooden rails and trimmings. It has a patio with flowers and a fountain.

Basilica of the Virgin of Suyapa. Newly built in honor of the miracle-working Virgin of Suyapa, it is situated on a mountain-side on the outskirts of Tegucigalpa; a carved wooden image approximately eight inches high is housed in a silver, gold, and glass case. The old wooden church nearby was much sweeter and more appealing. Each year on February 2 and 3, Indians walk from all sections of Honduras and from other Central American countries to pay her homage.

Santa Lucía. A very quaint and ancient little mining village near Tegucigalpa, it is perched precipitously on a steep slope, with a small church founded early in the sixteenth century. Drive east to the end of Avenida de los Próceres, left across the bridge, and follow the road up through pine forest; at the fork in the road, take the right. Drive for about fifteen minutes. If the church is closed, knock on adjacent doors; somebody will have the key. There is a story about the crucifix over the altar. Some years ago, when the vein of silver ran thin in Santa Lucía, some of the village leaders decided to move the church's most beautiful possessions to a church in Tegucigalpa. When moving men started down the hill carrying the crucifix, it became so heavy that they had to put it down; they could not carry it at all. When they started back toward the church, the crucifix became light as air. And so the crucifix never went to Tegucigalpa but to this day remains in Santa Lucía.

AROUND THE COUNTRY

El Zamorano and Environs

It's a two-hour drive from Tegucigalpa over a curving, rough clay road through mountains reaching an altitude of 5100 feet before descending to the Río Yeguare Valley and El Zamorano at 2400 feet. Yet hundreds of visitors sign the guest book at the

Pan-American Agricultural College there each year. The setting is beautiful, proudly groomed. White plaster buildings with tiled roofs are joined by walks on emerald green lawns, with flowers and trees close to the campus and fields full of prize-winning cattle, horses, sheep, hogs, and poultry in neatly fenced meadows in peripheral acres.

Unique in education anywhere in the world, the school was founded and endowed by the United Fruit Company to train bright boys in agricultural economics. They are trained to run the family *finca* brilliantly or to spearhead agricultural projects for government and private industry.

Since it opened its doors in 1942 with Dr. Wilson Popenoe as its first president, the school has graduated between fifty and sixty young men a year; they have taken the most advanced techniques in agronomy and animal husbandry back to their communities.

There is terrific competition for admittance. Dr. Arthur Mueller, the director, told us that in 1969 only 77 out of 905 candidates were accepted. There is no tuition; the school pays all of a student's expenses including travel, board, room, clothing, even haircuts. The three-year program stresses horticulture the first year, field crops the second (the boys work with over eighteen crops), animal husbandry the third. The motto is "Learning by Doing": the boys get going early each morning. According to Dr. Mueller, "This is the only school in the world at this level that does field work."

The Western Hemisphere's most critical problem, as yet little apprehended, is more food production; as far away as Zamorano seems, its teaching is vital to all the Americas.

It's fun to visit Zamorano. It has a cheerful, constructive environment; one heart-warming touch—on a pedestal on the lawn, frozen for posterity like a pair of baby shoes, is the first farm tractor used by the students.

Zamorano has been such a success that it has served as a model for the Instituto Técnico de Agricultura, an agricultural school near Guatemala City financed by the government. After a modest beginning, the Instituto moved in 1947 to its present spacious site with modern facilities and hundreds of acres, and is now building more dormitories and classrooms to accommodate 500 students instead of the present 125. The director, Guillermo Vadilla, is snowed under by young men seeking to qualify for admittance, and each graduate has his pick of good jobs in agriculture and animal husbandry.

Worth a trip from El Zamorano is San Antonio de Oriente, a picturesque village stepping down the slope of a steep mountain, with a beautiful view. You can ride it in a four-wheel drive vehicle, hike, or ride horses or burros (for two and a half hours) from Zamorano. Take your lunch and a Thermos of water.

Comayagua

From Tegucigalpa north on Route 1 (Carretera del Norte). Prior to 1880, when Tegucigalpa became the permanent seat of government, this was the capital. It has a 300-year-old cathedral with a solid silver tabernacle and candelabra that were gifts of King Philip IV of Spain, a clock from the Alhambra, a painting by Murillo. Worth seeing.

Copán: The Ruins of a Great Mayan Ceremonial Center

Although it is possible to drive to Copán in the dry season (May through November) from Honduras, Guatemala, and El Salvador, the roads are very rough; it is considered best to fly in. SAHSA charges $37 round trip from Tegucigalpa, and we noticed two-day excursions for $45, covering all expenses, posted in the lobby of the Savoy Hotel. There are many such package trips to Copán.

The extensive ruins of this ancient ceremonial center, believed to have been the second largest city of Mayan society, with a population of 50,000, contain archaeological wonders unique among Old Empire constructions. More hieroglyphic inscriptions are found in Copán than in any other Mayan ruins. Astronomy reached its highest development here.

The largest archaeological cross-section in the world is an exposed portion of the Acropolis, 118 feet high, 1000 feet long at the base, which has been excavated by the flowing of the Copán River over centuries. Layers of building going back to the beginning of Mayan culture can be seen clearly. Archaeologists consider that Copán has more outstanding sculpture than any other center of Mayan civilization. Their media was greenish volcanic tuff with flinty deposits. The ruins are situated in a protected valley, now a Honduran National Park. The main structures cover seventy-five acres.

The first whisper of the existence of Copán came from a Spanish colonial foreign-service official, en route from Guatemala to a new post at San Pedro Sula, in 1576. He wrote to King Philip II of Spain: ". . . within the province of Honduras, called Copán, are . . . superb edifices, of such skill and splendor that it appears that they could never have been built by natives of that province."

The first expedition to Copán, in 1834, was headed by an Irishman, John Gallagher (known locally as "Galindo"). He told the world about the exciting archaeological prospects there but did not excavate or renovate.

Fifty years later, Alfred P. Maudslay, an Englishman, brought a well-equipped expedition and began the work of discovery and repair that was carried on by the Peabody Museum of Harvard, and since 1935 by the Carnegie Institute of Washington, D.C.

Copán has been lived in more recently than other Mayan ruins. To this day, candles and *pom* are burned on an altar in the East Court (northeast corner of Mound 16) before a gigantic sculpture of a masklike face. Chorti Indians, descendants of the inhabitants of Copán during the ages of its glory, continue to worship there. While the abandonment of Tikal, Guatemala, remains a mystery, the story of the end of a society in Copán is known. Chorti Indians say that it was a plague that finally emptied the city; all but seven residents died. They moved, but not very far away from the site of death and disease.

The Main Group of courts and temples at Copán is the most important for sightseers. The Acropolis covers approximately twelve acres. The five courts or plazas are connected. The most interesting carved stelae and altars are found in the Great Court, or Amphitheater. Under Stela H, the only metal ever found in an Old Empire city (four gold legs) was unearthed. On Stela 15, dedicated in A.D. 524, can be seen the earliest use of head variant numbers. Stela 12 (east) and Stela 10 (west) are thought to have served a uniquely predictive purpose. If, from the vantage point at Stela 12, the sun set behind Stela 10 on April 12, runners advised farmers that the conditions were right for burning their cornfields the next day.

The carvings of sixteen figures on Altar Q, one of the most important monuments in Copán, apparently represent an early scientific conference. Archaeologists believe that the leaders probably met to decide on the correction needed to bring the Maya year into accurate relation with the solar year. The date reads 6 Ahau 13 Kayab, or about A.D. 776.

The most beautiful structure is considered to be Temple 22, on the north side of the Eastern Court, the finest ever produced by Mayan architects and sculptors. Sculpted in the round on the upper façade is a famous figure known as the "Singing Girl." Like most Copán sculpture, in which individual characteristics are stressed, the girl seems to have been a portrait of a real person. The Eastern Court also has the famous staircase, steeper than New England steps to the attic, flanked by rampant jaguars whose spots were once disks of shining black obsidian.

There is a concentration of hieroglyphic inscriptions in two sites. One, the Hieroglyphic Stairway, completed in the eighth century after two hundred years of work, has sixty-two steps, each thirty feet wide, and their faces are sculptured with over 2500 glyphs, telling a story that no one archaeologist has as yet fully deciphered. The other site is the Temple of Inscriptions, Temple II, whose eight panels contain over 140 glyph blocks, showing a wonderful resourcefulness of design.

The cleared and partially restored acres of Copán represent only a beginning; for miles around there are uncovered sites and mounds to be excavated. Archaeologists feel that they are only on the verge of understanding the Mayan civilization, but the record left by those brilliant Indians in glyphs and sculptures will eventually make a breakthrough possible.

San Pedro Sula

San Pedro is the boom city of Central America. Twenty years ago the population was approximately 20,000; today it is more than 100,000. After a slow colonial beginning, it developed as a banana town in a country with a climate that was more agreeable to bananas than people—hot, humid, and rainy. Yet the boom took place here instead of in the naturally air-conditioned highlands. Of course, it's close to ports, convenient for shipping, and Central Americans very often seem to blossom best when they are bucking the climate.

You fly into La Mesa Airport over miles of intensely green banana trees, with aerial spray played on them for disease control. The airstrips are jet-sized; the old, green, somehow romantic wooden terminal has been replaced by a modern, excitingly designed building. Since San Pedro Sula is a crossroads for air traffic, a lot of hand-shaking goes on at La Mesa. Landing in jets and changing to prop planes for wilderness locations are missionaries, doctors, nurses, Peace Corps and CARE people. San Pedro Sula may be the first stop in Honduras for American tourists traveling to Tegucigalpa or the ruins at Copán; they will change from an international jet to a "local" here.

You don't need to fly into San Pedro Sula. It is possible to drive from Tegucigalpa, Guatemala City, or San Salvador, but it is difficult. These roads will improve in the near future, and their current condition should be checked by the prospective tourist. When we were there, they were rough gravel, full of bumps and chuck-holes and said to ruin a new tire on a truck in a couple of trips. Still, buses and trucks and private cars regularly travel between San Pedro and Tegucigalpa.

Or you can tramp-ship it to Puerto Cortés, La Ceiba, or Tela on a United Fruit or Grace Line ship, and travel by airplane, bus, or railroad to San Pedro Sula.

In 1968 the only thoroughly first-class hotel was the *Bolivar,* with comfortable, tastefully decorated rooms, handsome dining-room, and cocktail area in the swimming-pool patio. If a good dry martini is a measure of sophistication, you will be glad to know that the best dry martinis in Central America are made at the Bolivar. However, there were several other hotels that were reasonably comfortable, including the *San Pedro*. The best motel in the area was the *Vitanza* (single $10, double $15); very pleasant, with a restaurant, a cocktail lounge, a small pool.

A large high-rise hotel was being built overlooking the main plaza. Space gets very tight at the Bolivar; the hotel and motel situation will certainly improve as fast as cement blocks can be laid.

There are some first-class restaurants in the city and on the outskirts, including Vicente's, El Rincón Gaucho, the Country Club, and a couple of new night clubs. More night life in the near future is predictable.

Transportation in and out of the city is excellent. Taxis are plentiful, and you can travel by bus to Puerto Cortés or Lake Yojoa (details on pp. 216–217). You can get a Ferrobus (a one-car diesel that runs on tracks) at the railroad terminal to Tela and the coast; it's an interesting ride through the jungle and the banana and African-palm country.

As you cannot stand in a flower garden without being aware of color, you cannot be in San Pedro Sula without feeling the excitement of the boom. There's new construction going on all over the city; wherever you walk you'll pass wheelbarrows full of wet cement. And on the outskirts are miles of new plants and factory buildings.

Shirts are the best bargain in San Pedro Sula. There are shirt factories in the city—you can stand on the sidewalk and look into the plant and watch the people at work.

In this city you are always running into something that's about to change. A ramshackle old building was headquarters for the Cultural Center, whose Board of Directors are Hondurans and United States citizens. They were cramped for space for their adult-education English classes and cultural activities, which include a record library with a good hi-fi set and a large library of American books. Looking around the main room, I took a quick inventory of the jumble. A movie projector stood on a ping-pong table, aimed at a portable screen that was placed in front of a huge map. Close by was a large portable blackboard, a record player, a Coca-Cola dispenser, a model of a space capsule, a portrait of Benjamin Franklin, the Stars and Stripes and the Honduran flag, folding chairs. The director, Dick Murphy, told us that they expected to move into a new $500,000 building.

In contrast to Tegucigalpa, San Pedro Sula has been culturally backward. A Peace Corps volunteer told us that there *had* been an active chamber music group but that "when the Peace Corps guy who played the French horn went home, it folded." He was amused that "they are teaching a course at the university called 'Cultures of the World,' but there's nothing about Mayan culture."

The Peace Corps in that section is mainly involved in teaching inadequately educated teachers, putting them in touch with modern tools, and in helping bring small farmers into the money economy through cooperatives.

Peace Corps leaders have been watching with interest the progress of workers trained for jobs in the new plants. The turnover is rather rapid in the first year, we were told, running from 60 to 70 per cent, but subsides in the second year to 20 to 30 per cent.

There is nothing much to see in the city except for a large fountain in the main square, which is incredibly full of scrambling turtles, a sort of Exhibit A on the perils of overpopulation.

You can see Mayan ruins at nearby La Travesía, and there are three or four wonderful side trips to be made.

SIDE TRIPS FROM SAN PEDRO SULA

Puerto Cortés. 30 miles north on excellent paved road. Take a bus, rent a car, or fly. Beautiful beaches. The historic Castillo de San Fernando, built at Omoa in 1775 as a defense against pirates, can be visited. The *Ronassari Motel* offers fine accommodations; its La Cabaña Restaurant specializes in seafood.

Lake Yojoa. 50 miles south on paved highway, Route 1. Famous for bass fishing; hunting for jaguar, puma, and tapir in surrounding mountains. Inquire at hotel or tourist bureau in San Pedro Sula for hunting and fishing safari schedules.

Islas de la Bahía. Fly from La Mesa Airport in San Pedro Sula or from La Ceiba on scheduled flights. *Lundy's Boat Motel,* on Guanaja, has good accommodations; from $8 single. American investors are building new tourist accommodations. Crystal-clear waters, an undiscovered Caribbean heaven.

La Ceiba. Fly from La Mesa Airport in prop plane. Wide, clean beaches, pleasant surf; picturesque river inlets good for fishing, boating. *Hotel Paris,* from $8.

Tela — Lancetillo Station. Fly from San Pedro Sula or take the Ferrobus.

From our log: "Flew to coastal Tela in a prop plane. Came down over miles of bananas, went to a tiny wooden hangar to look for a taxi. A beat-up little taxi turned up and brought us to the United Fruit dock, where a car would take us out to the experimental station at Lancetillo. The taxi took off right through fields and around houses. The "banana division" residences were neat wooden dormitory-like buildings up on stilts. There's a lot of flooding here at times. Of course it is dead sea-level and it rains and rains.

"The long United Fruit Company warehouse is green and beside it is a track leading out to a long dock where a banana boat is being loaded. The dock is beautifully situated, in a palm-tree-circled harbor with clear turquoise water and a great quietness about it despite the banana loading. Alongside the dock, the usual enterprising vendors had set up hot charcoal tables with lunch dishes for the dock workers.

"The 'car' that called for us was actually on tracks; it was like a streetcar, used for ferrying workers out to the growing areas. Canvas flaps were rolled up at the sides to be lowered in case of a storm. We went crisscrossing the back shambly streets of Tela and ducked into the jungle. The jungle reached out close to both sides of the car, all ropy vines, big sprouting bamboo trees, just a big snaggle of growing things, so dense that the shadows were black and no sun got through.

"The experimental station, in a jungle clearing, includes acres of rare trees, clipped lawn, a large wooden, screened administration building. I noticed a dead hummingbird with its beak wedged in the screen.

"At the moment a group of foreign students was studying tropical trees; the administrator had tables full of oblong cross-sections of important ones. There were teak, balsa, mahogany, rosewood, ebony, well over five hundred kinds of trees. The living Arboretum Collection, the trees themselves, were growing up in the groves—litchi nut, gardenia, etc. The station also had special collections of varieties of avocado, bamboo, citrus, cacao, coffee, grass, heliconia, mango, palm, and sugar cane.

"I was beguiled by a decorating idea on the porch of the administration building, which some clever gardener had thought up. Bamboo poles were ranged in columns between the tile floor and the roof on the porch. In pockets cut in the bamboo poles, tropical plants were growing.

"The driver of the 'car' that took us back stopped in a criss-crossing jumble of tracks near Tela, jumped out, and went to find us a taxi. The taxi set off over sandy roads through what seemed relatively untraveled wheeltracks, marshes, and grass to the Paradise Hotel, where we would have lunch and dinner and spend the night.

"Paradise Hotel was beautifully situated, right on the Caribbean, with breakers pulsing slowly up on a white clean beach, and palm trees bending this way and that as if bowing to a partner. The reception building was a large open shell, where there were tables for dining. The bedrooms were all in cottages, some of which were palm-thatched. Plumbing was modern, beds were comfortable, food was delicious. We learned that one can play golf at the American Club in Tela.

"We went out on the beach and played catch with a coconut shell. Gray pelicans were flying. Some fishermen were catching some small pink fish; a very old man was pushing a small dugout canoe up the beach toward San Juan, a fishermen's village on the beach near the hotel.

"We went to see San Juan; the homes, palm thatched, high on stilts, under the palm trees and close to the breakers, made us think of the South Sea Islands. One beautiful woman, sitting on the ladder to her house on stilts, was wearing a purple cotton dress, open at the throat and to her breast, and a red cotton turban on her head. She was something to remember.

"That night there was a thunderstorm with teeming rain; next damp morning when shining puddles were in the roads, we returned to San Pedro Sula on the Ferrobus, a car of the Ferrocarril Nacional de Honduras. It was a two-hour ride on a swaying trolley through banana plantations and jungles. It was great fun. Houses all along the way faced the tracks and were close to them. We passed many small schoolhouses and could see the children sitting there, stopping their work to watch the train. Once, at an intersection of tracks, we passed an old-fashioned choo-choo train pulling freight. I had forgotten how that labored chuffing sounds, how it shakes the air when it goes by, and how plaintive is the sound of an engine hooting. We passed the Ulúa River, the quiet winding river that gives its name to the valley of the bananalands.

"We debarked at San Pedro Sula in the pouring rain and stood on the platform waiting for the deluge to let up. It was fun to watch a family of children with their chickens next to us. The roosters and the hens were waiting patiently on the platform; the children were dragging one another about by the heels for fun."

MARKET DAYS

Tegucigalpa	Daily
San Pedro Sula	Daily
Choluteca	Daily

The crafts of Honduras are brought by bus to city markets, which is the best place to shop for them.

FIESTAS

One patron saint, the Virgin of Suyapa, serves for all Honduras. The country honors her with local fiestas in all cities and pueblos for two weeks beginning February 2. The celebration is particularly interesting in Tegucigalpa, where the saint's effigy is kept in her basilica on the outskirts of the city.

15 / Nicaragua

Land of Fresh-Water Sharks and Fresh-Water Pirates

> *Rica vergel es mi suelo*
> *y copio en dulces halagos,*
> *en el azul de mis lagos*
> *el esplendor de mi cielo.*
> —Rubén Darío

> A happy garden is my earth
> and full of sweet delights.
> In the blue of my lakes
> Is the radiance of the sky.

The largest of Central American nations, Nicaragua has hundreds and hundreds of unpopulated miles. And yet she has the greatest number of small, interesting, historical cities, intact in their colonial architecture and atmosphere. Absolutely unique to Nicaragua are the horse-drawn black *coches* with red wheels, which still, at ten córdobas an hour, serve as taxis on the streets of Granada, Masaya, and Chinandega.

There is an excellent highway system, offering more alternate routes than anywhere else in Central America. The scenery on all sides is magnificent. Flying into Managua can be an unforgettable experience. Lex wrote about one trip: "Beautiful, with the mountains shooting up above the scattered clouds. You could see the volcanic range from Momotombo on Lake Managua down to Consegüina on its Gulf of Fonseca peninsula. The inlets of the Gulf of Fonseca reach inland like fingers. Consegüina is quite a sight; it occupies all of the peninsula but has very little peak due to the big blow-off. We came in over the *isletas* in Lake Nicaragua . . . so green and beautiful."

Part of the beauty from the air is the checkerboard of fields, all shades of green and yellow and off-white and buff. The money crops are cotton, coffee, rice, beans, corn, and sugar. Cattle-raising is of increasing importance; Brahma cattle thrive in the climate. At every fair you'll see gentle, humped Brahma bulls with names like Cacique (chief) or Muy-Muy (very-very).

There's less Indian influence in contemporary life in Nicaragua than in any of the other republics except Costa Rica. Rarely, except during folk dances at fiestas, do you see old-time Indian costumes. But there is a "native" dress for women—an embroidered, sleeveless blouse, a draped skirt, Grecian in its fall, and sandals. Hair is worn in a single braid, falling over one shoulder to the breast.

Nicaraguans are cheerful, sometimes contagiously merry. They can make a fast trip from a somber, brooding expression to a dazzling grin. This may be partly due to their standard of living: Nicaragua is second only to Costa Rica in its level of income and literacy.

They are a sociable people; even the poorest families make a fiesta of an evening. It is customary to carry rocking chairs to the sidewalk, watch the goings-on and chat with passers-by, while the stars come out and the moon rises and a fresh breeze springs up.

Driving at night through Nicaragua, one comes upon wonderfully sociable scenes. In Rivas, we passed a number of lit-up barbershops in the early darkness. There were mirrors, old-fashioned sumptuous chairs, mahogany bureaus, and men with bibs on, leaning back; on the doorstep the youths were gathered. It wasn't merely a shave; it was somehow a party. And there too, in a birthday-cake, columned, and sculptured bandstand in the central square, we saw the children of the area convivially gathered around a community television set.

Even animals feel a cozy relatedness to human life. Once, in Diriamba, on the poorer outskirts of town, we stopped to talk to a woman known as "Doña Milla" (short for Camilla), who was a knowledgeable member of the community. Her daughters were cleaning house at the time. A large black sow wandered in and out and nobody thought anything of it. Doña Milla invited us both to a party sometime. We would come and there would be a party—no other reason.

Nicaraguans are given to reciting poetry; no wonder this was the birthplace of the world-famous Rubén Darío. We once heard an American boy at the American school in Managua recite Darío in Spanish with such a sense of the beauty of the phrases, with such passion, that we could feel the Nicaraguan influence.

DRIVING THROUGH

It is 238 miles through Nicaragua from the border of Honduras to the border of Costa Rica on CA-1 (Inter-American Highway), which ends in Managua, and then on CA-2.

El Espino. Border station. The exchange is 7 córdobas to the dollar.

If you are carrying firearms, you must show a permit, available in advance of the trip from the Ministerio de Defensa, Managua.

Somoto. Altitude increases from here to Estelí.

Estelí. Las Pintades ruins lie west of the city; carved stone figures of pre-Columbian origin. Good motel, restaurant.

San Isidro. From here you can go straight on CA-1 to Managua, or take the fork that goes southwestward to Telica, where you pick up Route 12 east to Managua, via León.

From San Isidro to Managua via León

Telica. See its active volcano.
León. Take Route 12 east from Telica. León is the second oldest city in Nicaragua.(For details, see p. 234.) Twelve miles southwest on Route 14 is Poneloya, a favorite beach.
Chinandega. Continue westward on Route 12 from Telica. Look for the San Cristóbal volcano on your right along the way. Nearby are the port and beaches of Corinto.(See p. 236.)

From San Isidro to Managua on CA-1

Sébaco. From here, if you want to make a side trip into the mountains, take Route 3 to Matagalpa (17 miles), Santa María Ostuma, and Jinotega. (For details, see p. 241.)
Ciudad Darío. Birthplace of the poet Rubén Darío. From here on, watch for views of Lake Managua to the right; ahead at night, the lights of Managua can be seen 40 miles away. Restaurant, hotel.
San Benito (230 feet). This is the turn-off for getting to Bluefields (see p. 242) on the Caribbean coast.
Tipitapa (164 feet). See p. 233.
Managua. See p. 225.

Managua to the border of Costa Rica

It is 92 miles to the border. The first stretch can be made either on Route 2 or 4. Route 4, the more scenic and interesting, meets Route 2 at Nandaime. From Nandaime, continue on Route 2 to the border.
Route 2: San Marcos, Diriamba, Jinotepe. The beaches of Casares and La Boquita are 20 miles from Diriamba (see p. 234).
Route 4: Masaya, Granada. The ancient and destructive volcano Santiago is on Masaya's lagoon. On the way to Nandaime from Granada, look left for the formidable volcano Mombacho. (See p. 48.)
Nandaime. From here to the Costa Rican border, Route 2 is close to the shores of Lake Nicaragua, 100 miles long, 45 miles wide.

Light and water can be very dramatic here. You can see volcanoes Madera and Concepción on the island of Ometepe. Once, close to the lake, we tried to capture the way it looked. From our log: "It is just after sunset. The clouds are pearly, tinged with pink, the water is steel gray with whitecaps, the sky placid by contrast, a very pale blue. The big volcanoes are sooty shadows."

Rivas (197 feet). Scene of the historic battle in which William Walker and his mercenaries fought Costa Rican troops.

San Juan del Sur. Turn south on Route 16 to this Pacific seaport and nearby beaches. This road was once a section of the famous Vanderbilt Road that conveyed Forty-Niners over the isthmian short cut that preceded the Panama Canal. Good hotel, meals (see p. 234).

Peñas Blancas. Border station.

Managua

Our favorite view of Managua is at kilometer 10 on the Carretera Sur (Route 2), driving north from Diriamba. It is high and windy there, with leaves sparkling like water in the sun and wind. Far ahead and below, beside the blue pewter Lake Managua, is the capital city, its tall new buildings rising in a shimmering heat haze, as if they were behind a gauze curtain. It is reminiscent of Mediterranean or Adriatic seaports, of Piraeus, Casa Blanca, Tel Aviv. And putting its long, shapely foot out into the lake beyond the city is the peninsula that is the base of tall, conical volcano Momotombo and, at a respectful distance, its small echoing shadow, Momotombito. This backdrop of peninsula and volcanoes across the lake gives the city its absolutely unforgettable and unique look.

At kilometer 12, there is a distracting sight—the most madly beautiful hedge of bougainvillaea. It blooms in a quartet of colors, apricot, American Beauty red, pink, purple; though the colors sing together loudly, they combine without discord.

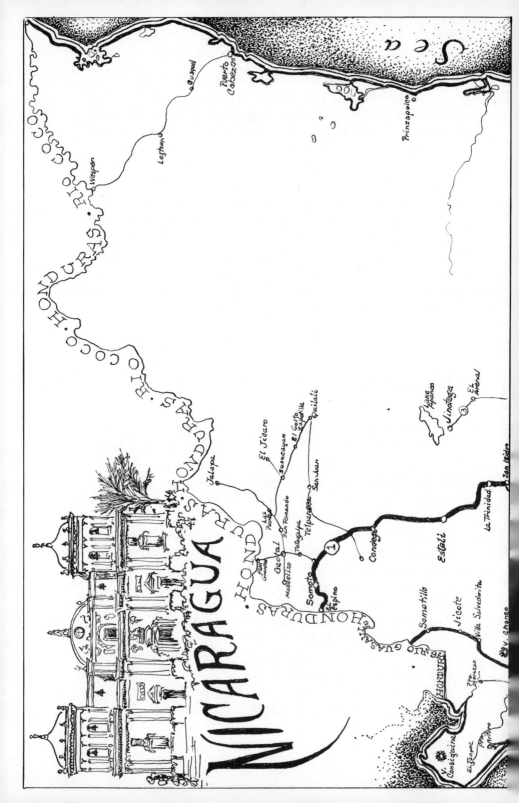

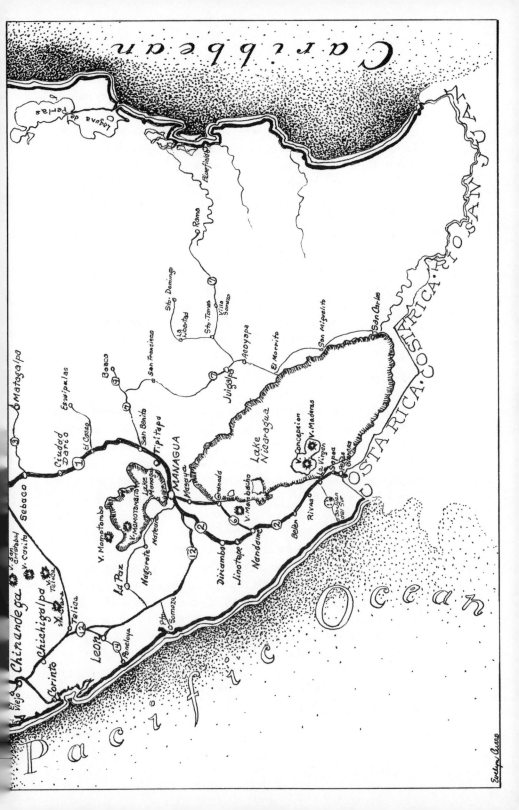

Managua has more crater lakes in and around it than any other Central American city; all shades of blue crystal are Tiscapa, Asososca, Nejapa, Apoyeque, Acahualinca, and Jiloá.

Downtown, old government buildings are stately, palatial. Then there are high-rise office buildings and hotels that incorporate in their stunning designs the latest architectural ideas.

The city sprawls into attractive residential sections known as *colonias*. An idiosyncrasy of charming Managua is that few of the houses have numbers. Addresses are invariably given as if you were about to hunt for pirate treasure: nine paces to the right, three to the left, etc. Usually the directions specify how far you go *abajo* (down) or *arriba* (up), or *al lago* (toward the lake) or *a la montaña* (toward the mountain).

Landmarks that are used by direction-givers can be quite amusing. A familiar orientation is "the house with the eagle on it," and once Lex was told how to find his way to a home by locating a wrecked red car in front of it. The wrecked car was apparently expected to remain where it had come to grief, indefinitely.

A friend sent me a note, inviting me to visit him, and he enclosed just such an address, using the *"arbolito"* as a landmark. Lex, who drove me to the house, glanced at the address as my friend had written it and went zipping purposefully down streets and around corners without any hesitation. When he fetched up at the house, miles from any of the places we usually went, I marveled.

"I know *arbolito* means 'little tree,'" I said, "but since Managua is burgeoning with trees, how did you know which one?"

"Everyone knows the *arbolito*," Lex replied offhandedly. "Of course it's gotten a lot bigger since we called it 'a little tree.'"

Lex's own address is rather unusual, come to think of it. "Take dirt road opposite kilometer post 14 on Carretera Sur. Proceed to white house with blue trim on left, opposite large tree with a white horse tied underneath it."

You can't feel lonesome in Managua. The people are friendly and gregarious; even if you don't know any of them you somehow are part of the scene. And of course you never pass a stranger without saying *"Buenos días."* In Managua it's enough to say *"Buenos."*

Perhaps the easy sociability begins with family togetherness, for the family, and not the community with its institutions, is still the important unit in Central America. On a Saturday night you may see a young man whizzing by on a small motorcycle with a child on the handlebars. Behind him perches his wife, sitting sidesaddle and holding an infant. Central American children seldom cry or appear to be fidgety, and we have often discussed this. There is no reason that we can see why they should not yell and whine even louder than gringo kids, because gringo kids have everything while those black-eyed youngsters patiently endure everything. Perhaps they are always so close to their mothers that they never feel neglected; or their placidity may be due to malnutrition and consequently lack of spunk. Shall we have a swifter degree of progress but little peace when and if the children open up? Teen-agers are never in evidence as a dominant sector of society in Central America. It would be easy to believe that there are no teen-agers, except that they can be seen in the daytime, crisscrossing plazas in various school uniforms.

There is the most dramatic change of climate in Managua from one mile to another. It can be steaming and soggy *al centro* (downtown), and a few miles south, up the mountain toward Diriamba, cool, windy, and sparkling.

On the outskirts of this city, I learned to appreciate tropical foliage. Around Lex's house there was a mob of plants, not only the tall and profuse stands of red and pink and white poinsettias, but all shapes and colors of leaves; many were multicolored, fun to use in flower arrangements because of their shape and texture. There was so much tossing green, making swishing movements and shadows, that there was an aqueous effect at times I felt as if I must be underwater, like a goldfish.

There is something else that's very special about Managua. It has the Gran Hotel, and there is no hotel in Central America to match it. A polestar for all newcomers to Managua, it is downtown, around the corner from the main square. It is a pale-green

stucco building with a small semicircular porte-cochère supported by white columns. Near the entrance crouch men from
Masaya, selling hammocks, or women from the mountains and
the jungles, selling kinkajous, baby wildcats, or young parrots.
At night, vendors are on hand near the Gran with charcoal-
heated stands, selling the typically Nicaraguan *carne asada* (beef
barbecued on an *asador,* or stick), and *gallo pinto* (red beans).

The lobby, a huge dim room with very high ceilings and
tiled floors and ceiling fans like oversize propellers, immediately
looks like the crossroads that it is. Except for the wood-paneled
reception desk and cashier's cage to the left of the entrance, and
the counters of Sophie's gift shop beyond, the lobby is filled with
tables and chairs, a welcome oasis for all downtown Managua.
Men are constantly walking in and out, wearing the typically
Managuan uniform—neat, dark slacks, short-sleeved white shirts,
and perhaps a necktie. You very rarely see a jacket—or a man
without a briefcase.

To the right of the lobby is a bar, known as the "Rumor
Room," and straight ahead as you enter, beyond the bandstand
with its piano for the cocktail hour, is a stand of tall tropical
plants, and beyond that the brightness of a large open patio with
a swimming pool in it. The dining-room, which serves American-
style meals, is on the other side of the pool.

It is infinitely entertaining to sit in this lobby because the
people who come in and out are seldom in Managua for merely
routine errands and you can feel the excitement. There are a
lot of big deals pending, much writing on napkins with ballpoint
pens. There is usually a group of insecticide pilots with their
girl friends. They are practically unmistakable, as Lex has
pointed out, with their jaunty "live dangerously but live it up"
air.

Sophie, perky, small, with crisp gray hair, watches the panorama from the lobby counter of her gift shop. She sells travelers
alligator purses and watches, embroidered blouses, ceramics, local
handicrafts, and pre-Columbian pottery. She was born and
brought up in Nicaragua; the daughter of a British diplomat,

she is married to an American and is one of the moving spirits of the lively American Society.

Traditional are the Saturday and Sunday afternoon *tertulias,* or gatherings, and anybody is welcome as long as he can find a place to sit down. There is free entertainment, generally consisting of a band and a personality-plus woman singer with long hair and a tight dress cut low in front. She jazzes around the dance floor, singing into a portable microphone, sometimes to a particular man at a table. Meanwhile the musicians shake maracas and hit metallic resonators that go *clank,* while they play loudly enunciated Latin rhythms. You have to shout at your friends, but it's like a party, and the only ones that aren't enjoying themselves are a few poor souls who, up in their rooms, are trying to take a siesta.

New hotels and motels will soon be open for business, but the Gran Hotel will remain dear to all visitors to Managua.

Transportation is cheap and plentiful. You can go anywhere by taxi in downtown Managua for one córdoba (less than 15 cents). Buses will ride you indefinitely for one córdoba. You can hire an English-speaking driver who will double as guide and will carry up to four people for $10 an hour.

The train station is near the Lido Palace Hotel; tracks skirt the lake; terminal is across the tracks and near the shore. You can travel very cheaply by rail to Granada, Masaya, León, Chinandega, and Corinto. Managua to Corinto, "Pullman" (first-class), is 10 córdobas, or about $1.40.

WHERE TO STAY, EAT

In this humid climate all hotels are air-conditioned.

Hotels

Balmoral: single $11-$14, double $16-$20.
Gran: single $11-$13, double $16-$20.
Lido Palace: single $11, double $16.

Managua Intercontinental: single $12-$14, double $16-$20; in-spired by Mayan temples.
Roma: single $8-$10, double $13-$16; comfortable surroundings.

Pensions

Tala Inn: $8; air-conditioned.
Pensión Romero: $4.50-$6 per person.
Casa Vargas: $7 per person.
La Residencia: $4-$6.

Restaurants

Los Ranchos: $3.50-$5; steaks; open air.
Gambrinus: $2.50-$6; beer and hearty food.
Mandarin: $3-$4.50; Chinese cuisine.
Coliseo: $2-$4; Italian, baked clams a specialty.

WHAT TO DO

Night Clubs

Tortuga Morada: discothèque; $1 drinks.
Club 113: orchestra, dancing, stage show; $6 per person.
Versailles: dancing in open-air overlooking Lake Managua; $5 per person.
Adalon: orchestra and dancing; $5.50 per person.

Sports Facilities

Your hotel manager or tour director will arrange for a guest card to the Nejapa Country Club, which offers golf, swimming, bowling—dining and dancing too.

Baseball, the favorite sport of Nicaragua, is played at the National Stadium (capacity for 40,000).

For deep-sea fishing, contact Alfred Bequillard, phone 4522. For hunting safaris, inquire at Junta Nacional de Turismo de Nicaragua.

WHAT TO SEE IN MANAGUA

National Palace. Opposite the Central Plaza; houses government offices. Public is welcome.

El Paseo de Tiscapa. Promenade around Lake Tiscapa and Presidential Palace. Beautiful view of three lakes and volcano Momotombo.

Footprints of Acahualinca. This National Park on the western outskirts of the city contains a building sheltering a section of lava containing petrified human and animal footprints, thought to be two thousand years old; a record of ancients who fled from a fierce volcanic eruption and left the story of their desperate haste in the lava.

National Museum. A representative and instructive collection of pre-Columbian artifacts. Some natural history exhibits.

Rubén Darío Arts Center. Inaugurated in December 1969, this is one of the most modern of such centers in the world.

Las Piedrecitas Park. On shores of Lake Asososca. On the faces of the cliffs overlooking the lake are pre-Columbian paintings. Section for entertaining children has playground equipment. Restaurant.

Jiloá Lagoon. A peaceful, happy Sunday place just outside Managua on the lake. There is a terrace with tables, a band under a shell, and a long look at blue water and dark blue to green encircling heights. A monster called the "Apoyeque," which has golden scales and enormous ears, is said to inhabit this lagoon and to surface at the full moon. The waters of Jiloá are salty, they say, because an Indian maiden lost her lover and cried and cried.

Tipitapa. From Managua, it is just 14 miles north on CA-1; it is on the Tipitapa River, which connects Lake Managua with Lake Nicaragua, and is known for its hot mineral springs and for *guapotes,* fried fresh-water fish.

AROUND THE COUNTRY

Pacific Coast Beaches

Within eighty miles of Managua (south and west) there are wide, clean beaches with restaurants and hotels at hand. They are fun to visit for a day or longer. Bus from Managua or drive your own car. (See also Poneloya, Corinto, p. 236.)

San Juan del Sur. From Managua, south on Route 2; beyond Rivas, turn right on Route 16. There is a daily morning bus from Managua. The beach is in a picturesque crescent harbor ringed by mountains. Wonderful fishing. *Barlovento Hotel* has first-class accommodations, food. The hotel will arrange for boat rentals, fishing trips.

Masachapa. From Managua, south on Route 2, right on Route 8. Smooth sands, gentle surf, beaches fading into infinity to left and right. Pleasant old hotel, the *Terraza.*

Pochomil. South on Route 2 to Route 8, right on Route 8. Thatched refreshment huts are under the trees that stand back from the bare, beautiful shores. You can buy clothes, turtle eggs, *conchas negras* (black clams). Once we left Pochomil late in the afternoon; the tide was just going out, the sand was wet and mirrored the gentle blue sky; black seabirds planed over the beach, and the wind had a light touch. Unforgettable.

Casares and La Boquita. South on Route 2; inquire in Diriamba for road to Casares and La Boquita. Traditionally visited by the wealthier "society" families. These beaches are reminiscent of some in California, with jutting piles of rocks over which crabs scramble at low tide. At Casares, there's an old hotel with an open pavilion on the beach where people drink Flor de Caña, a Nicaraguan rum, on Sunday afternoons. Nearby Diriamba, up from sea level at a cooler, crisper altitude, has a very comfortable hotel, the *Majestic.*

León and Environs

Old León. From Managua, take Route 12 toward León, turn right at the La Paz Centro sign, and continue on the road to a small village with shabby adobe houses and narrow streets. This is La Paz Centro: inquire there for the way to León Viejo (Old León). You can be sure that you are headed in the right direction when you cross the railroad tracks. Make a right turn and pass the ancient railroad terminal. Old León is the next village, on the shore of Lake Managua. Park your car and walk to the beach. Across a small inlet the volcano Momotombo, the most beautiful one in Central America, rises from the opposite shore. You can see it smoking. The recently excavated ruins of León Viejo, one of the earliest colonial towns in Central America, are on the outskirts of the present village, to the left as you drive away from the lake. Signs approaching the ruins read, "Nicaraguans, here is your history." There is a thriving restaurant for visitors, run by a family in a roof-covered pavilion next to their home. Cold drinks are served as well as sandwiches and hot food.

As you drive or walk, you will notice that the streets are composed of gray volcanic ash from Momotombo's eruptions. Dug out from under centuries of volcanic ash, the walls, stone floors, and steps of the church, the governor's palace, and other of the original buildings can be seen. Excavations are continuing as a project of the Nicaraguan Government, and in time all the foundations of the original León Viejo will be uncovered. Exquisite little wildflowers blossom in the grasses around the excavations.

The skeletons of several of the early colonial residents can be seen under glass. They did not perish as a result of disaster but were buried near the church when the town was an important colonial outpost in the sixteenth century. It is said that the residents suddenly abandoned León Viejo for the present city of León because of a scandal involving the murder of a priest. The colonists feared that reprisals from the Almighty through eruptions of Momotombo might come, and so they fled.

León. To reach this mellow and charming colonial city 60 miles from Managua, drive or take a bus over Route 12 toward Chinandega and the Honduras border.

Bell towers rise left and right of the main section. We heard them ring and were surprised. They should have been lugubrious, sonorous, and important, but the clangs were light as little clock chimes, almost merry.

From our log: "Lions everywhere in León; there is no end to couchant lions. A statue of Jérez in the middle of the main square is guarded by four stone lions. There were lions on either side of the dusty mosaic steps leading to the cathedral door."

Inside the cathedral we saw the famous topaz shrine, sent to the new world by Philip II of Spain. We gazed at the bronze Christ of Esquipulas, at the marble Altar of Sacrifices with its golden ornaments, once profaned by a private. He is said to have struck at the clutter of golden arms and legs and hands with his pistol to make sure that they were really undentable gold.

We don't know what he did after he found out; history often leaves one wondering. We imagine that he promptly copped them and that they have since been replaced with other golden arms, hands, legs, and feet donated by parishioners in gratitude for miraculously cured parts of their bodies.

Poneloya. From Managua on Route 12 to León, then west on Route 14. This golden and azure beach is one of the loveliest in Central America. The surf is gentle. Resort hotels serve delicious seafood.

Corinto. From Managua on Route 12 down through León and then on toward Chinandega. On the outskirts of the city, turn sharp left for the highway to Corinto. One of the world's most modern ports, Corinto has nearby beaches, harbor, and inlets that are gorgeous, backed up by tropical plants and trees. There is a softness and a subtlety to the views. There are good seafood restaurants, partly due to the active shrimp fleet. Boats may be rented; the fishing is good. There is also a yacht club. Nearby islands have crystal-clear waters, are fun for excursions. El Cardón Island is a favorite for skin diving.

On the Way to Lake Nicaragua

Masaya. South from Managua on Route 2, it is noted for crafts of all kinds, particularly for its hammocks, hats, purses, and rugs. There are a few shops, but you are welcome in the homes where the crafts are produced by individual families. Hire a horse-drawn *coche* for a sightseeing tour of the picturesque little city. The driver will take you to a small park with a balcony looking out over the lagoon with the volcano Santiago rising from the opposite shore. For overnight there is the *Motel Texas,* which is fairly nearby.

Granada. South from Managua on Route 4, on the north shore of Lake Nicaragua, this historical colonial port has an unusually picturesque central park surrounded by buildings that are Moorish in character. *Coches* serve as taxis and are fun for sightseeing tours of the city and the waterfront. For overnight, the *Hotel Alhambra* is old-fashioned but reasonably comfortable. Visit the venerable Church of San Francisco with the emblem of its founder, Fernández de Córdoba, carved on the façade.

Lake Nicaragua's Isletas

These can be toured inexpensively in large launches that serve the islands. The excursion is great fun. Each island is small; the volcanic rock is covered with tropical greenery. Many have been bought by wealthy Nicaraguans who have built imaginative summer homes on them. So far there are no hotel accommodations but the tourist bureau is working on the idea.

To reach the embarkation point for the isletas, turn right on the shore at Granada. You will find a little harbor on an inlet from the lake; as well as launch service, there are small boats to rent. Refreshments are served at tables under giant shade trees by a family who live in a rambling house on the shore.

Early one Sunday afternoon we waited near the embarkation point for a launch to come in so that we could visit friends of Lex's on one of the isletas. We sat under the trees and watched naked little boys paddle small dugout canoes in the dark-green satin lagoon; we saw a monkey snoozing on the railing of the shabby, rambling house.

From our log: "This is a very Nicaraguan place, casual, friendly, cheerful. It is located on a miniature peninsula that juts into the lagoon, with towering trees whose branches reach out over the water. It accommodates the family's house and a terrace with tables for visitors. This is where we are sitting and watching the family.

"Behind the house, on bare earth between the house and the water, the woman who runs this refreshment stand [she was our waitress, then went back to being housewife] is cooking on a charcoal stove made out of an up-ended industrial metal container. Around her there are turkeys, chickens, children, and a fawn with a red collar. The fawn is tiptoeing around on fairy hoofs as if afraid of waking children. She eagerly nibbles up tortillas that the woman gives her. One very small little naked boy comes up to his mother, and she reaches out like a magician and holds out a clean pair of shorts for him to step into. His name is José. We know that because his mother keeps saying 'José, José.' José is very busy. No sooner has he stepped into clean shorts than he gets hold of a large rag, squats near the lagoon so that he can saturate it, comes up with it dripping wet, and slaps it happily against the stove. A teen-aged boy passes us; he has his dinner on a plate, and Lex identifies what he is eating: cornbread, white cheese, yucca, chopped, cooked cabbage, and *chicharrones* (pork cracklings). Typical, Lex says."

When the launch came in and it was time for us to get aboard, we left this cozy and peaceful spot rather reluctantly.

The isleta on which we spent the afternoon was small, rocky, tropical in its shade trees, cool, beautiful. Toucans and other exotic birds fly from island to island.

From our log: "There's a crowd of people, some lying in hammocks, some sitting in chairs, some breast deep in the swimming pool. The house itself is a joy, made of wood that looks like our redwood, open to the winds, with an unwalled sweep-through living area in the middle, full of tables and chairs, a well-equipped kitchen in an adjacent cubicle, lawns and terraces close to the water.

"Took a ride in a motor launch with other guests. It was a good-sized boat and so it was possible to appreciate the belly-whopper roughness of Lake Nicaragua. We came hammering down on the turbulent waters. Got soaked from the spray that flew in over the bow.

"At the end of the day, our hostess assembled her household for the return to Managua after the weekend. We piled into launches and headed for the shore over the rocking water."

Steamship Trip on Lake Nicaragua. The *Somoza* and *Jenotepe* (principally cargo ships of approximately 5000 tons) leave the port of Granada on Mondays and Wednesdays for a four-day circuit of islands and lake ports, such as San Carlos, San Jorge. Accommodations are poor on board, but views and quaint ports are worth the discomfort. At every stop vendors come aboard with foods, but you might prefer to take a stock of your own, plus a large Thermos of drinking water. At San Carlos you can board a smaller boat to Castillo Viejo, a historic Spanish fort near the mouth of the San Juan River.

Diriamba

This unique and lovely city in the coffee-growing highlands is south of Managua on Route 2. Diriamba has a champagne climate; cool and dry and sunny, absolutely effervescent. The buildings are of traditional colonial architecture; they seem to have been bleached by the sun, so that they are the color of sand. The city is not only beach-colored but beach-clean. There is not a garish commercial sign or modern display window to break the spell of antiquity; Diriamba seems to have become a national monument before its time.

Unlike most of Nicaragua, the residents do not gregariously crowd the streets; there are no noisy motorcycles or honking taxis. Men on well-mannered, beautiful horses ride into Diriamba, and horse-drawn water carts ply the streets. The windows fronting the sidewalks are shuttered, the handsome doors closed.

Yet, despite Diriamba's nothing-ever-happens-here appearance, it has the most exciting folk-dance group in Central America. The Diriamba Dancers perform just once a year, on January 19, during the festival of San Sebastián, the city's patron saint.

The annual performances began almost four hundred years ago. At that time a Spaniard archbishop, Manuel de Santa Cruz, visited Diriamba during the fiesta of San Sebastián. The colonists wished to demonstrate to their distinguished visitor the methods they had used to convert the neighboring Indians to Christianity, how they had encouraged them to "act out" Bible stories in song and dance.

Prior to the Archbishop's visit, they recruited the best dancers from the Indian community on the outskirts of the city. The magic number of those rounded up was seventeen. Fancy costumes for the dancers were fabricated from the goods at hand; it was like rummaging through an attic and coming up with a shoe buckle here, a sequin there. The result of this improvisation was necessarily different—nothing like it had been seen before. The crowns of the dancers' hats spurted ostrich feathers; they wore white shirts with long billowing sleeves, velvet knickers and felt boots, covered with sequins, bright bits of mirrors, and all sorts of ribbons and bangles.

On the day of the feast, the proudly attired Indians turned up with their accompanist, a man who played two instruments simultaneously; he blew a reed pipe and beat a drum. As they danced for the Archbishop the Indians sang out a Biblical story. Their language was a mixture of Nahuatl and Azteca. The Archbishop was charmed and impressed; it was such beautiful dancing and expressed a total involvement with the Bible. He was particularly delighted by the dancers' interpretation of the story of David and Goliath (El Gigante). All of Diriamba was moved by the unusual performance. The Indians themselves were aware of how much they had stirred Diriamba, how unexpectedly they had converted the colonists. And so they and their descendants haven't stopped dancing since. Not one dance, not one phrase of story-telling, has changed for almost four centuries.

The costumes, the masks, the music, and the dialogue have been handed down, generation to generation. Until recently, none of the performers knew how to read, and so everything always had to be learned all over again through memorization.

There are still exactly seventeen Diriamba dancers. When one dancer gets too old for the vigorous steps, his place is taken by a carefully selected youth. When a new dancer joins the group he makes a vow to perform only for the glory of God. Diriamba dancers will not accept any payment for their efforts. They rehearse the year around, on the third Sunday of each month, with a brief recess between Ash Wednesday and Easter, when a halt is called out of piety.

Each January 19 they dance joyously and generously on request; they dance in front of the church, in front of houses, in parks; they dance all over the town. And it's as wonderful an experience to be there in Diriamba as it was for the Archbishop all those centuries ago.

The Mountains

Matagalpa. Resort renowned for beautiful flowers. Fine hotel. Closest to the eastern wilderness, this is a take-off place for hunting safaris. Jaguar, ocelot, puma, and other game are found in this area.

Santa María Ostuma. There is not a more charming hotel in Central America than the *Santa María Ostuma* in the Sierra Madre mountains. From Managua, take Route 1 north to Sébaco, then head for Matagalpa on Route 3. Santa María Ostuma is approximately 5 miles north of Matagalpa en route to Jinotega. Sign on left reads "Santa María Ostuma"; there is a short steep driveway to the hotel.

Suggesting an alpine chalet, the garden-surrounded building was once the private home of the hospitable Salazars, who are the hosts. They speak English, which is a help if the traveler knows little or no Spanish. Originally their business was raising coffee, and Santa María Ostuma is still an active *finca*.

The atmosphere is cheerful and homelike. An upper-porch sitting-room, with windows that pivot to let in the delicious mountain breezes, runs the full length of the main building and overlooks the immediate gardens and distant giants of mountains beyond the valley below. The view is gorgeous and spell-binding.

The dining-room is below the viewing porch; it occupies the

entire first floor. Wooden beams are decorated with evergreen boughs, and there are pitchers of pink-veined Easter lilies on the tables.

A bell is rung to announce meals. The day we were there for lunch, there was steak in roulades, served with a tasty gravy that had vegetables cut in slivers swimming in it, tossed salad, fried *plátanos*, mashed potatoes, *frijoles* with sour cream, rice, local white cheese. We discovered that the food was as good as it looked. You could have as many helpings as you liked. After the meal, waitresses came around with fresh pineapple pie and filled our demitasses with a brew of home-grown coffee.

The rates for overnight guests are reasonable—$10, meals included. We, who were only there for lunch, paid about $3.50 apiece.

Jinotega. North of Matagalpa on Route 3, this picturesque town, colonial in character, is surrounded by mountains and has a cool climate.

The Caribbean Coast

Bluefields. This is to be developed into a major Caribbean port in the near future. At present, it is picturesque, lovely, natural. Fishing is excellent, and side trips by launch to such little communities as Pearl Lagoon are fun.

You can fly to Bluefields, or reach it via an interesting and scenic combination of highway and river boat. From Managua, north on Route 1 toward San Benito; turn right on Route 7, known as the "Rama Road" because land's end is the important port of Rama, on the Río Escondido. The Rama Road is now being improved; it is perfectly negotiable but unpaved and rough at present. From Rama, you transfer to a river boat for Bluefields. Recently an excursion, called "Bluefields Express," was operating out of Managua. You leave by bus from the Gran Hotel at 7 A.M., arrive at Rama at 12:30 P.M., transfer to river boat and reach Bluefields at 6 P.M.

Bluefields has fair hotel accommodations and marvelous seafood.

Corn Island. The Isletas del Maíz (Great Corn Island and Little Corn Island) are 40 miles offshore of Bluefields. The largest island, on which the *Playacoco Hotel* is situated, is the one usually referred to as Corn Island. It is an idyllic spot, with crystal-clear, calm Caribbean waters, white sandy beaches, and palm trees. Reefs are ideal for skin-diving, and the water is calm enough for water-skiing. Sailing and boating are excellent. Fishing is great; you can catch groupers, yellow tails, red snappers. (Bring your own tackle.) It is a shell hunters' dream come true. The hotel is owned and managed by an American couple, Mr. and Mrs. John Cussen (AP 2787, Managua, Nicaragua). Mr. Cussen is co-owner of the 113 Club in Managua.

A couple of years ago, on a plane trip, Mr. Cussen's plane landed on Corn Island for repairs. He walked around to kill time, was struck by the beauty of the island, saw a large summer home for sale, and immediately "went in with a bid." Renovated, the Playacoco has ten bedrooms, seven with private baths; American-style food is served, with an emphasis on seafood (broiled lobster, shrimp, sea turtle soup, red snapper). Mrs. Cussen, who "does the kitchen end," has tropical fruits and fresh vegetables flown to the island from Costa Rica. For entertainment, Playacoco offers a native band that improvises gaily on such instruments as a washboard. It costs about $20 a day for two with meals.

The natives on the island are descendants of the six or seven British families that moved there from Bluefields and intermarried, and of later Jamaican immigrants. They are lobster and shrimp fishermen. Some work for the Producto Del Mar shrimp plant, some for the lobster plant operated by Booth Fisheries. Their hand-woven lobster pots are unique, light as a feather.

You can fly direct to Corn Island from Miami ($175 round trip) via Lanica. From Managua, Lanica flies to Corn Island three times a week. The 2900-foot landing strip is located just behind the Playacoco Hotel.

Getting to Corn Island by road and boat is more of an adventure: five hours by car or bus to Rama (Route 1, Route 7 from San Benito); then by river boat to Bluefields, where you get the boat for Corn Island (leaves Bluefields at 5 P.M., arrives at 3 A.M.). It can get rough between Nicaraguan and island shores, so anyone taking the boat trip should be a good sailor, or be well equipped with motion-sickness pills. You land at the Municipal Wharf on the island, now being rebuilt. However you come in, Playacoco will meet you and bring you to the hotel.

There are several small pensions that are less expensive than the Playacoco, but they serve *típico* food only—that is, rice, beans, and *plátano*.

Game-Fishing Safari

Tarpon Camp is the comfortable rustic base for Alfred Bequillard's fishing safaris on the San Juan River. You fly from Managua to San Carlos, on the southeast shore of Lake Nicaragua (about 65 minutes), change to a large dugout canoe propelled by a 20-horsepower outboard motor, and travel for two hours toward the Caribbean on the river, which is close to the Costa Rican border, to the landing at Tarpon Camp.

Fishermen are guaranteed to hook a tarpon. Tarpons average forty to fifty pounds, though up to ninety-pounders are not uncommon. Golden dolphin and swordfish are often caught. Light tackle enthusiasts love to battle the native *guapote, guabina, roncador, gaspar, mojabra, chulin,* and *machaca.*

The camp building is entirely screened. The drinking water is purified. Food is good, somewhat adventurous. Sometimes the cook serves chicken from the tree (iguana), sea turtle, or armadillo—and always beans and rice. Meals are buffet style; breakfast between 6:30 and 8, lunch at 1:30, dinner at 7:30.

The following arrangements can be made, leaving from Managua and returning from San Carlos:

Four-day tours: leave Fridays at 10:30 A.M., return Mondays at 2 P.M.; $420.

Six-day tours: leave Fridays at 10:30 A.M., return Wednesdays; $480.

Eight-day tours: leave Fridays at 10:30 A.M., return the following Friday at 11:30 A.M.; $540.

The fee is all-inclusive; covers round trip, bedroom, meals, boats, and guides. For reservations, write: Safaris Company, Ltd., Managua, Nicaragua.

Bring your own fishing tackle, or buy or rent it in Managua. Terminal tackle and lures can be purchased at the camp, but prices run approximately 30 per cent more than in the United States.

Mr. Bequillard, who speaks English with the smallest trace of an accent, is very good about briefing his guests. Mimeographed sheets sent well in advance tell what to wear, what safety measures should be observed, and, more for fun than out of necessity, how to speak Camp Tarpon Spanish.

Many fishermen—even more frequently, fishermen's wives—double as bird-watchers during visits to Camp Tarpon, for a wonderful variety of birds can be seen on the water, on the edge of the jungle. It *is* real jungle territory; howler monkeys can be heard spookily in the night, going *hoo, hoo, hoo.*

We asked Mr. Bequillard how fishermen while away the evenings at the quiet camp. Generally they sit around with drinks, talk fishing, tell jokes, and inspect their gear, he told us. Before nine o'clock everybody is yawning, and anyone shooting the breeze after that would be advised to whisper.

"Have you heard any good jokes about fishing?" we asked him.

He said no, he'd never heard any on that subject. Evidently fishermen do not see themselves as funny.

MARKET DAYS

Daily throughout the country. Crafts from each area gravitate to the central markets of the cities.

The nation's craft center is Masaya (see p. 112); a colorful variety of goods is on sale daily in individual homes fronting the streets.

FIESTA CALENDAR

DATE	PLACE	CELEBRATION
Jan.		
15	*Tipitapa*	Esquipulas
19	*Diriamba*	Jesús de Rescate
Sixth Friday in Lent	*Rivas, Popoyuapa*	Feast of San Sebastián
April		
25	*San Marcos*	Feast of San Marcos
May		
3	*La Boquita*	Feast of Santa Cruz
July		
25	*Jinotepe*	Santiago
26	*Chinandega, Nandaime*	Santa Ana
Aug.		
1–10	*Managua*	Santo Domingo
15	*Granada*	Virgen de Asunción
Sept.		
30	*Masaya*	San Gerónimo
Dec.		
7	*León*	Virgen de Concepción
8	*El Viejo*	Virgen de Concepción
	Everywhere	Purísima

16 / Costa Rica

The Tico Charm

People from the United States transplant easily to Costa Rica. A greater number of Americans live there than in any other country south of the border. There is an all-American Quaker colony of almost a hundred persons at Monteverde; in all, there are about 20,000 residents from the States, or one American to every seventy-five Costa Ricans. Many Americans have moved to Costa Rica because of the government's attractive Retirement Plan (see p. 286).

It is interesting that in Costa Rica, on the southern extreme of the Central American complex of nations, 95 per cent of the people are of Caucasian stock and tend to be blond and blue-eyed, while in Guatemala, on the northern end, close to 90 per cent of the people are of pure Indian stock, direct descendants of the Mayas and Aztecs. The Indians in the southern part of the isthmus simply withdrew to the wilderness and declined to fight with the colonists or to mix with them in any way. The hard-working settlers of Costa Rica, unlike those elsewhere, were more self-contained and had less missionary zeal. Also, where elsewhere the Spanish overlords brought pomp and cere-mony to their cities, Costa Rica was too far away from the important center, first Antigua, then Guatemala City, to be swayed by European tradition and formalism. Costa Rica developed autonomously with fewer outside influences than any Central American country.

This beautiful little country (288 miles long, never wider than 175 miles) is unique in immediately recognizable ways. Once you cross the border, the homes are predominantly of wood rather than adobe, and they suggest Swiss chalets, with detailed overhang, balconies with wood-worked railings, reminiscent of gingerbread carving, and beautiful paneling. Then there is a noticeably greater variety of cultivated flowers in front yards and gardens; elsewhere the honors may be left to poinsettias and bougainvillaea. Especially in the dry season, you are aware of the abiding brilliance of the green. It stays green in Costa Rica between November and May, whereas in other countries the slopes and valleys grow brown and dusty.

You see more shoes (sign of middle-class prosperity) and eyeglasses (Costa Ricans are educated and like to read). As one friend said, "Even on country roads, you'll see them going home in ox-carts, reading their paper."

There is an ambiance about Costa Rica that causes visitors to choose the word "happy" to describe it. When we first drove across the border into Costa Rica, Lex said, "The people are so friendly here, so gentle and so happy with what they have, that you couldn't be rude about anything."

Ingredients of this lightness of heart include the climate. Except in a few tropical areas, the climate of the major cities is rightfully described as "eternal spring"; the average temperature is about 70 degrees.

You don't see extremes of wealth and poverty as you do elsewhere in Central America. The poorest homes in Costa Rica have a sort of hope and pride about them. There is one type, a sort of synthesis of all the homes of its poor families, that has insinuated itself into my memory. It is small, wooden, steep-roofed, with a balcony. It is not painted but weather-beaten silver. On the railings of the front porch and against the front wall of the house, flanking either side of the door, are plants;

those on the wall hang in brightly painted, tastefully arranged tin cans. Children sit on the steps or play in the yard. There are a couple of brightly feathered roosters and scampering little black pigs.

Costa Rica is at present the only country in the world without an army. Its budget is concentrated instead on education, and there is a higher rate of literacy than in any other Central American country. Its police are notoriously gentle; the only weapon they carry is a whistle. Once Lex pointed out a little group in the middle of the road; we bypassed it, looking back. Several smiling men in uniform were surrounding a male citizen and clapping him on the shoulder. "See them babying that guy?" Lex said. "He's drunk."

Sixty per cent of the population of Costa Rica is under fifteen. If youth is a buoyant time of life, and if this particular youth, being educated and growing up in an atmosphere where the class structure is not restrictive, can afford to dream, to work toward accomplishments, then the high incidence of youth must add to the nation's lightheartedness.

"Tico" is the nickname for the Costa Rican national; he is neither ostentatiously patriotic nor self-consciously gay, but reserved and gentle in his joys. In fact, instead of being bombastic and know-it-all, he has a way of speaking in diminutives. It is part of his manner, his attitude, reflected in his speech, as when a friend, explaining the geography of his country, said, "We are just a little bridge." Where most Spanish-speaking peoples might add *tito* for the diminutive, as in *momentito* (one little minute), Costa Ricans will say *momentico*. Thus they are Ticos.

Even the siesta in Costa Rica is different. Here a whole community knocks off from eleven to one, or from half-past eleven to half-past one; elsewhere the siesta is from twelve to two. Men's sun hats are also different, usually of fabric, with brims turned down, and smaller.

The Ticos' capital, San José, is, as you will see, quite different from any other. Lights blaze far past the onset of darkness, which elsewhere signals the closing of shutters, the blacking out of shops, and deserted streets.

Costa Rica is the only country in Central America where you can drive all the way to the craters of active volcanoes (Irazú and Poás) on smoothly paved roads.

Botanists have a literal field day in the mountain meadows, volcanoes, lush valleys, rain forests, jungle areas, and seashores. Since altitudes vary from mile to mile, there are infinite varieties of plant life, from giant "elephant ears" to exquisite alpine plants. Many of the blossoming trees and shrubs are unknown on the North American continent. And ornithologists report 728 kinds of birds in this little nation. (The United States has about 800.)

Hunting safaris are booming in the wilderness provinces of Guanacaste, Alajuela, and Heredia. The quarry ranges from pumas and jaguars to game birds; white-tailed deer, wild boar, armadillo, tapir, and alligator are plentiful. Safaris cost between $40 and $50 per day; you travel in a four-wheel-drive vehicle with a guide; meals are cooked over a campfire.

Fishing safaris are on the increase; rivers and ocean water off both coasts yield game fish, from 14-pound fresh-water *guapote* (trout) to salt-water swordfish and tarpon.

DRIVING THROUGH

It is 292 miles from Managua to San José (Route 2 to the border, then Route 1). Although the two-lane highway is in poor condition, now being improved, count on a full day for the trip, because of the curving mountain roads from Esparta to the capital. Not hair-raising, but not for the straight-away drag race either.

Peñas Blancas. Border stations. A visitor may not bring in a pet without a permit. Dogs are prohibited from entering the country by car.

One *colón* is approximately equal to 15 cents; figure 7 colones to the dollar.

Liberia. From our log: "Now in the dry season, we are passing miles and miles of tall trees with yellow blossoms; groves of these are lit up in the sun for miles."

Look for the *Bramadero,* an excellent restaurant and satisfactory motel on the highway. This is an enjoyable luncheon
stop with a plain but pleasant porch dining-room.

Liberia is a good jumping-off place for flora-and-fauna-sighting
or for a fishing trip to lakes Arenal and Cote, and it is within
easy driving distance of fabulous Pacific beaches with calm seas
and beautiful vistas, such as Playa El Coco (see p. 260) and
Playa de Tamarindo. These are in a state of pristine beauty but
no doubt will eventually be developed.

Las Cañas. Lowest elevation of the journey (315 feet). Iguanas
jump in the Cañas River and swim vertically, propelling themselves by their tails, like sea horses.

Puntarenas. Right on Route 17 from the Inter-American Highway. San José's favorite resort is on a long, narrow peninsula
with the ocean on one side and an inlet-river on the other, providing a shelter for shrimp boats and pleasure craft. There is a
beautiful beach, shaped like a new moon; back from the sunny
sands there are groves of palm trees to shade the sunburn-prone.
A long drive and promenade follow the beach, close to the
breakers, and along this stretch there are fine hotels, motels,
restaurants, and *refresco* pavilions.

Motel Tioga is particularly comfortable and attractively furnished; it has a dining-room four flights up, overlooking the bay,
and you can see the mountains rising from the farthest shore.

At the Santa Rita Yacht Club and the Pacific Marina, it is
possible to rent boats for fishing and for trips to offshore islands.

Puntarenas is a swinging place during the "season" (February
and March), and it always picks up on weekends. (See p. 260
for details.)

Esparta. From 751 feet you climb approximately 73 miles to the
capital at 3870 feet. It is a beautiful trip with vistas of giant
green mountains. There are fields of tasseled sugar cane from
which light seems to emanate. Sometimes a field worker, walking along the road, will peel sugar cane with a machete and
slake his thirst with its juice. We sucked a fibrous section of
cane once; the juice was not cloyingly sweet; it was rather like
fruit juice. Glossy coffee trees, with fragrant azalea-like blos-

soms or cranberry-red berries, thrive in the cool mountains. The land is very green and bright; in certain lights it almost glitters. Now and then, in a village, there are glimpses of human beauty. I noted in our log: "A group of girls on a corner, all laughing, under a pink parasol. Lex says, 'They don't have those serious Indian faces.'"

Sarchi. Craftsmen are building ox-carts for coffee in open sheds on the road. The wheels are made from sixteen wedges of seasoned alligator wood, fitted to make resonant "music" as the wheels turn. A workman says that a cart must be capable of carrying a 3000-pound load without changing "the song of the axle."

Grecia. If you want to take the time, you can stop and visit a modern sugar mill, watch the cane as it is pressed into juice, the juice reduced by cooking in big moving vats to brown rock candy, and the rock candy piled in a storehouse in an incredibly high candy mountain. A sugar-mill manager, showing us a towering candy mountain, told us that for some reason the rats did not touch it. It was literally "too much for them." Just looking at it killed their appetite, and they had to leave before they had a dizzy spell.

From our log: "The mountains are very high, but there are so many, all rising up together, that they look like a London audience standing for 'God Save the Queen.'

"In the car ahead of us is a green parrot perched near the back window, riding along as companionably as a dog. As the afternoon shadows lengthen, it is a beautiful time to be in the mountains. They are deep green in the shadows, jasmine yellow where the golden light glows. The clouds that were high and billowing earlier have turned into wisps of scarves below the peaks—the mountains are getting chilly and it seems that they need something around their necks when the sun is setting. Near San José the little houses along the road are charming. Their gardens blaze with color. Nobody plants flowers in rows— that's for vegetables or Marines."

Alajuela. Here's where you find a trailer park, if that's what you're looking for. Start watching as you approach. We can report on one, the Yeluka Trailer Park, which is run as a sideline and eventual retirement project by a Swiss dentist, Dr. Kurt Sluter. (A fine place to have a toothache, if you must.) You can park for $1.50 a night or rent a three-bedroom cottage with a kitchen for $6 to $8, depending on the season (dry or rainy). The camp has a restaurant-recreation room (European-style food) and a swimming hole in the river. There were signs heralding other trailer camps, but we did not look into them. (For other details, see p. 259.)

San José

San José is the most cosmopolitan of Central American cities. There are more first-rate hotels and pensions to choose from than elsewhere on the isthmus, and there are fine international restaurants. There are art galleries, record shops, book stores, and a baker's dozen of good movie theaters. If you have been away from a real city for a long time, the first night in San José is a dazzling experience.

Though much about San José is as it would be in a North American city, including the electric current, San José has a special beauty and individuality. There are the fruit carts on every corner, each one an artistic display of produce. There are many parks with fountains and shade trees and flowers, and in the Parque Central the traditional Spanish *retreta*, which has virtually been abandoned elsewhere, is still observed. After Sunday Mass and during the evenings, young men walk clockwise around the park, young women counter-clockwise, looking one another over. It's more romantic when a band is playing.

The shopping center is great fun, and there are actually women's dress shops with smart ready-to-wear apparel. You do not generally see women's dress shops in Central America. Women customarily buy "yard goods," show a picture to a seamstress, and say, "Make me that." You become more clothes-conscious in San José, partly because the year-around cool

climate makes you think more of putting clothes on than of taking them off. And then, whereas in many of Central America's tropical communities men customarily go about in shirt sleeves, this is a jacket-and-tie city, and you would feel conspicuous in any smart restaurant dressed too casually.

Transportation: Buses crisscross the city at twenty centimos, or about three cents, a ride. For longer journeys or *viajes*, check the schedules at Coca-Cola Station, the bus terminal.

Taxis will take you anywhere within the city limits for three colones, approximately forty-five cents. They charge approximately $1.30 an hour for more extensive sightseeing. Three or four passengers can share the cost.

Taxi hops by plane cost very little. We suggest checking LACSA (the national airline) for schedules to resorts.

WHERE TO STAY, EAT

Hotels

Pays Bas: $10 single, $20 double.
Gran Hotel Costa Rica: $10 single, $20 double.
Europa: $10 single, $20 double.
Royal Dutch: $10 single, $20 double.

Motels

Motor Crystal: $9-$11 single, $15-$16 double; swimming pool.
Motor Bemo: $7-$9 single, $14-$15 double.
Holland House: $7 single, $12 double.

Pensions

(All charge single rate per person, whether double room is taken or not. Food is included.)
Costa Rica Inn: $3.50
Villa Verde: $3.50
Otoya: $2.

Restaurants

Swiss Chalet: $3-$6; fondue a specialty.
El Chicote: $1.50-$3; American style.
La Bastille: $3-$6; steaks.
Vesuvio: $3-$6; Italian and Hungarian dishes.

WHAT TO DO

Night Clubs

(No cover charge. Count on $1 drinks.)
Zorba's: discothèque; interesting lighting effects.
La Orquídea: strip show, combo.
Y Pub: beer, records.
Balmoral Bar: orchestra, dancing, floor show.
La Tranquera: orchestra, dancing.

Sports Facilities

Obtain a tourist card from the Tennis Club of San José or Country Club of suburban Escazú. Both places serve meals and have swimming pools.

The favorite sport of Costa Rica is soccer, or "futbol," played in stadiums and fields throughout the republic. If you watch a soccer game, you will be among wildly enthusiastic spectators. The generally gentle Costa Ricans get all fired up about this game and take sides with gusto.

WHAT TO SEE IN SAN JOSE

Bolivar Park. North end Calle 11. Zoo has collection of representative native wildlife, such as parrots, tapirs, *tepeizcuinte,* monkeys, snakes.

Carrillo Park. Faces City Hall. This green, restful park contains ancient Indian monolith.

Metropolitan Cathedral. Calle Central and Avenida 2. Very grand. Sunday, 8 A.M. Mass is interesting; military band attends in full uniform.

Parque Central. Mosaic pavements, gardens; military band plays Sundays at 5 P.M., Wednesdays at 8 P.M. National Symphony also gives concerts here.

Parque Morazán. Concerts in circular bandstand, Mondays and Fridays 8-9 P.M. Japanese garden, pagodas, bridges, ducks, geese, swans.

National Museum. Avenida Central. Open daily (except Monday), 9-11 A.M., 2-5 P.M. Formerly the Bella Vista Fort, this museum is situated on a height, within walking distance of the center of town. It has a spacious and beautiful green patio, and archway views of the city below. A serene place, one of its most fascinating wings is the archaeological section, with pre-Columbian pottery and jewelry on display. There are several replicas of excavated graves, showing how artifacts look when they are found. The archaeological periods are classified in an interesting and engaging manner. There are also cultural and historical exhibits. Well worth a leisurely visit.

National Palace. Legislature sits daily at 3 P.M., May through January. Visitors welcome.

National Theater. A copy of the Renaissance-designed Paris Opera, built in 1898. Foyer, public rooms, stairways, and balconies of Carrara marble. Gold and bronze decorations, crystal chandeliers, Venetian plate mirrors; gorgeous rose garden out front. Concerts, opera, ballet, drama are presented here.

Mercado Central. Calle 6, between Avenida 1 and Avenida Central.

Galerías Forma. Calle 9, Avenida Central and Avenida 2. Exhibits the works of contemporary Central American artists from all five republics.

National Stadium. Soccer, or "futbol," played on Sunday afternoons.

Banco Central. A collection of pre-Columbian gold artifacts is displayed. Visitors welcome.

SHORT SIDE TRIPS FROM SAN JOSE

Ojo de Agua (Eye of Water). To reach this beautifully land-scaped and planned recreation center near San José, take the freeway north toward the airport. Watch left, for a large church with a spacious green lawn. This is the Church of San Antonio and it is the only church to the left of the freeway as you pro-ceed from San José. Here, turn left off the freeway and take the road that crosses directly in front of the church. Turn left at the crossroad and continue north to Ojo de Agua.

The "eye of water" is a lively, copious spring that feeds swim-ming pools and the boating lake. The spring, which is above the pools, spills over in a waterfall, where swimmers can enjoy a cold shower by sitting under it. Monkeys romp in the trees. Good restaurant and refreshment stands. Tennis courts, soccer fields, dressing-rooms, acres for strolling or lolling. Open daily from 8 A.M. to 5 P.M.

Alajuela. CA-1 northwest of San José. El Coco, the international airport, is located here. Bus service. A colorful cattle fair is held each week; gaily painted ox-carts come to town. It is possible to combine this fair with a visit to a coffee *beneficio,* or processing plant, at El Brasil, on the outskirts. Alajuela's Central Park is surrounded by ancient mango trees. Here you will find the statue of Juan Santamaría, a native of Alajuela, hero of the rout-ing of William Walker. Ask to see the famous orchid-covered tree, which is particularly spectacular during March and April. (It is on private property.)

Lago de Lindora. Take Route 7 west to Santa Ana. Bus service from Coca-Cola Station. Festive straw hats in beautiful land-scape. Restaurant and bar service. Dance hall. Horseback riding, canoes and rowboats, gocart racing.

Patarra. Bus from Coca-Cola Station takes 25 minutes. Swimming pool, lake, dancing, rowing, food. Open until 5.

San Pedro. Roller-skating at "Patines Music." Bus or taxi. 7–10 P.M.

Escazú. On Route 7. Rollerama. Bus from Coca-Cola Station.

San Isidro de Coronado. Bus from Coca-Cola Station. See Gregorio Litwin's collection of tropical birds, macaws, toucans, quetzals, etc. It sells to zoos all over the world.

AROUND THE COUNTRY

Playa El Coco. A recent discovery by Central Americans, it is the avant-garde beach and water playground. To get here from San José, take CA-1 northwest to Liberia. At Liberia, take Route 21 southwestward (it is a beautiful road) for approximately 25 kilometers. Turn north on a dirt road for about 11 kilometers to reach the crescent beach with its white sand and clear water. The little bay has mountains on one of its arms. There is a small, adequate hotel and a restaurant that serves deliciously cooked seafood. Fishing is excellent and boats are for hire. Bring your own skin-diving equipment. No bus service as of this writing. Check tourist bureau and travel agencies for scheduled trips.

Puntarenas. This exciting beach resort can be reached by plane, bus, or train. The train has a gala atmosphere. By car from San José, west on Route 1 to Esparta. Shortly thereafter watch the road signs; turn left on the spur (Route 17) to Puntarenas (see p. 251 for description). Many interesting side trips can be arranged from Puntarenas. If you are interested in archaeology, one of the best sites for unearthing pre-Columbian artifacts in Central America is on the nearby peninsula of Nicoya. (Ask your hotel manager how to arrange for transportation and for an experienced guide with digging equipment.) Amateur archaeologists dig all the time on Nicoya but this hobby is officially frowned upon. What it amounts to is that, as yet, you will not be prevented from digging for ancient pottery and jewelry, but it can appear, to the ethical-minded visitor, a little like swiping his. hostess's engagement ring.

There are wonderful daily fishing expeditions from Puntarenas. You can also take a launch to Jesusita Island and fish from there; there are comfortable accommodations on the island at $15 a day, meals included. Other offshore islands are being developed for ardent fishermen.

Playas de Jacó. By air, 20 minutes from San José. You land on the beach at low tide, on the runway of the Amstel Hotel. Beautiful beaches, water sports, horseback riding. Excellent food and some new adventures in eating, such as *cambote,* a shellfish similar to abalone. Rates from December to April are $8 and up; from May to November, $6.50 and up.

Golfito. Reach this banana division on the Pacific Coast by plane. But first write the United Fruit Company, and you will be welcomed and shown around.

Heredia. From San José, north on Route 3.

This "City of the Flowers" is Costa Rica's fourth largest city and is located in the coffee country. An unusually comfortable and attractive mountain resort stopover, *La Catalina Motel,* offers Swiss chalets, modern comforts, swimming, tennis, and horseback riding. This is a good base for nature walks; it is recommended for resting after the pressures of an always-on-the-go trip.

In the Parque Central there is a cathedral built in 1787, and north of it, the ruins of a fort. Otherwise this happy little city is unsensational, but continue on to see the Poás volcano.

Poás Volcano. Better inquire for the road to Poás at a service station in Heredia. It is smoothly paved and leads to the active crater at 9500 feet. Blue hydrangeas and calla lilies grow wild along the way, and ravines are filled with giant ferns. For several miles as you approach the summit, you may smell sulphur and see white vapor escaping from the earth. This is subdued

volcanic activity indicating restlessness below the earth. At the
end of the road, park your car and walk a short distance forward
to look into the crater. At all times Poás emits churning clouds
of steam from fissures in the bottom of the crater; sometimes it
erupts more forcefully, shooting out black clouds of ash. Beyond
the active crater there is an "extinct" crater, now filled by a
vividly blue lake that is surrounded by flowering shrubs with
waxy rose-colored blossoms (*Cavendishia Gaultheria*) and ever-
greens. You should not try to find your way to Blue Lake without
a guide. If you wish to make a day of it, ask the tourist bureau
how to locate a guide to take you there. Bring your lunch and
a Thermos of water.

Cartago and Environs

By bus, guided tour, or your own car, 14 miles east on Route 2.
For a leisurely visit to this exhilarating and beautiful place, to
the nearby volcano Irazú, and to interesting sites on the outskirts,
you may elect to spend the night at the *Motel Río*. Here you will
find comfortable rooms, a swimming pool, and fresh-water fish
dinners. (For a different meal of fresh-water fish, try the Palomo
Restaurant on the Reventazón River.)

Cartago is a miniature colonial city. The earliest building dates
from 1564. Look for the stone shell of Iglesia del Convento de
los Padres Capuchinos; it appears to be in ruins, roof open to
the sky, but some say it is a church that was never finished;
there is a romantic legend about a young priest, a love affair,
and a murder. Whatever the past, stone walls are now standing
and there is no roof. Once, somebody had the inspiration of using
the four walls to enclose a garden. Vines climb the walls; paths
meander through triangular and rectangular pots full of blossoming plants. All paths converge on a central pool teeming with
gleaming iridescent tropical fish flashing brilliant reds, greens,
blues, golds.

The central fact about this garden is that you want to sit on
a bench, let your shoulders sag, perhaps stay there forever. It

casts a spell over you; you want to bask and contemplate indefinitely; you hate to be rushed off.

The effigy of Costa Rica's patron saint, Our Lady of the Angels, can be seen in the basilica, an elaborate building in the Moorish style of architecture. It is kept in a shrine below the church. It is said that if the saint does not wish to be moved, nobody can lift her.

On the southernmost outskirts of Cartago, on either side of Route 2, you will see miles of barren, mud-colored mesas. These are the congealed avalanches of rain-soggy volcanic ash that flowed with bull-dozing might from the volcano Irazú in 1963, covering prosperous farmlands for over twenty miles between the crater and Cartago.

Irazú Volcano. In Cartago, ask for the road to Irazú, left of Route 2. A smoothly paved road, on the outskirts of town, will take you to the crater, which is 11,325 feet above sea level. It is a beautiful drive, winding up through green alpine pastures. As you gain altitude the views are breath-taking. But there's a more stunning view ahead from the summit of Irazú: if the day is clear, you can see both the Atlantic and the Pacific Oceans.

At the end of the road you will find a cement lookout station near Irazú's active crater. You are advised not to venture beyond this point without a guide; a government guide is stationed there and will turn up if you wait. (He may be escorting other visitors to the edge of the active crater.) Irazú has two craters, one which is now quiescent and one which is active. The latter erupted strenuously in 1963; at this writing it is exhaling turbulent clouds of steam and gases. It is a thrill to look into the depths of the crater and watch the smoke come boiling up from the fissures at the bottom. (See also p. 53.)

Orosi. From San José, take Route 2 east to Cartago to paved road A-52. Here there is an active mission that was built two hundred years ago and that has an interesting exhibit of colonial relics.

Turrialba

From San José, Route 2 past Cartago, left on Route 10. This is one of the most beautiful drives in Central America, on an excellent road. The views of the valleys below and of the distant mountains beyond are not to be missed. Turrialba has a bright sun that does not burn, a climate that is heavenly—cool but not cold. There are good restaurants.

The Instituto Americano de Ciencias Agrícolas, an important agricultural research and teaching station, is situated in the valley at Turrialba. The buildings are attractive, surrounded by landscaped acres. Visitors are welcome, and it is fun to visit.

You can make arrangements to ride from San José to the Institute in its own station wagon. The charge is seventy cents each way, and you are invited to eat in the Institute dining-room for approximately $1.25.

The Institute is a research center for tropical agriculture and has the world's largest library on that subject. It trains specialists for Latin America. When we were there, they were exploring ideas for diversification of crops on coffee *fincas;* there is presently an overproduction of coffee.

A tourist need not be agriculturally oriented to enjoy a visit. It is fun to chat with some of the international types who are working there on projects. We talked to one young man, a biologist, a Harvard University graduate student, whose hobby is bird-watching; he had identified over 331 species within a half mile on the Institute grounds. He also told us that botanists looking for plant life on Turrialba volcano often find as many as sixty species of epiphytes (or air plants) in one cluster.

The crater of Turrialba volcano can be reached by road plus a short walk.

Puerto Limón

Discovered by Columbus on his last voyage, it later became a banana-boat port. It is located in a beautiful underdeveloped jungle and seashore setting on the Atlantic, or Caribbean, Coast.

There is no road to Puerto Limón. Go by train, return by plane. Time: two days. Cost: approximately $10-$15, which includes transportation, meals, hotel room, taxi, and refreshments. We recommend taking the train one way because the six-hour ride is gorgeous. The narrow-gauge track skirts abysses as it hugs the shoulders of mountains, goes through jungles, runs alongside the dramatic Reventazón River, whose rapids froth over rocks, and finally parallels white sand, blue seas, and palm trees, whose fronds swish in the balmy, soughing Caribbean wind like giant feather dusters.

You couldn't ask for more of a bargain. Coach fare from San José to Puerto Limón is $2; it costs $3 to return (25 minutes) on a LACSA flight. We had three hearty and well-cooked meals for a total of $1.95 apiece; a single room at the *Park Hotel*, which overlooks the harbor, costs $3 a night and is scrupulously clean, though not air-conditioned.

Board the train for Puerto Limón at the Great Northern Depot in San José. From our log: "The station is wooden, dark green, rectangular, the sort of stark structure one might have expected at any prosperous prairie railroad station in the States at the turn of the century; inside are wooden floors, benches, high ceilings, a cage for the ticket salesman, and gloomy dimness that is part of the character of an old railroad station anywhere. Outside, on the platform, there is a huge brass bell attached to one of the pillars that supports the roof. It sets up a great clanging when rung by hand on the arrival and departure of trains. This creates excitement; children shout with joy and mothers raise their voices and give orders in case anybody should be going to pieces. We heard one mother of five call out, 'Heads and hands inside.'

"When the train pulls in, you climb up steep iron-grille steps to the old-fashioned coach with worn leather seats. (The noon train has a fancy parlor car of Victorian elegance; we, however, took the morning coach train at 9:30 A.M.) It is best to sit on the right side, because the stunning views are out those windows. The windows are open, incidentally; the wind is welcome, fresh, sweet and clean, and you can feel changes in climate, as when, descending from the mountains, you smell the moist warm green of the jungle."

The railroad is still the hub of life for the cacao farmers who live beside the tracks, descendants of the Jamaicans who were hired to work on the railroad because they seemed to be able to resist the depredations of tropical diseases. They now live in tiny, unpainted, weathered-silver cabins on stilts along the tracks. There are jewel-bright roosters and little black pigs in front yards, trays of cacao beans drying alongside or underneath the houses. The porches and front walls are decorated with various sizes of tin cans converted into planters; these have the subdued silvery look of pewter vases.

At first the train creaks like a ship in a heavy sea as it toils up the grades from Cartago to Turrialba. On this stretch the vistas are extraordinary. You look deep down into valleys, beyond them to green mountains with their heads in the clouds, and the colors on the slopes, from bright lemon to deep Killarney green, are lovely. Whenever the train goes through a tunnel, it is pitch-black for a long moment, and all the children scream.

The train stops often to let people on and off at places called Azul, Guayabo, Cimarrones, Matina—also, Buffalo, Liverpool, and Boston. At every stop people lean out the windows and hail friends. Those who dwell along the tracks belong to one long, strung-out community.

Impatiens, pink to scarlet blossoms with encircling, corsage-shaped leaves, grow wild in big splotches along the steep banks. Horticulturist Claude Hope believes that early Spanish colonists planted the first impatiens, which has now become a native wild-flower.

At Cartago and Turrialba, small boys jump on the train and follow one another up and down the aisles, selling bags of peanuts, ice cream, and *papas calientes* (hot potatoes). "*Quiere papas?*" they call. A barefooted woman wearing an apron offers hot fish and yucca; a man comes through holding high, like a torch, a paper cone filled with shaved ice, berry-red with fruit juice.

After Turrialba, the train descends to the jungle, which smells like a hothouse full of growing things. For miles and miles the tracks run alongside the wide and wild Reventazón River. The last lovely stretch is along the Caribbean coast, and, through palm trees leading every which way, you can see the blue-green water, stretches of white sand with gentle breakers frothing on the beach.

From our log: "Puerto Limón is a town of one-story frame buildings with the paint worn off. Has the look of one of our western frontier towns. Taking inventory on a taxi ride, we find that the town is an amazingly complete civic complex; stadium, post office, hospital, schools, governor's mansion. Its most unusual buildings are the Chinese school and the red enamel Chinese Nationalist Party headquarters. At the shore the city is surrounded by a high stone sea wall; it is fun to walk on it, or sit on it and look out to sea."

It is generally agreed that the best place to stay is the *Park Hotel,* which overlooks the water. Food is served family style and there is plenty of it. You don't order: they bring you what they've got, which includes the invariable rice and beans and such native vegetables as *cheyote,* a type of squash.

There are good restaurants also. The *International Bar* is recommended for lobster in season; there we had a first course of the tiniest oysters I have ever seen, delicious too, swimming in sauce.

Close to the water is a most unusual tropical park. Parque Vargas has tall trees with wide-spreading branches that almost shut out the sky. As you walk through it you are in deep green shadows. The trunks of the trees are covered with intertwining ropes of parasitic plants. Up in the branches live three-toed sloths. We went sloth-spotting our first evening there, squinting up into the branches in the shadows, without seeing a single sloth. Then, early in the morning, we tried again. At last, against the bright early light, we saw one up high in the branches, turning his slothful head. As our eyes became more attuned we saw other sloths up in the treetops.

Sloth-spotting is not by any means the only entertaining pastime of Puerto Limón. You can walk out to the modern docks and watch the banana boats being loaded. The hotel manager can make a deal for you to take a taxi tour and the driver will be your guide. He speaks English. He'll show you the old United Fruit compound on a jetty near the sea; the neat bungalows have pruned lawns and shrubs and the look of miraculous well-being. The directors of the Limón division of the United Fruit Company lived there several decades ago; then Panama disease blighted miles of bananas and they pulled out. Now the Standard Fruit Company has moved in with a Panama disease-resistant banana, the Cavendish, and that company is developing brave new areas of cleared jungle for the banana crop.

Our driver showed us local flora—pointed out breadfruit, cashew, water apple, avocado, mango, apple, and cacao trees. He was full of odds and ends of information or misinformation. ("If you eat Chinese bananas with butter, you'll die.") Once, when we passed a cave alongside the curving road to the beach, he said, "If you go in there, you'll never come out."

We visited two incredibly lovely coves. One was the lobster fisherman's harbor; their dugout canoes were pulled up along the shore under palm trees; nearby were little huts where they stored their gear. Playa Bonita, a cave with crystal-clear water and a little crescent beach, has a large, covered dining pavilion with tables; an orchestra plays for dancing on Saturday nights.

The airport at Puerto Limón has a landing strip on the beach, next to the breakers. Our LACSA plane was a B-47, built for flying over "the Hump" in World War II and still an excellent sturdy ship. While it was unloading luggage and freight, the passengers all went out and stood chummily around before boarding. A little boy used his boarding pass as a shovel and dug in the gravel under a wing.

A friend, who had been down visiting banana-boxing plants for his company, told us that the last time he had flown from Puerto Limón to San José the door to the hangar had jammed and they could not bring out the steep boarding ladder. The crew had finally fetched an ordinary wooden carpenter's ladder, and the passengers got aboard by a means at least more civilized than planting a bean and climbing up a vine, like Jack the Giant Killer.

Isla Cocos. 180 miles offshore in the Pacific. Inquire at the tourist bureau in San José for port of embarkation and rental of ocean-going launch. The attraction of Isla Cocos is legitimate "buried treasure"; pirate Henry Morgan logged that he had buried gold on the island to avoid surrendering it to a rival pirate. So far, none of the expeditions has found a whisper of it.

A trip to Isla Cocos would be a major adventure; there are no accommodations. You would need to bring camping supplies along.

TO PANAMA

Having gotten as far as Costa Rica, many tourists want to see the country 222 miles southward, Panama. It's a short hop by plane, but, as of now, a very arduous drive. From San José, take Route 2 east to Cartago. Shortly thereafter, there is a steep climb (6000 feet in 20 miles) to the pass at Cerro Buena Vista (formerly called Cerro de la Muerte, mountain of death) at 11,000 feet.

We recently drove from San José to David, Panama, and were shocked by the condition of the highway. From our log: "Except for one sign reading *peligro* (dangerous)—and such signs are common during minor road repairs—there was no warning of how perilous conditions would actually be. We found ourselves on a steep dirt road so awesomely unfinished that we would certainly have turned around had there been any room to turn around in.

"As we climbed, we drove into thick fog, and it became damper and chillier. Sometimes the unpaved muddy roadbed was deeply rutted, where the treads of heavy construction equipment had churned it up. On some stretches the earth was hard-surfaced but slithery; it set your teeth on edge because it would have been easy to skid off into an abyss. We jolted in and out of deep pot-holes, scraping the bottom of the car. Fallen rocks would strike, whacking or clanging against the chassis or the under-pinnings, making us fear for the gasoline tank. There were no flares or lights to warn us of the almost infinite variety of hazards. The only light was the fast-fading and ominous glow that lingered after sunset. This weather seemed to have no connection with that we had left in Cartago. The boiling fog was luridly yellow, and the mountains loomed up on all sides, jagged and black; they were like exaggerations; threatening, black-ink peaks out of a nightmare.

"To add to the dismal *ambiente,* it became so clammy and chilly that we rolled up the windows and turned on the heater. Always to our left and sometimes simultaneously to our right, the road fell steeply off into gaping abysses. 'Look at that,' we would marvel in carefully controlled voices—we might be referring to a whole hunk of road that had fallen away, leaving a very narrow passage, or to a pile of rock from an avalanche.

"At one time we were actually above the clouds, which lay in a dimly fluffy carpet below us, as if seen from a plane. On the descent from Cerro Buena Vista thick fog absolutely enveloped us. We said that in a way it was merciful that we could not see beyond the windshield, because the drops were so hair-raising. After what felt like years later, we suddenly drove out of the fog on a downward slope, and there, in a valley below us, were sprinkled the lights of San Isidro. It had taken us over four hours to drive seventy-one miles."

The border station is a short drive from Villa Neilly, Costa Rica, southward on Route 2, to the border at Paso de Canoas. Your passport should be visaed by the Panamanian Consulate in San José. If you are staying only forty-eight hours, you will be granted an "in transit" pass. From the border station to David, the first city in Panama of any consequence, it is 42 miles. It is 258 miles from David to Panama City.

MARKET DAYS

San José	Tuesday, Friday
Alajuela	Monday, Tuesday
Cartago	Sunday

Visit craft center at Sarchi (see p. 106) to buy from the workshop outlets a variety of unique Costa Rican woodcrafts, painted in the traditional designs used to decorate ox-carts and yokes.

FIESTA CALENDAR

DATE	PLACE	CELEBRATION
Jan.		
1	*San José*	New Year's Day (end of Fiestas Cívicas)
15	*San José*	Special Mass at Alajuelita Church
March		
2–9	*San José*	Feria de las Flores
19	*San José*	San José
Holy Thursday	*Everywhere*	Jueves Santo
Holy Friday	*Everywhere*	Viernes Santo
April		
11	*Everywhere*	Anniversary of the Battle of Rivas
May		
4	*Everywhere*	Corpus Christi Day
June		
29	*In all towns named San Pedro or San Pablo*	San Pedro, San Pablo
July		
16	*Puntarenas*	Fiesta de la Virgen del Carmen
Aug.		
2	*Cartago*	Fiesta de la Virgen de los Ángeles
15	*Everywhere*	Feria de la Asunción

DATE	PLACE	CELEBRATION
Sept.		
15	*Everywhere*	Independence Day
24	*Grecia*	Fiesta de la Virgen de Mercedes
Oct.		
12	*Everywhere*	Columbus Day
24	*Escazú*	San Juan
31	*Everywhere*	Halloween
Nov.		
2	*Everywhere*	All Souls' Day
Dec.		
8	*Everywhere*	Concepción
24–25	*Everywhere*	Christmas
29–Jan. 1	*Everywhere*	Fiestas Cívicas

III / The Long Haul

Settling Down for Months or Years in Central America

17 / Culture Shock

To settle down in a foreign country for a long haul instead of being a temporary visitor is the difference between having a date with a seemingly fascinating character and being married to him, or her. Culture shock is a painful disorientation; the sufferer reacts with hostility and panic to unfamiliar, stubbornly unfathomable surroundings.

The United States Government, private agencies, and business firms make a big thing of culture shock when briefing their foreign-service people. Retired persons, gravitating in ever larger numbers to Central American countries—and especially to Costa Rica, whose immigrant program is specifically designed to attract them—are well acquainted with the symptoms through pamphlets read in advance of their switch in residence.

It's a minimal risk in countries long visited by American tourists and chronicled in films, travel books, letters, postcards, and slides. If an American suddenly found himself on the Acropolis in Athens, he would probably recognize the Parthenon; it would be almost as familiar to him as the White House. Standing on a drizzly corner, seeing red double-decker buses reflected in a puddle, he'd guess that he was in London. But

Central America is as yet little known. A survey of business leaders in the United States has revealed that only one in a hundred could name all five republics on the isthmus!

A rat who has been deliberately befuddled in a lab, who has been conditioned to receive food when a bell rings and, instead, gets a sizzling shock on the nose, could not be more frustrated than a newcomer making a telephone call in Central America.

The dial tone is a shrill beep-beep-beep that could be a Disney sound effect. You dial over these tiny, frantic beeps and often they keep right on going. So you hang up and dial again. *Beep-beep-beep.*

Once, in Guatemala City, I was trying to reach Lex on a friend's telephone. Exasperated, I called to her, "I try and try but I can't get anything but those beeps."

"Dial a little faster," she suggested.

This somehow quelled the beeps, by beating them at their own game, and I got the number. If, in the States, you did not get your number, who in the world would suggest dialing *faster?* And if you did, would it *work?*

In Central America the trouble often starts with locating the number of the party you wish to call. Generally there isn't any telephone book on the premises. Telephone books are privately published but nobody seems to know where to buy them. If you can lay hands on a telephone, this is by no means the end of the trouble.

The Spanish tradition of putting one's mother's name last makes listings as mysterious to the average gringo as if they were printed in Mayan hieroglyphics. Thus Juan García Solano's last name is not Solano but García; Solano is his mother's maiden name. Compilers of Central American directories list his last name as García. But what about the gringo whose name happens to be John Hubbard Fox? What compatriot would expect to find him listed under Hubbard, if indeed he even knew his friend's middle name?

Lex did not have a telephone book either in his office or in his house. I discovered that he considered it subversive literature.

One day I asked him if he could recommend a doctor.

"Dr. Blanco has an office three blocks *abajo* from the barbershop side of the Gran Hotel. Drop in there around four this afternoon," he replied.

"Can't I call and make an appointment?" I asked.

"That would be all right if you knew the number," Lex said coldly.

"Why can't I look in the telephone book under 'B' for 'Blanco' and *find* the number?"

"I don't have a telephone book." His tone of controlled indignation suggested that nobody'd had one since the days of the horseless carriage.

"Why not?"

"I used to try calling numbers in the telephone book and I never got anybody I wanted. Why don't you do as I suggest and drop by his office around four?"

I did—if you can call riding for eight miles in a crowded bus and walking three long ones *abajo* "dropping in." The receptionist told me that Dr. Blanco was vacationing in Europe, which was a long way to go for a shot.

As I stayed longer I began to see why it was possible to develop an allergy to the telephone. Even if you did get a number, the voice on the other end might keep shouting, "*Hola!*" (hello) or "*Cómo?*" (what?) in a fortissimo that would put to shame the muezzin's call to prayer.

I was told about a recent experience of a resident American couple in Guatemala. One night the husband dialed his home from down town Guatemala City to tell his wife that he would be late to dinner. He kept getting a strange señora. Finally he intercepted the operator. She was gone a long time on a dead wire but returned to inform him that his number had been changed. He hadn't been notified, he said; there must be some mistake. How could his number have been changed without notification? Nobody was more mystified than the operator. He asked her to find out what his number had been changed to. He shifted from one foot to the other while, in the *oficina* of the telephone company, people scurried around but did not succeed in finding his number. He got home as fast as possible.

For a few days the couple could make outgoing calls, but none of their friends knew how to get through to them. Then, one night, their telephone rang. The *muchacha* (maid) answered and had the wit to ask, "What number are you calling, *por favor?*" She jotted it down and the cliff-hanger was over. Next morning the couple called the telephone company so that it too would know what their number was.

It is generally felt that American women are more prone to culture shock than the men. Of course business brings the men into closer touch with the community faster; they have more practice speaking the language and so feel surer of themselves in the environment.

What triggers anxiety or exasperation is that nothing goes as you expect it to; no previously acquired wisdom about how to live with life seems to work. You become edgy, easily upset, close to tears or rage. After a whole series of things have gone wrong—your refrigerator has been broken for days in this climate, the landlady keeps promising to send a repair man, and the repair man keeps promising the landlady, but nothing happens—it doesn't take much more to make you fall apart.

Once I was picking flowers when I felt terrible stabs of pain near my elbow, where I had been reaching into the bushes. It was as if I had been stung by a legion of hornets. I flew into a panic, jumped to the conclusion that I had been bitten by a poisonous snake or a tarantula. Lex looked at my arm, where big blisters were ballooning, and told me I'd touched a pica-pica plant. The pain would wear off in a half hour or so. If he had not been there to reassure me, I would have gone to pieces.

And once, before I was the least bit acclimatized, Lex left me in the Gran Hotel in Managua, saying he'd be back in a few minutes. I ordered a Coke and watched the goings and comings in the lobby. I began to watch the clock. An hour went by and no Lex. Two hours. I began to worry. I found myself remembering the way Lex crosses streets, as if he were participating in a *corrida* with madly charging Managuan taxis. How could I find out what had happened? I was shattered. Then Lex appeared, sat down and ordered a Coke. He had had to wait and wait for somebody who was late. He said to me, "You have to hang loose around here or you'll go crazy."

An American wife told me about the waiting game as it was played by Central American women. "If your husband goes out, you never ask him where he is going or what he is going to do or when he'll be back," she said. "You just wait until he turns up, and you still don't ask any questions, don't complain about holding dinner, don't expect him to explain."

You have to learn to use these unexpected gifts of time resourcefully. Have a backlog of things to do, books to read, puzzles to finish, letters to write.

I learned to play it by ear by watching Lex, who was seldom either dismayed or indignant over the unexpected.

In Puerto Limón, Costa Rica, there is a shadow-black park with three-toed sloths living in the trees, and a birthday-cake pink bandstand that has been converted into a barbershop. Lex went there one morning in quest of a shave. The barber lathered him, then began to dig up his face with an ill-wielded razor. Lex jumped up and asked him what he thought he was doing. The barber said, "I never could shave anybody. I'm nervous." This amused Lex, who walked over to the wall mirror and finished the shaving himself. He then paid the barber and left without rancor.

Once I was helping Lex decorate a booth for agricultural chemicals at the Managua Fair. Five carpenters had been hired to build graduated plywood boxes for display purposes, and when we arrived one hot Saturday morning I expected to find everything finished as promised. What we found were men drunk and nothing done. Lex and I began to paint the booth. I was furious at those feckless carpenters and, bitterly putting on the paint, kept muttering under my breath.

"Just look at the poor bastards," Lex said.

I turned around. One man with his hat falling off was trying to hit a nail with a hammer and missing it over and over again. I laughed. I got over my rage and began to enjoy the business of improvising, making do without the equipment that the boys we called "the Cinco Stinko" had promised us.

I watched Lex operate day after day with only general goals, a very loose framework of immediate hopes, and a thorough play-it-by-ear philosophy. It seemed to me that he usually got more accomplished by happenstance than by plan.

Once when we were driving back to Managua from Tegucigalpa, Honduras, he passed a car, waved and gestured to the driver. Several miles on, where there was a road leading off to a *finca*, Lex pulled up, and the gentleman to whom he had waved soon stopped too. Lex walked over, leaned in the window, and had a very important conference. He later told me that much had been accomplished, adding that if he had deliberately tried to reach the man, to track him down, he would have had a wild-goose chase.

From being prone to culture shock, I found that after a time I gradually acquired a more comfortable, resilient attitude. To become more at home in another world, follow its lead instead of trying to impose your pattern in the hope that it will fall into step with you.

Toward the end of four months in Central America, we were returning to Managua from San José one morning and stopped for breakfast in a place that, as it turned out, served *típico* food. My fried eggs came atop a mountain of rice and beans. I actually enjoyed this once unthinkable concoction. Lex said, "So now you like rice and beans." I replied that I was wild about them.

The ultimate in adjustment, of course, is to go home and, after a time, find yourself missing the Central American world that once made you homesick. You notice how brashly teen-agers talk to their parents, how billboards make the highways hideous, and you think what a rat race it all is. And you go to a place in the city where Spanish is spoken and order rice and beans.

18 / The Muchacha

In most of the world, legislation protects the individual against predatory practices of employers. The Central American *muchacha*—"the girl," or maid of all work—may be *theoretically* protected by government policies but, in actuality, she is unaware of her rights and would not know where to turn to protest abuses. Her pay is astonishingly low: thirty dollars a month is tops, at present; ten dollars, if an untrained youngster is hired by a middle-class family.

Usually she has Sunday, or part of Sunday, off, but she cannot even count on this. A yearly vacation is unheard of. She is helplessly dependent upon the whims of her employer. The *muchacha* has no way of knowing what goes on in the rest of the world; the newspapers she reads, if indeed she can read, are local and are not concerned with social reforms; she has no idea what she's missing.

Once Lex picked up an old woman who was walking up the mountain from Managua. She had just been fired from a job she had held for years as *muchacha* for a family. They had told her that she was too old to do the job. The woman told Lex that she intended to look for an unoccupied bit of land up on the

mountain and build herself a hut. She had no relatives, no resources. This was all she could think of—to find branches and
boards and odds and ends to improvise a hut. If she was lucky,
kind neighbors might give her a tortilla now and then. Her erst-
while employers had not concerned themselves with where she
would go or what she would do; she had no form of social se-
curity. There were charitable organizations in Managua, church
groups, but she had no way of knowing about them. She was
absolutely on her own. Lex, whom she met only by chance,
offered to help her.

Generally the attitude of the *muchacha* reflects no rebellious-
ness, not even such masked rebellion as pleading illness and not
showing up after her day off. On the job she is a paragon that
most newcomers can't believe. She is kind and cheerful to children and elderly people. She has charming manners and is
sweetly solicitous. She never complains or shows impatience and
fatigue. She doesn't clatter or bang as she works but gets everything done on softly slippered feet and with gentle hands; none
of that self-important display of energy that some maids flam-
boyantly affect in a busy household with children and a lot of
washing and ironing and dishes and picking up to do. She never
asks for anything as her right, and very, very seldom does she
request a favor. With shrewd affection, she studies her family
and knows the habits of its members well. Having been brought
up to do the wash kneeling on rocks by a river, she can remove
the most stubborn stains and spots in cold water without any
miracle product other than her own scrubbing and some old-
fashioned brown homemade soap. She can bargain cleverly at
the general market; give her five dollars and she'll return with
bulging brown paper bags full of fruit, vegetables, and meat.

I'll never forget my astonishment when Lex explained to me
why it might be difficult for me to teach his Nora how to cook.
This was the one thing she did not do beautifully, and I promised Lex I'd try to teach her.

"You see, it's hard for them to cook something if they don't
know what it ought to look like or taste like and if they never
eat it," Lex said.

"What do you *mean,* they never eat it?"

"They don't eat what the family eats," Lex said. "They eat rice, and *maíz* (flour for tortillas), and that's all.

I discovered that, indeed, maids rarely are allowed to eat the same food as the family. The boss supplies them with beans, rice, and *maíz* (flour for tortillas), and that's all.

When Lex hired Nora he was looking for a woman with a child, because he figured, kindly and accurately, that a single woman would be lonesome and unhappy up on the mountains in the blustering wind, fourteen kilometers outside Managua. He put an ad in the paper, Nora answered it, and he hired her. She moved into the maid's quarters, a small room with an adjacent shower and toilet, with her four-year-old son Iwo.

Iwo never gets in the way, never goes out of bounds into the main part of the house. He plays in the yard, or sleeps on his part of Nora's bed, or stays quietly in the kitchen with her. He is not allowed to whine or cry. When he starts, Nora spanks him uncompromisingly. Once I saw her standing in the kitchen, stirring something on the stove, holding a strap over her shoulder while Iwo eyed her respectfully but sorrowfully from the door.

When Nora is not busy with something else, she is wiping up the tile floors with a mop—one typical of Central America, long old rags clasped in a mop handle. She wipes up the tiles intermittently, over and over, during the day. Sometimes a niece comes to visit her and then Lex has two maids. The niece, Nora, and Iwo somehow fit into that one small bed in the room out back.

I have thought a lot about Nora. For one thing, I saw that she could not be dismissed as "simple and uncomplicated." All day she led the life of a quiet, orderly house mouse. She wiped the tiles; she spread clean sheets on the grass to dry; she chased horses who came through the yard. But at night, after she fell asleep, she led a life that made you think of the *Perils of Pauline.* Time and again, she brought Lex and me racing out from our rooms with her screams. She would be sobbing and gasping. Someone had just tried to choke her. A man had just chased her up a ladder with a knife. Sometimes she had palpitations at night and sobbed that she was afraid she would die and there would be nobody to take care of Iwo.

Then, while she was never mad at Lex when he was hours late for dinner, or at me for giving her cooking lessons in my faltering and inadequate Spanish—with long pauses while I looked up a word in a dictionary—she did get absolutely furious with chickens. She hated chickens with an unreasonable passion. They were always running through the yard too. "Ras-ras, ca-ca," she would say angrily, imitating their scratching (ras) and their clucking (ca). "They ruin everything."

Gradually I learned a little bit about her life.

Nora grew up in Nandaime, Nicaragua, in a one-room house built of sugar cane, with rice matting and mud and grass as wattle. The floor was tamped-down earth, the roof was thatch; the family slept on reed mats. They went barefooted, and during the rainy season they used big leaves for umbrellas. They cooked on a raised hearth in the corner, using wood they gathered on the ground. They had a kerosene lamp and candles for light. Water was the greatest problem. It was high and dry country and you had to walk a long way to find a brook. Or you could buy water from a man who came around with a tank in a cart pulled by a horse. A jug of water was very precious and you did not waste it.

There were no doctors in the pueblo, only someone called the *curandero*, who sometimes knew what to do. For a stomach ache they drank black coffee or an elixir which was made by salting and boiling the four top leaves of the *quelite de fraile* plant. For a cold they would render the fat of a chicken and take a teaspoon now and then. To clot the blood and heal a wound, they put coffee grounds on it and covered it with a tobacco leaf. There was a terrible stomach ache that people sometimes got called *cólico miserere,* and it could kill you (doubtless appendicitis). There was a fatal croup (probably diphtheria). You could rub in menthol and kerosene to no avail. Once four adolescent girls in Nora's family succumbed to the croup together, were laid out in white dresses, and buried at the same time.

Nora was a bright child. The one thing she was later told

about herself as a small child was that she "threw things in her hair, soup, beans—nobody knew why." A cousin, who was a nun, saw to it that Nora was enrolled in a nun's school. She went through kindergarten in half a year and won prizes right through the sixth grade, which was as far as the school went. At eleven and a half Nora was out in the world. As Lex observed, "The children of the poor have no adolescence. They skip it."

Lex admires Nora; he helps pay for Iwo's private school. And he is very lucky to have her on the job. Lex is away a great deal and she is resourceful during emergencies in his business. Lex has only to call her and explain the problem and she replies, "*Entendido*" (understood), and set forth on some trouble-shooting mission that an experienced secretary might not dare to undertake.

Nora's intelligence and sense of responsibility qualify her for jobs she has never dreamed of doing. Now what she wants more than anything is a good education for Iwo. He has her brightness and her generous responsiveness to life. Perhaps he'll know enough, when he grows up, to help improve the world that denied his mother the fulfillment of her potential.

19 / Gringos in Residence

UTOPIA FOR THE RETIRED

There are thousands of North American citizens living in Central America. Many, like Lex, are businessmen, working in the Central American economy. Many gringo farmers have bought land and are raising crops. In Guatemala there is such a large group of cotton farmers from Hastings, Nebraska, that the area they have settled is known as "Little Hastings." Then there are the retired Americans who have chosen to live in Central America; there are a number of them in every republic, but Costa Rica has attracted more *pensionados* (retirees) than any other country.

Costa Rica offers special incentives for the retired, allowing a tax exemption of $5000 on such heavily taxed goods as cars, refrigerators, washing machines, stoves. It is interesting that this small nation, in which 70 per cent of the populace is under twenty, should have thought up the best come-on for retired persons that exists anywhere in the world. You can retire there, incidentally, at any age—all you need is an income.

To settle down in Costa Rica and retain his American citizenship, a would-be *pensionado* enters in the same way as any other tourist, on a visaed passport or tourist card. He then applies for a special residence visa from immigration officials in San José. The *pensionado* is required to have a monthly income of $300, but he pays no taxes. He has all the rights of other citizens except that he cannot vote and he cannot take a salaried job away from a national. If he has a special skill that is lacking among nationals, then he may be hired on full salary. At present, an American *pensionado* is working at El Coco Airport on a traffic-control project.

But there are no strictures against private investments. Recently a *pensionado* bought land, discovered a large deposit of copper, and is now exporting it. Another is raising mushrooms for the market. And one bought a mountain-top mansion near Heredia, turned it into a guest house, and is adding twenty cottages.

Many *pensionados* do not have the money-making urge or do not need to augment their incomes, and they are doing valuable volunteer work.

The Instituto Costarricense de Turismo in San José puts out an excellent, comprehensive booklet on all the provisions of Law 3393 (which spells out the status of *pensionados*), including information that prospective retirees consistently request: current food prices, prices for land, houses for rent or for sale, etc.

The Retirees Club, which can be addressed in care of the Instituto, is extremely helpful, will correspond with a prospective *pensionado*, answer all questions, and make recommendations. A newcomer will be met on arrival by members of the club and given whatever assistance he needs in settling down.

One afternoon we visited Cecil Bellou, first president of the Retirees Club. Though now retired from that office, he is still a policy-maker, a lobbyist with the government, and a concerned, enthusiastic senior of the senior citizens.

Mr. Bellou, his wife, and his teen-aged daughter live in a spacious home in a suburb of San José with a magnificent view of the Santa Ana Valley. The view includes El Coco Airport, with tiny silver planes visible at a great distance, and mountains with cloud shadows chasing over them. The Bellous bought the land "very reasonably," he says, and lived in the little wooden gate house until their home was built. Their permanent home is Spanish colonial in character (white plaster walls, wooden beams, tiled floors, red-tiled roof) with modern picture windows and floor-to-ceiling glass walls. The furnishings are a pleasant mixture of favorites from the United States and Costa Rican pieces, such as the burnished coffee table, the top of which was once the wheel of an ox-cart, and large pre-Columbian ceramic vases and bowls near the hearth of the whitewashed brick fireplace.

The Bellous employ two maids, who have learned to cook and keep house gringo style. While we were visiting, Mr. Bellou ordered "Coffee and doughnuts, *también*."

The Bellous' daughter is one of 400 Americans at the Lincoln School, in which 500 nationals are also enrolled. Mr. Bellou confesses that they were worried about the girl's adjustment when they moved to Costa Rica, but he says, "She changed schools, she changed friends—that's all it was. And here she has her own horse."

He showed us around his sloping green grounds. "We have sixty-four pineapple plants coming up like the deuce," he said, beaming. "We grow our own coffee, vegetables, fruit."

We walked with him across the road to a nearby house that was being built for a retired American couple. Mr. Bellou helped them find the land and the builders. He is always being called upon for counsel and spends a great deal of time on correspondence. Some familiar advice:

Bring your appliances, your refrigerator and washing machine, but don't ship all your furniture. The woodcrafting here is extraordinary.

Don't come stocked up like the Swiss Family Robinson. Stores are organized differently from those in the States—you might have to get a needle in one place, the thread in another—but I have never failed to find anything I needed.

Try to forget how things are done in the States. You have to have patience and a sense of humor. Don't schedule too tightly. Let it go until tomorrow. It might work out better.

We asked Mr. Bellou at what juncture he had been able to forget how things were done in the States and had tackled the situation in a Central American style.

He recalled a night when he had brought his movie projector to a theater, to show a film that a number of people had requested. The hour for the showing was 7 P.M., but by 7:30 nobody had turned up. Bellou, remembering that he had once "heard a cannon fired to get people to church," went home, got his 12-gauge shotgun, and shot it off in front of the theater. "They came running," he told us.

We had never heard of the custom of firing off shotguns to get patrons to the movies, but perhaps there's nothing else to do with cannon and shotguns in Costa Rica, since the republic has no army.

After three years in Central America, Mr. Bellou went back to visit the oil-refining company where he had once raced between his four offices. He told them that he was actually busier in Costa Rica.

"Only there I can put something off," he said. "I can take a siesta."

YOUNG EXPATRIATES

Children, especially teen-agers, are doleful and stuffy about pulling up their roots. They hate to leave their familiar school and their good friends to move to a strange country. Parents on foreign service worry a great deal about this.

There are some pleasant surprises. There is an American school in each of the five capitals of Central America. Each one is slightly different in administrative structure, but the tuition is always far less than it would be in the States. In 1968, in Managua, tuition was $390 for kindergarten through sixth grade and $440 for grades seven through twelve. In San Salvador the

American school charged from $200 to $400 for the elementary grades and $710 for the high-school years. The Country Day School in San José, Costa Rica, costs $42.50 per month, plus refundable charges for books.

American schools generally observe the statewide school year, September through June, with some concessions to local weather. In Managua during March and April, when it is hottest, children get on their buses at 6:30 A.M. School begins at 7 A.M. and is out by 12:30. All American holidays, as well as the national holidays of the host country, are observed.

The curriculum is the same as in the top high schools and good preparatory schools in the States. However, it is usually easier for a graduate to be accepted by an American college or university, because of geographical distribution. That he is bilingual and that his travel has been broadening are advantages.

Approximately half the enrollment in an American school consists of sons and daughters of nationals. These boys and girls exert an important modifying influence on the social lives of the gringo kids. In Central America the world revolves around the family; children spend more time at home and there is no teen-age sub-culture. Teen-agers do not run everything; they do not even run *anything*.

J. B. Malone, director of the American school in Managua, told us: "Parents here do a tremendous job of supervising their daughters, which means, of course, that parents of boys do not need to concern themselves too much about their sons. No girl under college age is allowed to be escorted to and from a dance by a boy in a car. Her father brings her to the dance, leaves her there, picks her up and drives her home. For our Valentine party, we had a dance with an orchestra, and four adult chaperones. The children seem as uninhibited and free as at teen-age dances in the States, but there is actually a great difference in the control. Parents have abdicated in the United States. They are playing ostrich."

Charles Stemp, principal of the American school in San Salvador ("the only place in the city where touch football is played"), stressed the compensations to North American kids in the Central American social environment. "North American kids are lionized," he says. "The Salvadorans want to act like North Americans. North Americans are popular simply by being North Americans. There is no such thing as a wallflower."

Malone feels that the greatest disciplinary problem is tardiness. Keeping appointments promptly is not a Central American virtue. Stemp sees a disadvantage when a North American youngster has been "brought up by a maid in Central America. The attitude toward maids is different. American kids may treat them badly, and this is bad for the kids." This is part of an over-all danger of loss of identity as a North American, especially if a youngster has spent his life in Latin American countries. "He doesn't know who he is," Stemp says. "He doesn't know how much of a North American he is."

For most youngsters, this is not a problem. The average tour of duty for North American families in Central America is three years.

"And then," Stemp says, and Malone agrees, "they hate to leave."

TROPICAL CLIMATE, TROPICAL PETS

You rarely see a cat or a kitten in Central America. If there are any, they live within family compounds and are not seen prowling the streets and foraging in the garbage. You'd think that in Central America, where horses, dogs, cows, pigs, and chickens wander everywhere, there'd be a record number of half-wild cats. Yet you never hear the midnight yodeling that goes on elsewhere in the world.

However, there are stray mongrels everywhere, with their ribs sticking out, who are hysterically shy of people and quite unlike any that can be adopted at animal shelters in the States. Among the procession of animals through Lex's yard was a furtive dog who appeared to be part terrier. His black coat was wiry and his muzzle bristled. One ear was up and the other down and his tail was a question mark. Glimpsing him one day, Lex said, "You know, I'll bet that if somebody fed that dog, and talked to him, and gave him some affection, he might turn out to be lovable."

I began to put out food for him, first in the yard, then on the steps to the porch-terrace, then on the porch itself. Just to be silly, I called him "Pal." His trip to the porch for food was very nervous, and every time I tried to go out there when he was eating he would bolt in terror. After a while he would back away but not disappear entirely. I would keep holding my hand out to him and calling, "Here, Pal," and one day he cautiously came closer and touched his nose to my hand, but, when I tried to pat him, he was off like a shot. It was weeks before I could scratch him between the ears. After that, he took to lying beside me when I was typing on the terrace. About the time his ribs stopped sticking out and his coat began to shine, he began to play, putting his paws down, humping up his rear end, wagging his tail, and gamboling about like a puppy. He enjoyed romping with Lex. He began to watch the house with a great sense of responsibility and yipping officiousness. He adopted Lex.

A pet-prone American family, moving to Central America, can choose from among far more exotic natives. There are the kinkajous with their round eyes, Victorian lamb-chop sideburns, and long prehensile tails. There are varieties of gorgeous macaws, parrots, parakeets, and other jewel-like tropical birds. There are ocelots, beguiling spider monkeys, and members of the coati-mundi family, such as the *pizote*. Most of them, when young, are peddled in homemade cages along the highways, on street corners, or in front of popular hotels, and they cost less than a guinea pig would in a pet shop in the States.

We once played with a baby *pizote* on the Honduras side of the Honduras-Nicaragua border. The *pizote* has little hands, like a racoon, but its coat is brown and rough and short, and its face has the engaging quality of some comic-book character come to life. It has an exaggerated long nose, bright eyes, and an inquisitive, friendly manner. The nosy little one we met foraged in my purse, handling lipstick, keys, and pill bottles; he didn't seem to want to steal anything but simply to look at what was there. His curiosity and the fun he had exploring the purse reminded me of a human child. Finally the little creature, small as a guinea pig but a lot skinnier, snuggled its head in the palm of my hand and confidently curled up for a nap beside me on the bench at Customs. We reluctantly left the *pizote* behind, to his life as a border-station waif.

One afternoon in Managua, sitting near the back-yard pool of an American family, I held their new pet, an infant spider monkey. It was—as people are always saying about monkeys— "almost human"; the little thing drank from a bottle, wore diapers, was wrapped in a blanket, and peered up at me from where it lay happily in my cradling arms.

We talked to a family in San José who had raised a monkey named Jane. They named it Jane before they realized it was a male. Can't imagine how they missed the anatomy. As Jane got older, he took to cutting up, swinging on the drapes, leaping on the backs of guests, making faces out of the window. His monkey business became so disruptive that they decided to keep him out-of-doors most of the time; they put a collar on him, attached a long leash, and tied him to a post under a shade tree in the back yard. Jane became hysterical, fought the collar, yanked at the leash, threw bananas, moped, chattered, screamed, and refused to adjust to the new restrictions.

When they saw how persistently inconsolable the monkey was, they decided to take him to a simian colony that was known to live in a jungle area up a river near Puntarenas. They drove to the peninsula from San José, rented a motorboat, and went put-putting up the river. When they reached the jungle they tossed Jane onto the bank and raced away full throttle.

For the next few days they thought about Jane a great deal; they worried about him; they even missed him. So they decided to return to Puntarenas and check on Jane. With the motor idling, near the river back, they cupped their hands and called into the jungle, "Jane, Jane, Jane!" No Jane. Just as they decided that he might have met Miss Right and be leading an idyllic life in the monkey colony, there was a crashing sound in the trees and Jane jetted onto the deck with a thud. He threw his arms around his master's legs, chattering out a woeful monkey story.

They hadn't the heart to put him ashore again, so Jane rode home with the family. As they opened the car door in front of their house, Jane leaped out, raced to the back yard, and was trying to put his old collar over his head when they caught up with him.

After that, Jane was mostly a model monkey.

COST OF LIVING

Throughout the isthmus, goods are either ridiculously high or ridiculously low.

The cost of food is a good example. The Costa Rican Tourist Bureau, which is naturally not disposed to stress the difficulties, warns that imported foodstuffs often cost "five times the original price when duties have been added," points out that a well-cured T-bone steak can be bought for 36 cents a pound (American money) but that an imported can of peas costs upward to 75 cents. We have bought bulging bags full of fruits and vegetables for 50 cents at the central market in Guatemala City, but we have seen a can of sauerkraut priced at $1.25 at *supermercado* in San Salvador. The first rule is to live "on the economy."

Ready-made imported clothing is sky high and difficult to find. However, for $1.50 a day an expert seamstress will copy any dress you point to in a fashion magazine, and make it up for you in beautiful hand-woven materials, which are very cheap at local markets.

Unless you go to a beauty parlor in a hotel that caters to American travelers, you can have "the works" in a beauty shop for $2. However, an imported playpen that might cost $15 in the States costs $70, a small refrigerator is priced at $475.

Housing in the capital cities is not much cheaper than it would be at home for comparable accommodations. The American school at Managua, in its briefing pamphlet for new teachers, states: "Housing is neither easy to find nor inexpensive." The school itself rents several apartments and sublets them to teachers, pricing them as low as possible as an inducement. They run from $180 to $200 a month.

While the Costa Rican Tourist Bureau estimates that furnished homes throughout the nation may average from $135 to $200 a month, the American Embassy in San José estimates that housing in the capital runs considerably more, averaging from $250 to $500 a month. The Embassy residence originally cost $750 a month; recently the rent was raised to $1000.

The only person who seemed to feel that housing was a bargain was a young woman from San Salvador who was interning at the First National City Bank in New York City. She said, "You can get a whole house for what you pay for an apartment in New York." But New York rentals have always been notoriously high. And the figure she named was $300 a month.

Private clubs are often cheap. We spent an afternoon at the Bello Horizonte Club in Costa Rica, which has a beautiful swimming pool and grounds, tennis courts, swings and seesaws for the children, dressing-rooms and refreshment service. This costs $6 a month for an entire family, and it's open seven days a week.

It is outlandishly expensive to bring in a car on a permanent basis. Unless you are a retiree, it costs from $3000 to $4000 to bring a car of American make into Costa Rica. Cars are taxed according to weight. It would cost some 90,000 colones, or $10,000, to bring in a Mercedes Benz.

There *is* a way of ducking the high tariff. Bring your car in on a temporary tourist basis. Then, when the time is up, drive it over the border and back again, renewing the tourist status.

We understand that staying in a hospital is a real bargain. A week costs what a day does in the States—if getting sick is ever a bargain.

The quality of medical care in the capital cities is generally good to excellent. Central American doctors are usually graduates of medical schools in the United States. The American Embassy can recommend a doctor or a clinic. That is how I found the excellent Clínica Bíblica in San José when I needed to get a shot of gamma globulin.

Sometimes the small private hospitals in the capital cities are staffed, not by registered nurses or even practical nurses, but by local young women trained by the doctor or doctors operating the hospital. A friend who was operated on in just such a hospital saw the nurse who came to change her dressing drop the gauze pad on the floor and pick it up with a pair of sterile calipers. "The doctor told her not to touch anything with her hands, you see," the woman explained, "and she took him literally. The fact that the dressing had fallen on the floor did not worry her—as long as she did not use her hands to pick it up. I had to demand another dressing."

We heard no other stories of this kind during our travels. Generally American residents seem to be satisfied with doctors and medical facilities in the cities.

THE BIG DREAMERS

Of course it is very difficult for a gringo to find a paying job in Central America unless he is a technical specialist in work for which a national is not qualified. And a woman cannot count on landing a secretarial job because there is a plethora of bilingual secretaries. As a rule, the girls from well-to-do families go to college in the United States, speak English beautifully, and almost always come home with secretarial skills. This is the work they invariably choose, and the isthmus is full of attractive señoritas who work for Pan Am or the National City Bank or any number of other American organizations.

If any non-national wants to earn money, he must invent a business of his own. Consequently there is an epidemic of dreaming among American men who live, even temporarily, in Central America. You will see those who have come down with it writing on paper napkins in the cocktail lounges of the big hotels in the capital cities. They are figuring out how, by investing relatively little money, they can buy a snow machine and put a ski jump on the slope of Momotombo volcano; or open a chain of luxurious weight-reducing salons—Central Americans tend to put on weight in very early middle age, when it's not yet too late to save their looks.

We met a man who had gotten all fired up over the incidence of sharks in Lake Managua, the San Juan River, and off both coasts. "There is not a bit of a shark that cannot be marketed," he told us. "Shark meat is tasty, full of vitamins. Of course, an education job is needed, as at first you freeze the meat you don't sell. You use the teeth for jewelry, the viscera for fertilizer, the skin for beautiful sharkskin bags."

He actually went into business too; what lost him his shirt was that the sharkskin spoiled before he could get it to the tannery, and the education program was so costly that the frozen meat went begging and had to be jettisoned. We never found out what happened to the shark-tooth jewelry but we can guess.

A retired ex-resident of San Francisco, California, came cruising to the Bay Islands on a 43-foot cutter, was struck by their paradisiacal climate and scenery, bought land on Guanaja, built a pier, vacation cottages, and a lodge for cocktails and food. He has been trying to maintain it against the onslaughts of a tropical climate and sea weather and has hopes that "the whole thing will pick up."

Some of the big dreams have materialized. J. I. Bealle, now a resident of La Ceiba, Honduras, came to Central America on vacation via a banana boat from New Orleans twenty-five years ago. He loved coastal Honduras and resolved to find a way to make a living there. Mr. Bealle bought an ice-cream machine that made five gallons every eight minutes. Now his company supplies the whole coast of Honduras. His two sons are managing the business, which includes a dairy and many head of cattle, while Mr. Bealle is taking a somewhat delayed vacation.

Once I was sitting with a friend of Lex's, in the lobby of the Gran Hotel in Managua, Nicaragua, when he got to shaking his head at the men huddled around nearby tables. "I've seen more big deals worked out around here on paper," he said. "They always want to cut you in. They tell you they've got this and they've got that—and they don't any more have anything. I work for a salary," he said firmly, and paused.

"Americans down here are dreamers," he continued. "They are crazy. Ask them why they're not making a living in the States. They say, 'I could have a comfortable house, two cars, back home. But here I will be a millionaire.' They will never be millionaires."

I told him that I understood the dream bug because I had been bitten by it myself. Here was all this water—more lakes to the mile than anywhere in the world, two coasts—full of beautiful islands and inlets and bays, but there were no sailboats to buy. I could see manufacturing a good little all-weather sailing dinghy.

He nodded and a gleam came into his eyes. The muscles around his jaw tightened and he found a pencil and began to write on a napkin. "You'd have your assembly boathouse over near Granada," he said. "Much cheaper than you could operate here in Managua. Now, say you need enough to meet a payroll for two months. You wouldn't need more than $10,000. . . ."

20 / Adelante

One gray August morning I flew back to Managua, having been away for five months. The passengers on the non-stop Lanica flight offset the cloudy skies by clapping and singing folk songs and dancing in the aisles. I thought, "This is Nicaragua," and I felt as if I were coming home. As we lost altitude to land I looked down on a gorgeous patchwork quilt of earth colors made by the cultivated fields below.

Back in Putnam Valley, New York, where I had come from, it was late summer, and here it was late spring, the time of emerging rice and cotton, the time of the frogs. Frogs sound different in Central America; they laugh loudly and derisively, "gek, gek, gek." A *sapo* vocalized nightly near Lex's pool, cleverly using it as an echo chamber. I had thought frogs went "chug-a-rum," or whatever it is that gringo frogs say. Again I was to learn that everybody is not like us.

Many of the things were exactly the same as when I had left. Lex's shower still had its alarming attachment for making hot water. Above the spigot was a metal container. You started the water running and shoved up a big switch. The thing let out a bolt of lightning that would have frightened Moses. If you did not run away, electing to take a gutsy kill-me-if-you-can attitude, the apparatus made a percolating sound and sprayed out warm water.

The houses we visited in outlying cities were the same, with the well-remembered Central American decor. The framed photographs around the high-ceilinged rooms were far above eye level, as usual. Some had mustaches and some had doe eyes and patient mouths. All had apparently been photographed at funerals. The tile floors were beautiful and shining, and in the middle of each *sala* was a suite of varnished furniture; the coffee table was the magnet for chairs; matching rockers were common. There would be a huge vase of artificial flowers in this land where the real ones were apparently too common to be either interesting or elegant. Opening out from the *sala* was the *comedor*, featuring a long refectory table covered with a plastic cloth. There would be a huge refrigerator, standing like a statue, a monument to middle-class prosperity. And the people who lived there would be kind, perceptive, humorous, warm, with quick smiles. You never shake hands with the women (it took me some time to get over this habit). You put your hand on your hostess's arm, near her shoulder, and press it reassuringly. If you have always shaken hands and it has become so automatic as to have lost all meaning, try patting a shoulder.

I loved getting back to all the beautiful sounds, the bells, the wind in the trees, the clopping of horses, the calling of vendors' voices in the quiet streets, *Quiere bananos?*, the life that was lived so close to the roads. Driving to San Marcos, we passed a procession escorting the town's patron saint home from a fiesta. He was a tall effigy on a pedestal, wearing a spiky golden halo, clad in colorful plaster robes. He was surrounded by dancers in costumes and masks, women carrying babies, children running, men on horseback. They were taking their saint back to his own church. There had been ages of idols in Mayan times, and things hadn't changed much during the centuries of Christianity. With a pang, I realized that the people have the very qualities they attribute to their saint, but they still have not learned to believe in themselves, or in their ability to perform the miracles that can change their world. It was San Marcos, not they, who could do anything.

As always, life had that flowing, unscheduled quality I have seen nowhere else in the world. I took to dreaming as I always do there. I stood for moments, for instance, watching a fleet of ants, with green mainsails that they had chewed out of leaves, going into the wind on a definite tack up a tree trunk.

And I found that if you were inclined to grumpiness for any reason, it was practically impossible to stay grumpy. Once, when I was waiting for interminable periods on a hot day for Lex to do errands in León, he came out of a warehouse and handed me his business card. It normally read, "Lex Creamer, Jr., International Technical Consultant." He had crossed out "International Technical Consultant." The card now read, "Lex Creamer, Jr., International Fool."

I got to tapping my foot outside a *finca,* and Lex, after some absence, handed me a grasshopper. It was an extraordinary, gorgeous creature, with a helmet and waistcoat of Chinese red. I admired it as it waved its red antennae at me, and I smiled. Lex said, "This is one of those days when everybody is going to be home in five minutes but isn't. There are some days when you can't do anything. You can't even catch a grasshopper."

Always and everywhere there were unexpected vignettes of sight and sound. Driving from Tegucigalpa to San Salvador, we saw four cows trailing ropes, gallumphing wildly along with their eyes rolling. One cow had a dangling vine prettily and absurdly draped over her horns and ears and streaming out behind her; she had apparently adorned herself while butting her way through the bush. Soon we passed three *campesinos,* a boy, his father, his grandfather, trudging purposefully and gloomily uphill, carrying ropes. They were clearly after the cows, and it was going to be a long time before they caught them.

And once, in Managua, there was an unforgettable sequence of sounds. It was a bright moonlit night and all the dogs were yodeling. Nearby a candidate for the opera, who had remarkable soprano qualities, sang the "Bell Song" from *Lakmé.* He kept it up as if he were trying to please his teacher in one of those yodeler-packed buildings near Carnegie Hall in New York. (This time I'll hit every note, coach. I'm beginning to understand the intervals.) Suddenly we heard, "Ooooo-wooo, yowee, woo, woo-*woooo*, arrow, arrow, yi-yi-yi-yi," *pow*. Silence. Some hot-headed Latin insomniac had grabbed his *pistola* and put an end to his exasperation by removing the cause of it.

As ever, there was the infinity of mountains as far as you could see, and the pueblos and towns with their predominantly colonial character. But there were also some startling changes, which began at the Managua airport.

The last time I had flown in—only a matter of months before—I had approached Customs on a short, flower-bordered walk, a mere few steps away from the jet. It had been a low frame building, and beyond the counter where the men glanced at my luggage there had been a large window covered by a venetian blind. Lex had parted the slats of that blind and flapped his hand so that I would know that he was there.

The building I faced this time as I walked away from the Lanica jet was towering, very modern, with a sweeping ob-servation platform and lots of glass. Suddenly I thought I had somehow gotten on the wrong jet, or off at the wrong stop. This might be Zanzibar. I asked a man in uniform, in a sheepish, muffled voice of anxiety, "Is this Managua?" He said yes and waved me on. The big glass door opened without my touching it, so that I almost fell in, and the inside was beautifully re-frigerated.

During the next few weeks I found other changes throughout Central America; all had taken place in the brief while that I had turned my back. It gave me a Rip Van Winkle syndrome. There were new and beautiful airport terminals at San Pedro Sula and Guatemala City—art forms, like giant sculptures. Only a few miles from Lex's house, on the Carretera Sur out of Managua, there was a brand-new building, an extension of Harvard University. And downtown a new hotel, in the shape of a Mayan temple, was nearing completion. Motels were going up all over the isthmus at strategic places. Every capital had new, high-rise buildings, built to house international banks that were bringing "sophisticated economics" to these exciting, innocent lands.

On the outskirts of Tegucigalpa, close to the recently finished basilica for the Virgin of Suyapa, I saw the new, exciting, molded-looking shapes of buildings still under construction for the National University of Honduras. What was begun in 1845 as the Society of Learning and Good Taste had suddenly moved from yesterday right into tomorrow.

An exciting new development was the discovery of a pre-Columbian ceremonial center at Quelepa, El Salvador; the number of temples and palaces will not be known until excavations have been completed, but archaeologists believe that old Quelepa was one of the great ancient cities, as important as Tikal or Copán.

A new highway from Tegucigalpa to San Pedro Sula was almost finished. And Costa Rica, which, for all its progressiveness, has tended to have some stretches of pot-hole-ridden roads, was removing S-curves and resurfacing the poor highway from San José to Puntarenas.

Lex and I had changed too. Take the Spanish language. I hadn't spoken a word of it during my absence. I never had been fluent anyway, being mainly a good-morning and good-afternoon and how-are-you linguist. However, playing kick-the-can and baseball with some neighboring children up on the mountain where Lex lived, galloping around with Iwo, Chico, Armando, Sergio, Carmen, and Maritza, my inhibitions fled and I was yelling Spanish with the rest of them.

And Lex one day found that he could not speak English, which was a shock to him. It happened at the Customs House, where he was trying to get a shipment of rice seeds released. The man on duty spoke English to Lex in response to his gringo looks. Lex sputtered away in Spanish.

"I simply couldn't break into English," he told me. "Then I was throwing in a few English words. For a moment there, I absolutely couldn't speak English."

There are some changes that we long to see. Once on a rainy night in San Salvador, we came across a naked baby standing right smack in the middle of the highway, as unattended as a stray dog or a cow. While there is a lack of social services and community responsibility for the helpless, no Central American saints had better resign.

Here one age lives on with another. It is as if you had a dinosaur and a new breed of disease-resistant cattle foraging in the same small pasture.

Lex and I reminded ourselves how fast things jump ahead, how they can move along in seven-league boots. It's as the weather used to be described by old-timers on Cape Cod: "If you don't like it, wait a minute."

One businessman in Managua said to me, "We know what we should do. Now we must do it."

But that's the story of the human race, always lagging behind the dream.

Then Lex said, "But nature can't be changed too much here. And that's why it will always be special and why people will want to come back to it. It is not natural to be away from nature."

Yes, I thought, try changing Arenal or Telica. Try that, moon-shooters.

When they say good-by in Central America, it's often "Que le vaya bien"—"May it go well for you."

Time for Lex and me to say that.

Index

*Only capital cities are listed separately;
all others are listed under their countries.*

Date Due

Code 4386-04, CLS-4, Broadman Supplies, Nashville
Printed in U.S.A.